AN ONI PRESS PUBLICATION

ORCS IN SPACE*

WRITTEN BY
RASHAD GHEITH, ABED GHEITH & MICHAEL TANNER

ILLUSTRATED BY
FRANÇOIS VIGNEAULT

COLORS BY
DJ CHAVIS

COLOR FLATTING BY
DAVE PENDER

CO-CREATED BY
JUSTIN ROILAND

DESIGNED BY
SARAH ROCKWELL

EDITED BY
AMANDA MEADOWS

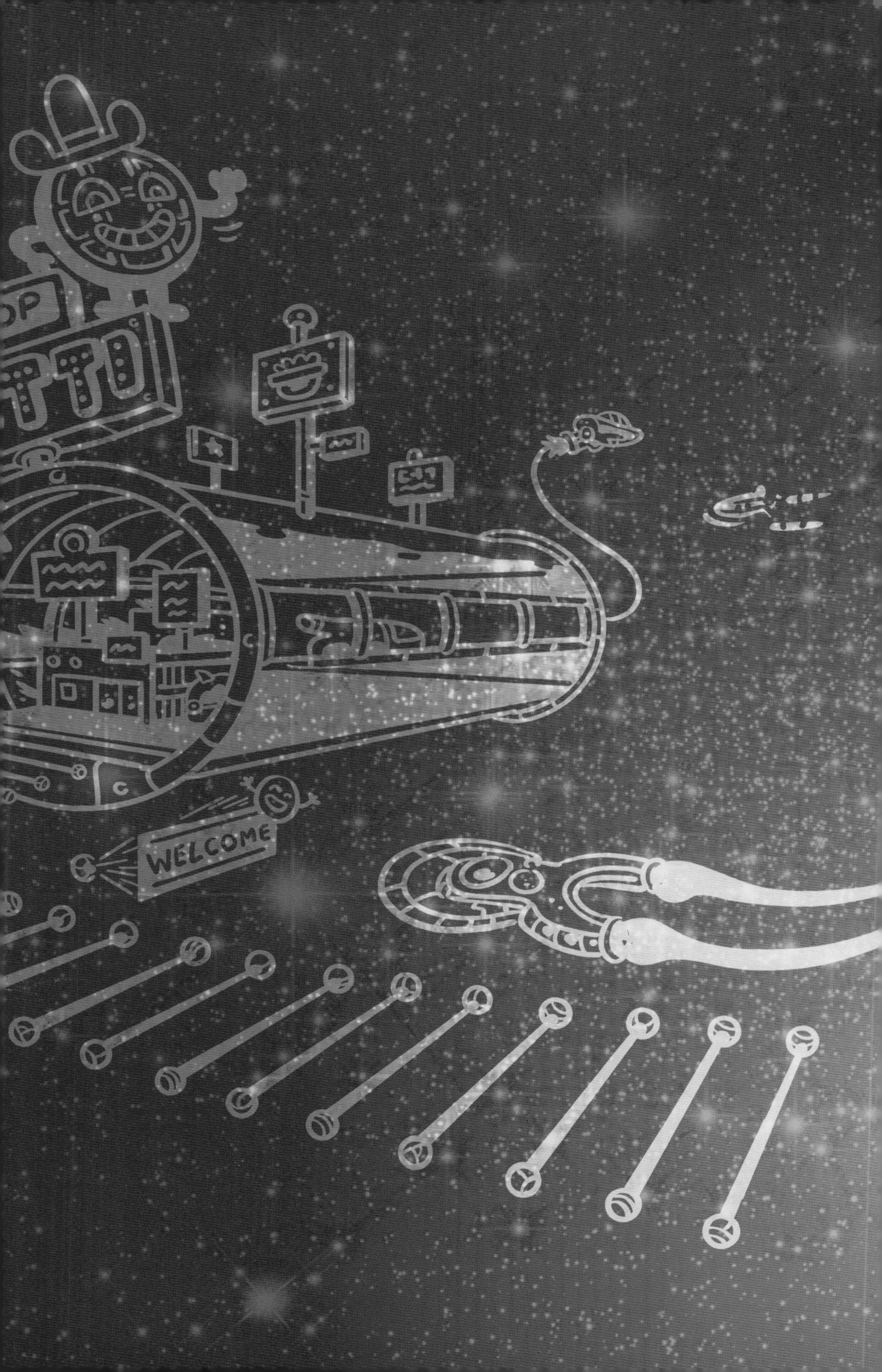
WELCOME

PUBLISHED BY
ONI-LION FORGE
PUBLISHING
GROUP, LLC.

JAMES LUCAS JONES, *PRESIDENT & PUBLISHER*
CHARLIE CHU, *E.V.P. OF CREATIVE & BUSINESS DEVELOPMENT* • **STEVE ELLIS,** *S.V.P. OF GAMES & OPERATIONS* • **ALEX SEGURA,** *S.V.P. OF MARKETING & SALES* • **MICHELLE NGUYEN,** *EXECUTIVE ASSISTANT*
BRAD ROOKS, *DIRECTOR OF OPERATIONS* • **AMBER O'NEILL,** *SPECIAL PROJECTS MANAGER* • **MARGOT WOOD,** *DIRECTOR OF MARKETING & SALES* • **KATIE SAINZ,** *MARKETING MANAGER* • **HENRY BARAJAS,** *SALES MANAGER* • **TARA LEHMANN,** *PUBLICIST*
HOLLY AITCHISON, *CONSUMER MARKETING MANAGER*
TROY LOOK, *DIRECTOR OF DESIGN & PRODUCTION*
ANGIE KNOWLES, *PRODUCTION MANAGER* • **KATE Z. STONE,** *SENIOR GRAPHIC DESIGNER* • **CAREY HALL,** *GRAPHIC DESIGNER* • **SARAH ROCKWELL,** *GRAPHIC DESIGNER* • **HILARY THOMPSON,** *GRAPHIC DESIGNER* • **VINCENT KUKUA,** *DIGITAL PREPRESS TECHNICIAN* • **CHRIS CERASI,** *MANAGING EDITOR*
JASMINE AMIRI, *SENIOR EDITOR* • **SHAWNA GORE,** *SENIOR EDITOR* • **AMANDA MEADOWS,** *SENIOR EDITOR* • **ROBERT MEYERS,** *SENIOR EDITOR, LICENSING* • **DESIREE RODRIGUEZ,** *EDITOR* • **GRACE SCHEIPETER,** *EDITOR*
ZACK SOTO, *EDITOR* • **BEN EISNER,** *GAME DEVELOPER* • **JUNG LEE,** *LOGISTICS COORDINATOR*
KUIAN KELLUM, *WAREHOUSE ASSISTANT*
• **JOE NOZEMACK,** *PUBLISHER EMERITUS* •

ONIPRESS.COM

/JUSTINROILAND
/MIKEISERNIE
/ABEDG
/FRANCOISVIGNEAULT
/DJCOLORSCOMICS
/WAYTOOMANYDAVES

FIRST EDITION: **APRIL 2022**
ISBN: **978-1-63715-017-7**
EISBN: **978-1-63715-026-9**
LIBRARY OF CONGRESS CONTROL NUMBER: **2020937772**

1 2 3 4 5 6 7 8 9 10

To my mom and dad for all their support, and to my cousin Rami for being a comic book copilot.

-ABED

To the Orc Lord Orcinacia.

-RASHAD

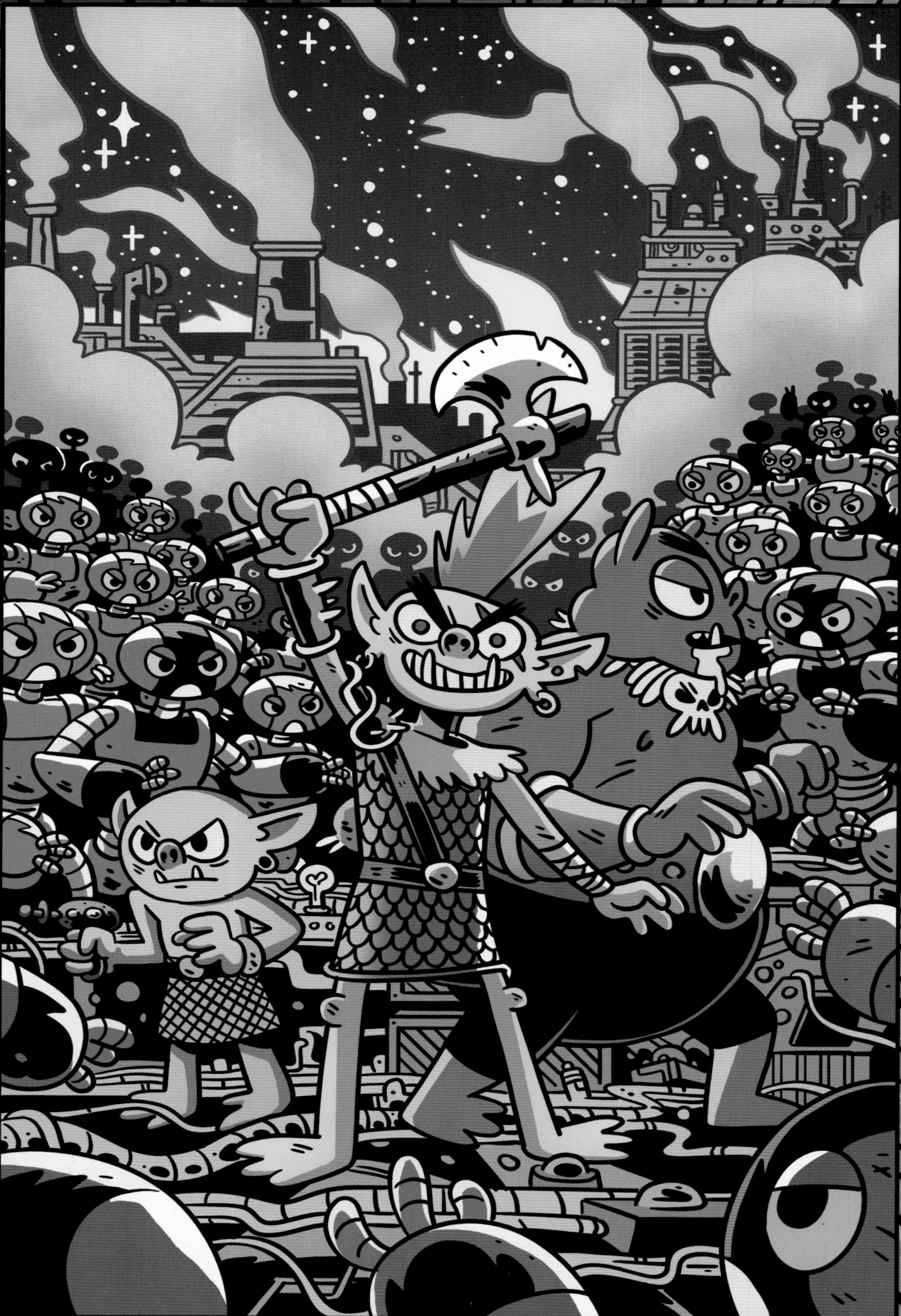

CHAPTER FIVE

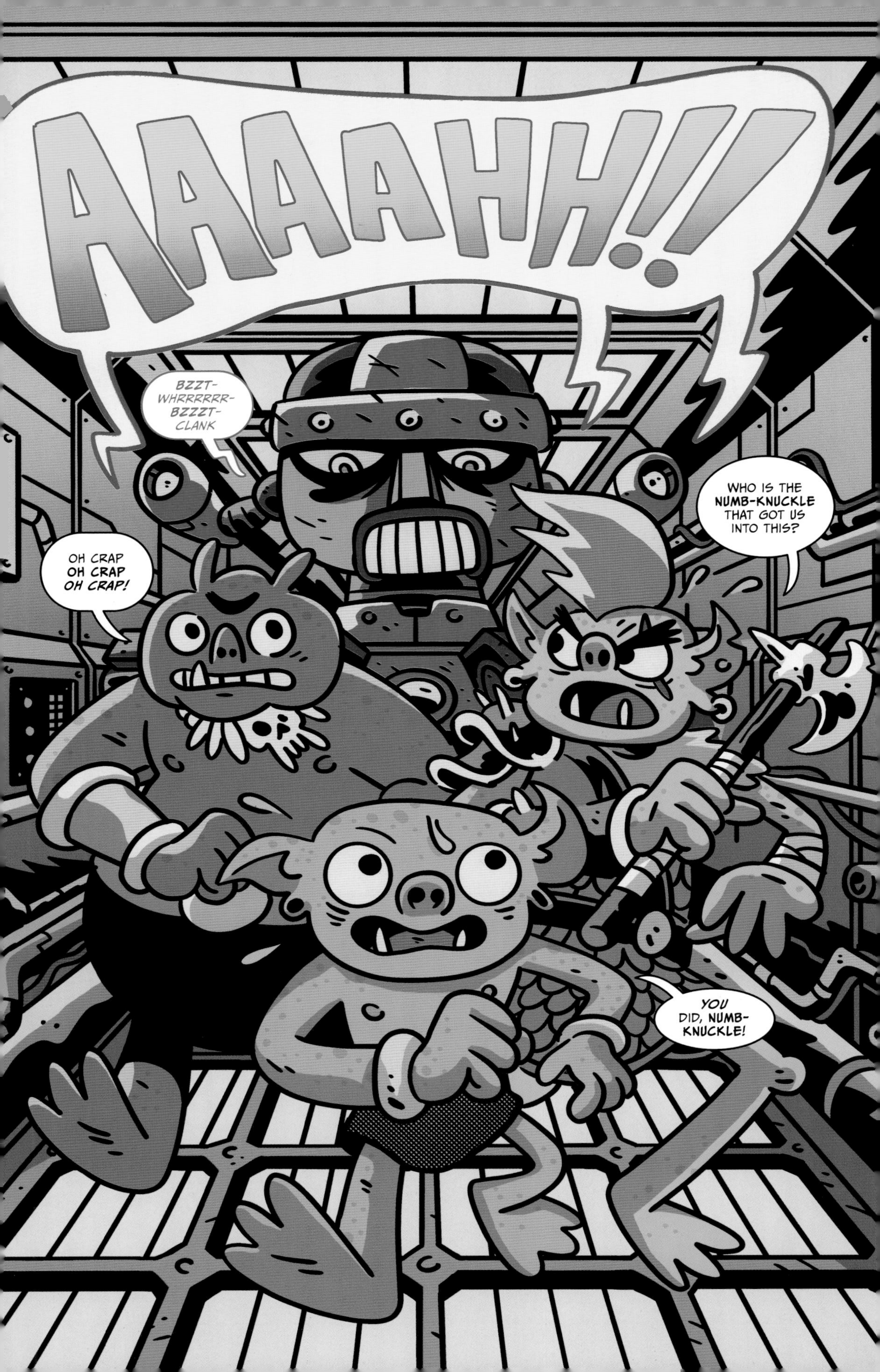
AAAAHH!!!
BZZT-WHRRRRRR-BZZZT-CLANK
OH CRAP OH CRAP OH CRAP!
WHO IS THE NUMB-KNUCKLE THAT GOT US INTO THIS?
YOU DID, NUMB-KNUCKLE!

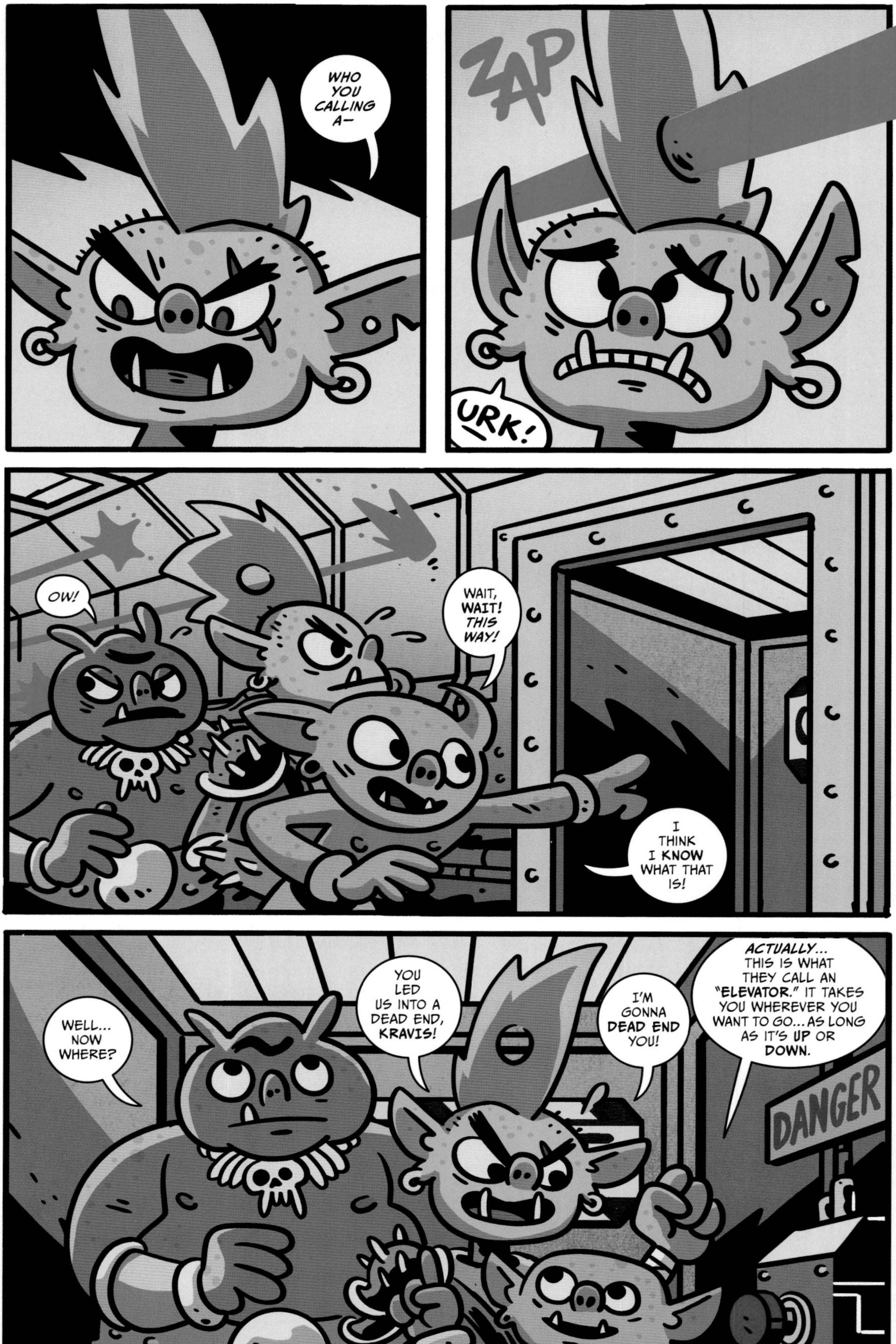
WHO YOU CALLING A—
ZAP
URK!
OW!
WAIT, WAIT! THIS WAY!
I THINK I KNOW WHAT THAT IS!
WELL... NOW WHERE?
YOU LED US INTO A DEAD END, KRAVIS!
I'M GONNA DEAD END YOU!
ACTUALLY... THIS IS WHAT THEY CALL AN "ELEVATOR." IT TAKES YOU WHEREVER YOU WANT TO GO... AS LONG AS IT'S UP OR DOWN.
DANGER

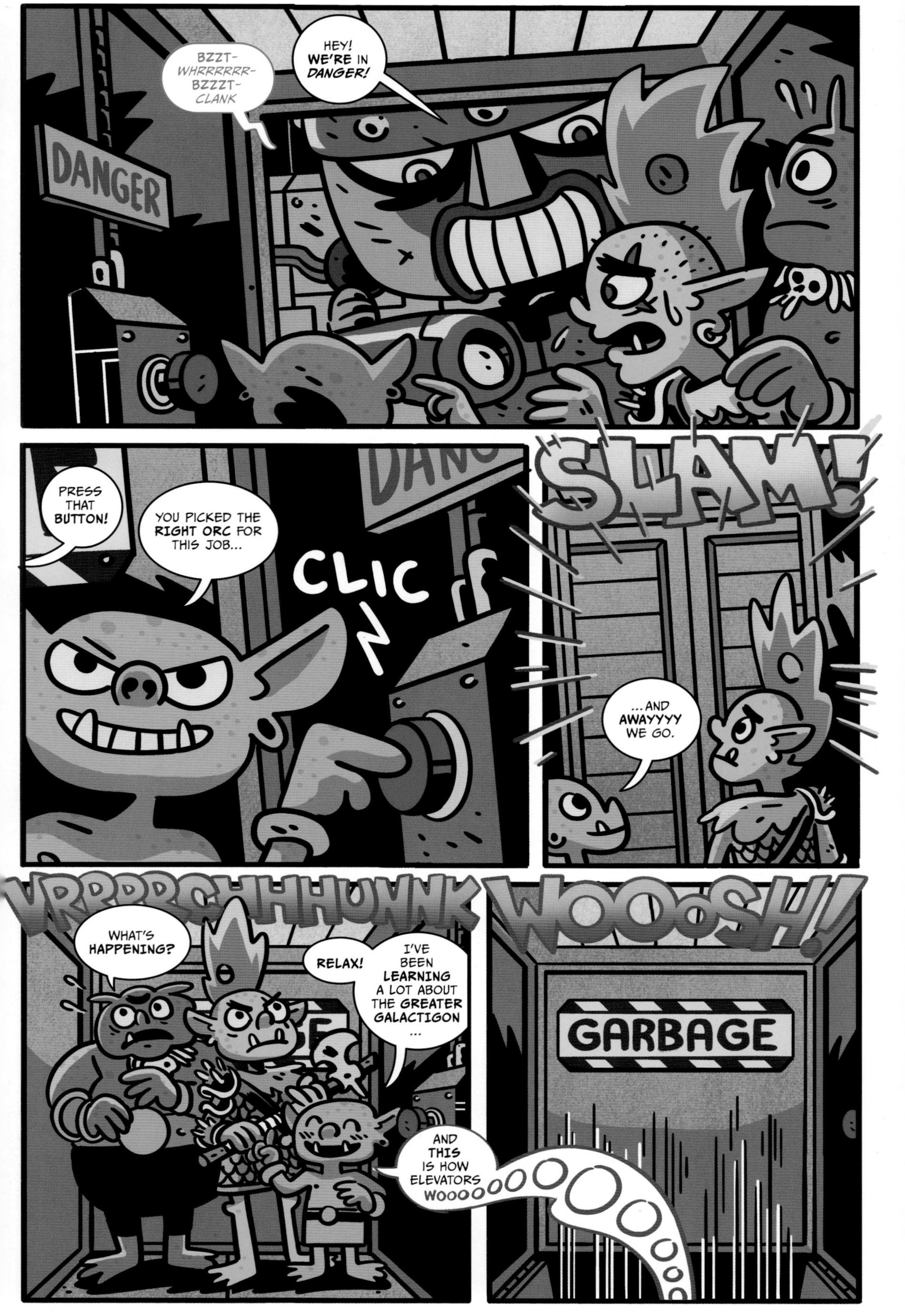
DANGER
BZZT-WHRRRRRR-BZZZT-CLANK
HEY! WE'RE IN DANGER!
DANG
PRESS THAT BUTTON!
YOU PICKED THE RIGHT ORC FOR THIS JOB...
CLIC
SLAM!
...AND AWAYYYY WE GO.
VRRRRCHHHUNNK
WHAT'S HAPPENING?
RELAX!
I'VE BEEN LEARNING A LOT ABOUT THE GREATER GALACTIGON ...
AND THIS IS HOW ELEVATORS WOOOOOOOOOOOOOO
WOOOSH!
GARBAGE

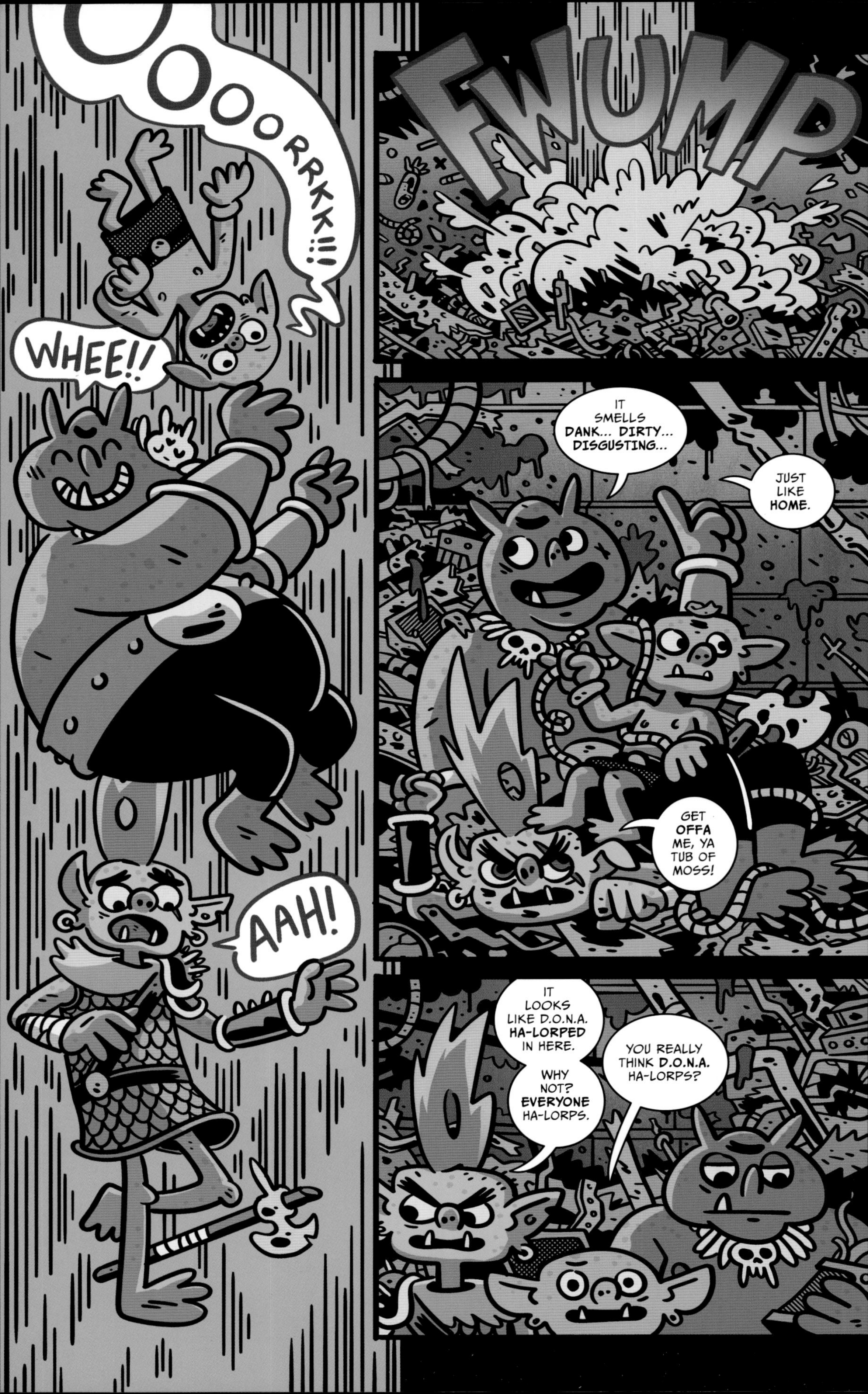
OOOOORRRKK!!!
WHEE!!
AAH!
FWUMP
IT SMELLS DANK... DIRTY... DISGUSTING...
JUST LIKE HOME.
GET OFFA ME, YA TUB OF MOSS!
IT LOOKS LIKE D.O.N.A. HA-LORPED IN HERE.
WHY NOT? EVERYONE HA-LORPS.
YOU REALLY THINK D.O.N.A. HA-LORPS?

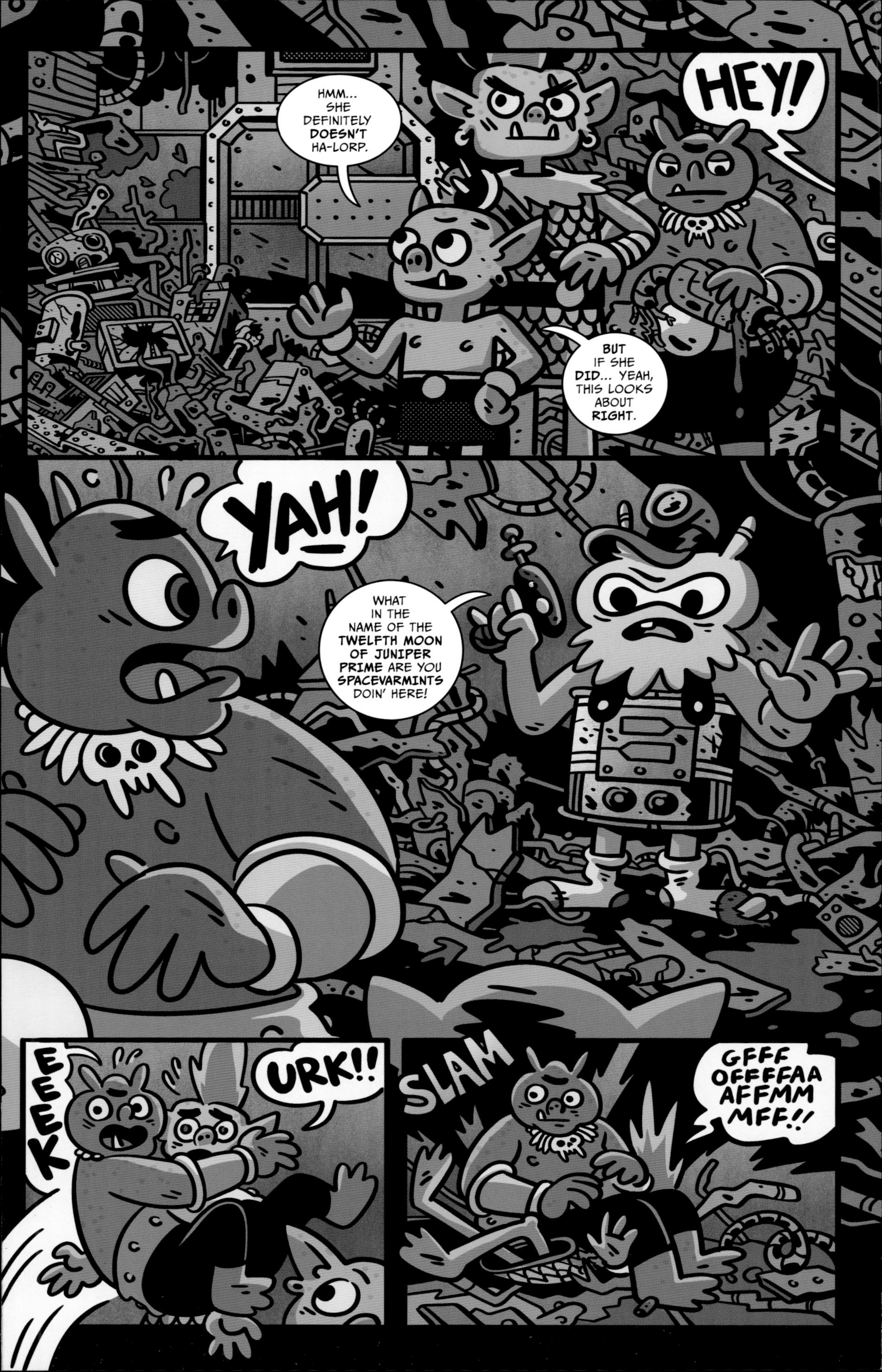
HMM... SHE DEFINITELY DOESN'T HA-LORP.
HEY!
BUT IF SHE DID... YEAH, THIS LOOKS ABOUT RIGHT.
YAH!
WHAT IN THE NAME OF THE TWELFTH MOON OF JUNIPER PRIME ARE YOU SPACEVARMINTS DOIN' HERE!
EEEK
URK!!
SLAM
GFFF OFFFFAA AFFMM MFF!!

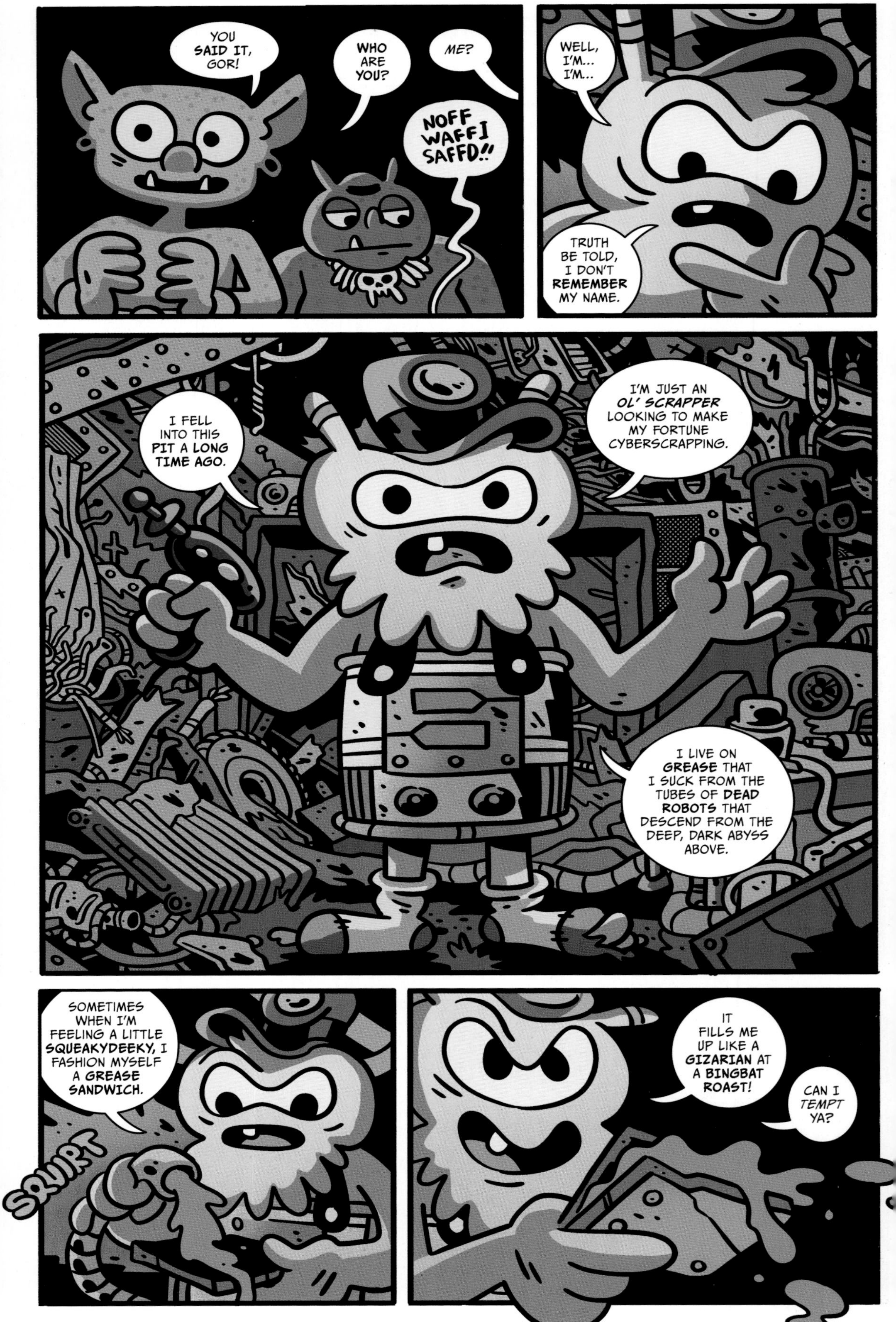
YOU SAID IT, GOR!
WHO ARE YOU?
ME?
NOFF WAFFI SAFFD!!
WELL, I'M... I'M...
TRUTH BE TOLD, I DON'T REMEMBER MY NAME.
I FELL INTO THIS PIT A LONG TIME AGO.
I'M JUST AN OL' SCRAPPER LOOKING TO MAKE MY FORTUNE CYBERSCRAPPING.
I LIVE ON GREASE THAT I SUCK FROM THE TUBES OF DEAD ROBOTS THAT DESCEND FROM THE DEEP, DARK ABYSS ABOVE.
SOMETIMES WHEN I'M FEELING A LITTLE SQUEAKYDEEKY, I FASHION MYSELF A GREASE SANDWICH.
SRURT
IT FILLS ME UP LIKE A GIZARIAN AT A BINGBAT ROAST!
CAN I TEMPT YA?

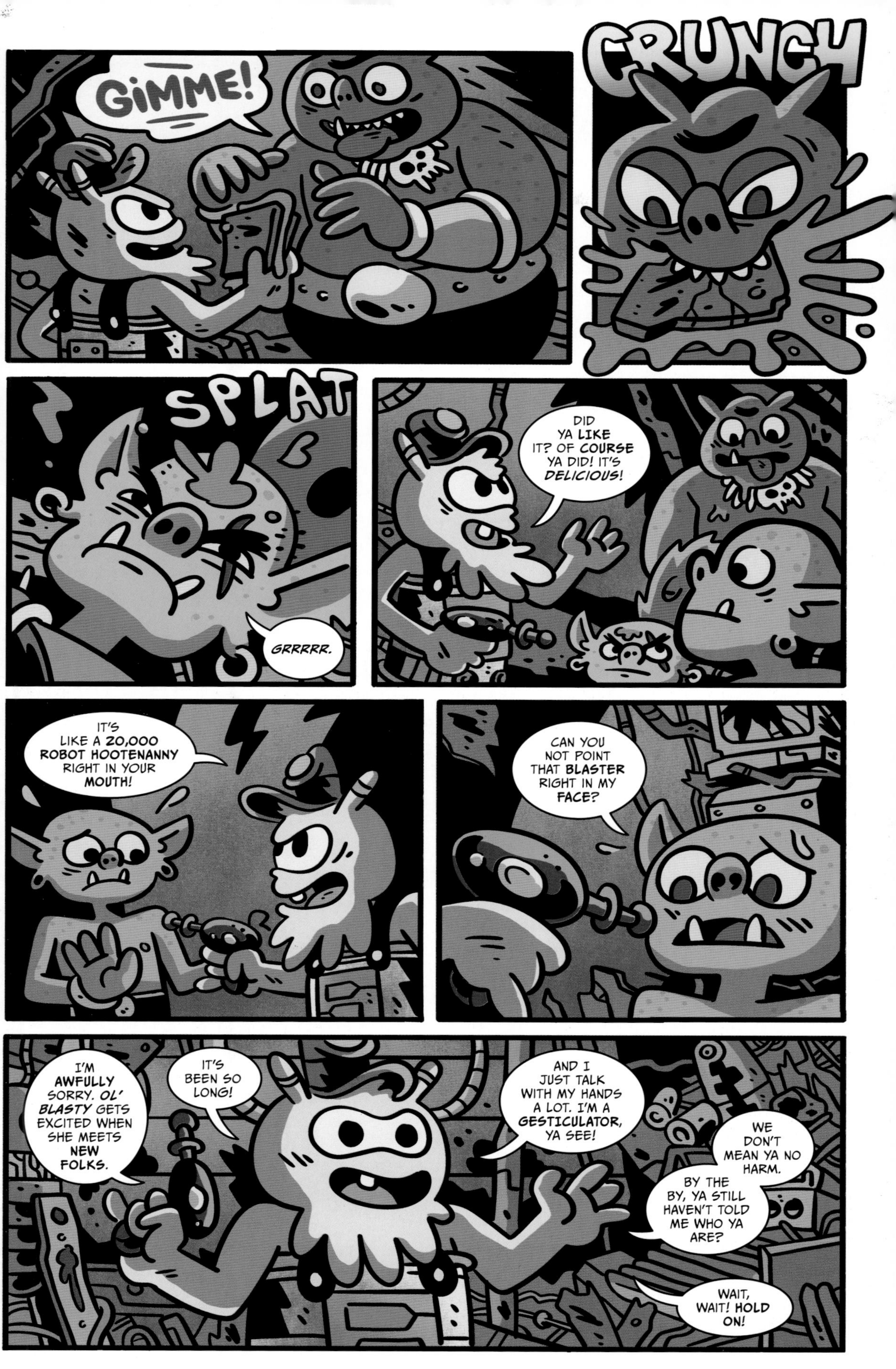
GIMME!
CRUNCH
SPLAT
GRRRRR.
DID YA LIKE IT? OF COURSE YA DID! IT'S DELICIOUS!
IT'S LIKE A 20,000 ROBOT HOOTENANNY RIGHT IN YOUR MOUTH!
CAN YOU NOT POINT THAT BLASTER RIGHT IN MY FACE?
I'M AWFULLY SORRY. OL' BLASTY GETS EXCITED WHEN SHE MEETS NEW FOLKS.
IT'S BEEN SO LONG!
AND I JUST TALK WITH MY HANDS A LOT. I'M A GESTICULATOR, YA SEE!
WE DON'T MEAN YA NO HARM.
BY THE BY, YA STILL HAVEN'T TOLD ME WHO YA ARE?
WAIT, WAIT! HOLD ON!

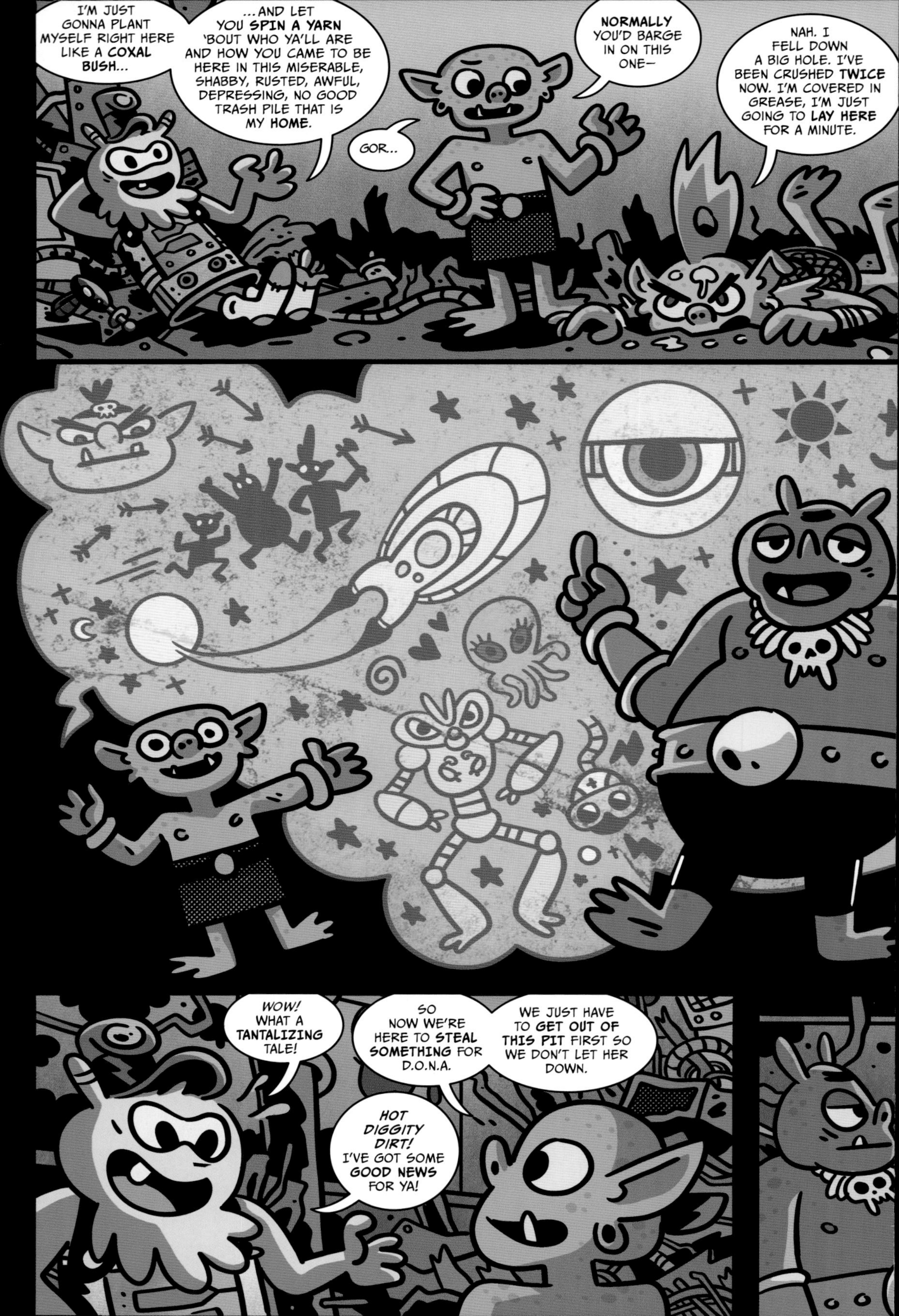

I'M JUST GONNA PLANT MYSELF RIGHT HERE LIKE A **COXAL BUSH**...
...AND LET YOU **SPIN A YARN** 'BOUT WHO YA'LL ARE AND HOW YOU CAME TO BE HERE IN THIS MISERABLE, SHABBY, RUSTED, AWFUL, DEPRESSING, NO GOOD TRASH PILE THAT IS MY **HOME**.
GOR...
NORMALLY YOU'D BARGE IN ON THIS ONE–
NAH. I FELL DOWN A BIG HOLE. I'VE BEEN CRUSHED **TWICE** NOW. I'M COVERED IN GREASE, I'M JUST GOING TO **LAY HERE** FOR A MINUTE.
WOW! WHAT A **TANTALIZING** TALE!
SO NOW WE'RE HERE TO **STEAL SOMETHING** FOR D.O.N.A.
WE JUST HAVE TO **GET OUT OF THIS PIT** FIRST SO WE DON'T LET HER DOWN.
HOT DIGGITY DIRT! I'VE GOT SOME **GOOD NEWS** FOR YA!

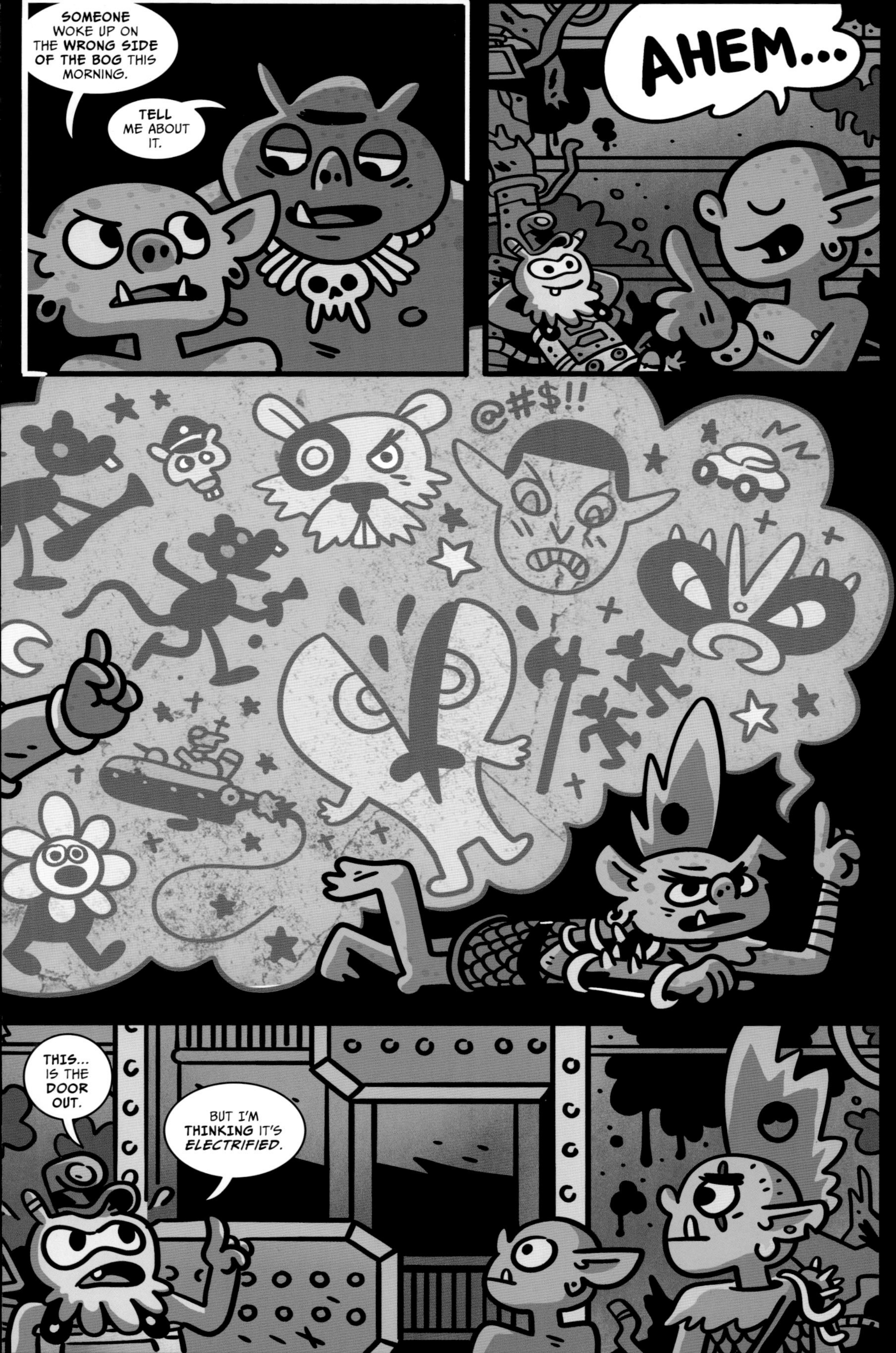
SOMEONE WOKE UP ON THE WRONG SIDE OF THE BOG THIS MORNING.
TELL ME ABOUT IT.
AHEM...
@#$!!
THIS... IS THE DOOR OUT.
BUT I'M THINKING IT'S *ELECTRIFIED*.

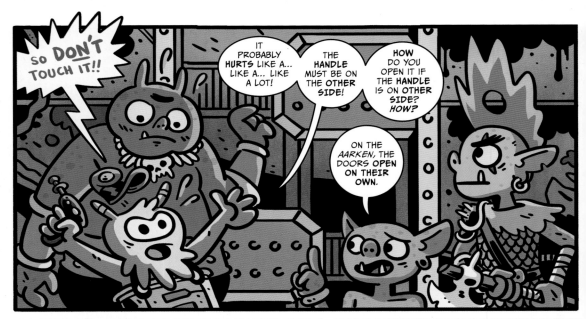

SO **DON'T** TOUCH IT!!

IT PROBABLY HURTS LIKE A... LIKE A... LIKE A LOT!

THE HANDLE MUST BE ON THE OTHER SIDE!

HOW DO YOU OPEN IT IF THE HANDLE IS ON OTHER SIDE? *HOW?*

ON THE *AARKEN,* THE DOORS OPEN ON THEIR OWN.

HAVE YOU TRIED JUST WALKING TOWARD—

I'LL TELL YOU HOW!

YOU NEED SOME GEN-U-INE INGENUITY, A BLASTER, AND *TWO* FRIENDS!

A BIG STRONG ONE ANNNNNND...

A SMALL SCRAWNY ONE.

HMMMF. ONLY "TWO," HUH?

16

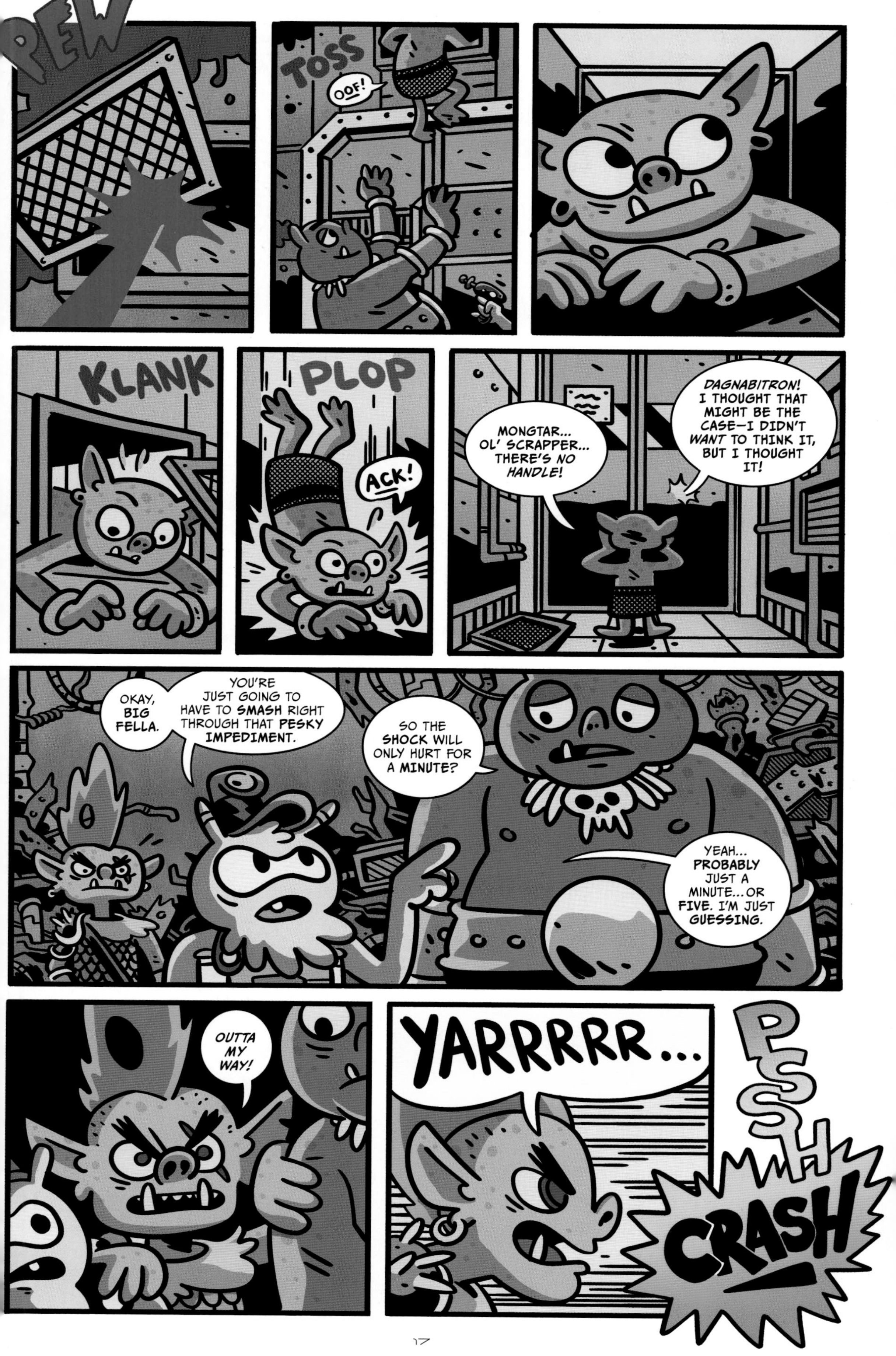
PEW
TOSS
OOF!
KLANK
PLOP
ACK!
MONGTAR... OL' SCRAPPER... THERE'S NO HANDLE!
DAGNABITRON! I THOUGHT THAT MIGHT BE THE CASE—I DIDN'T WANT TO THINK IT, BUT I THOUGHT IT!
OKAY, BIG FELLA.
YOU'RE JUST GOING TO HAVE TO SMASH RIGHT THROUGH THAT PESKY IMPEDIMENT.
SO THE SHOCK WILL ONLY HURT FOR A MINUTE?
YEAH... PROBABLY JUST A MINUTE... OR FIVE. I'M JUST GUESSING.
OUTTA MY WAY!
YARRRRR...
PSSH
CRASH

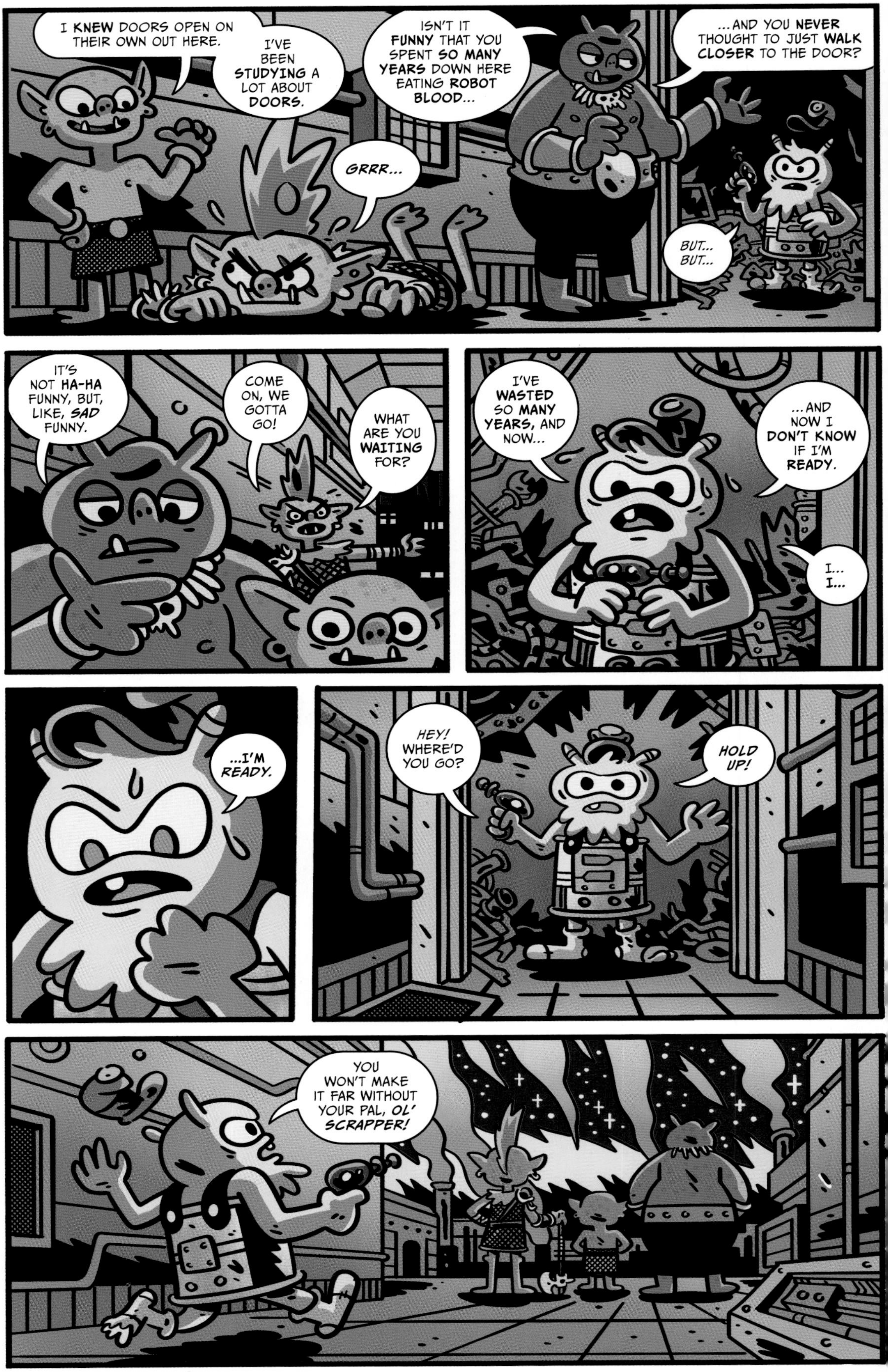
I KNEW DOORS OPEN ON THEIR OWN OUT HERE.
I'VE BEEN STUDYING A LOT ABOUT DOORS.
GRRR...
ISN'T IT FUNNY THAT YOU SPENT SO MANY YEARS DOWN HERE EATING ROBOT BLOOD...
...AND YOU NEVER THOUGHT TO JUST WALK CLOSER TO THE DOOR?
BUT... BUT...
IT'S NOT HA-HA FUNNY, BUT, LIKE, SAD FUNNY.
COME ON, WE GOTTA GO!
WHAT ARE YOU WAITING FOR?
I'VE WASTED SO MANY YEARS, AND NOW...
...AND NOW I DON'T KNOW IF I'M READY.
I... I...
...I'M READY.
HEY! WHERE'D YOU GO?
HOLD UP!
YOU WON'T MAKE IT FAR WITHOUT YOUR PAL, OL' SCRAPPER!

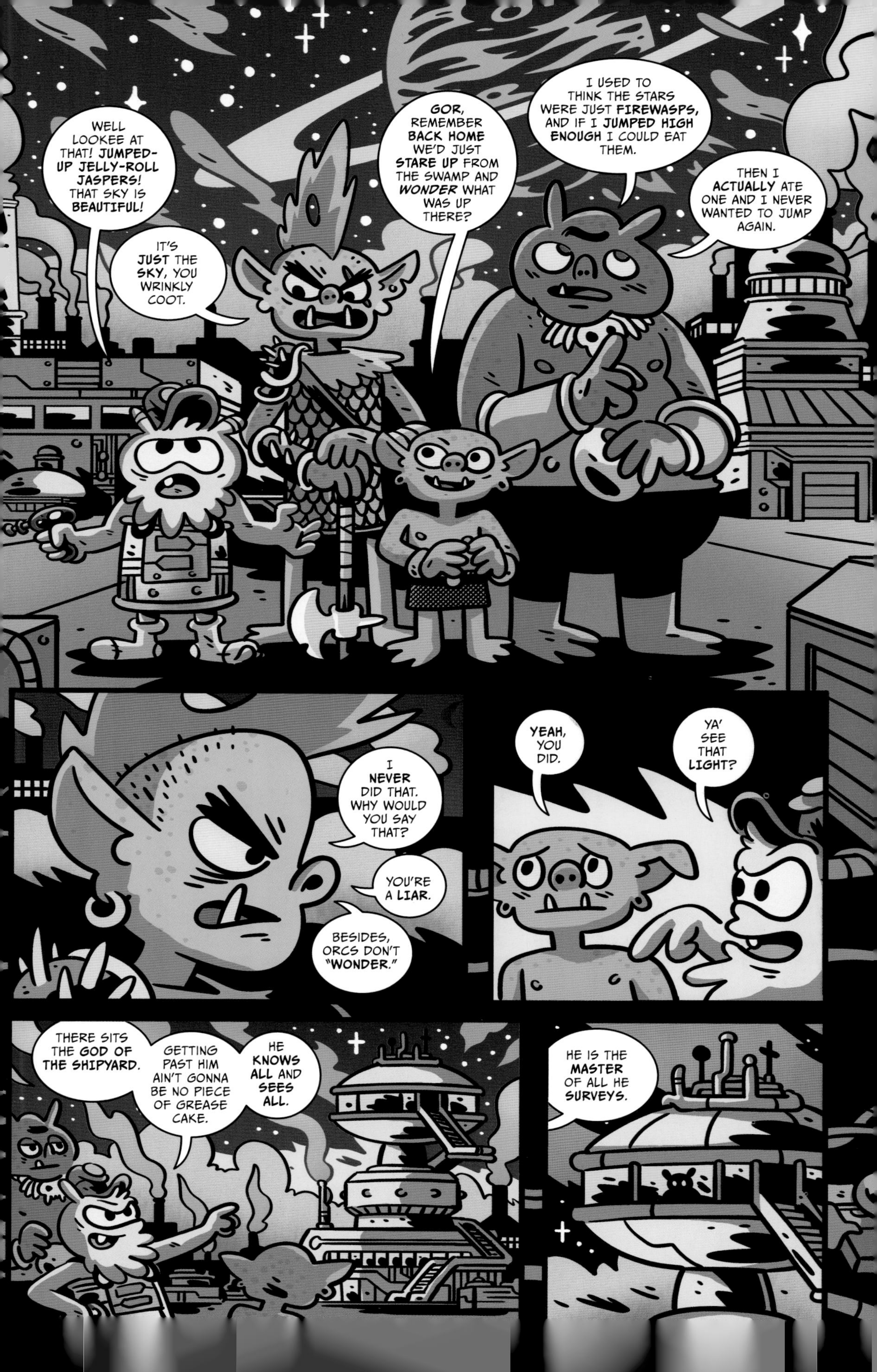

WELL LOOKEE AT THAT! JUMPED-UP JELLY-ROLL JASPERS! THAT SKY IS BEAUTIFUL!
IT'S JUST THE SKY, YOU WRINKLY COOT.
GOR, REMEMBER BACK HOME WE'D JUST STARE UP FROM THE SWAMP AND WONDER WHAT WAS UP THERE?
I USED TO THINK THE STARS WERE JUST FIREWASPS, AND IF I JUMPED HIGH ENOUGH I COULD EAT THEM.
THEN I ACTUALLY ATE ONE AND I NEVER WANTED TO JUMP AGAIN.
I NEVER DID THAT. WHY WOULD YOU SAY THAT?
YOU'RE A LIAR.
BESIDES, ORCS DON'T "WONDER."
YEAH, YOU DID.
YA' SEE THAT LIGHT?
THERE SITS THE GOD OF THE SHIPYARD.
GETTING PAST HIM AIN'T GONNA BE NO PIECE OF GREASE CAKE.
HE KNOWS ALL AND SEES ALL.
HE IS THE MASTER OF ALL HE SURVEYS.

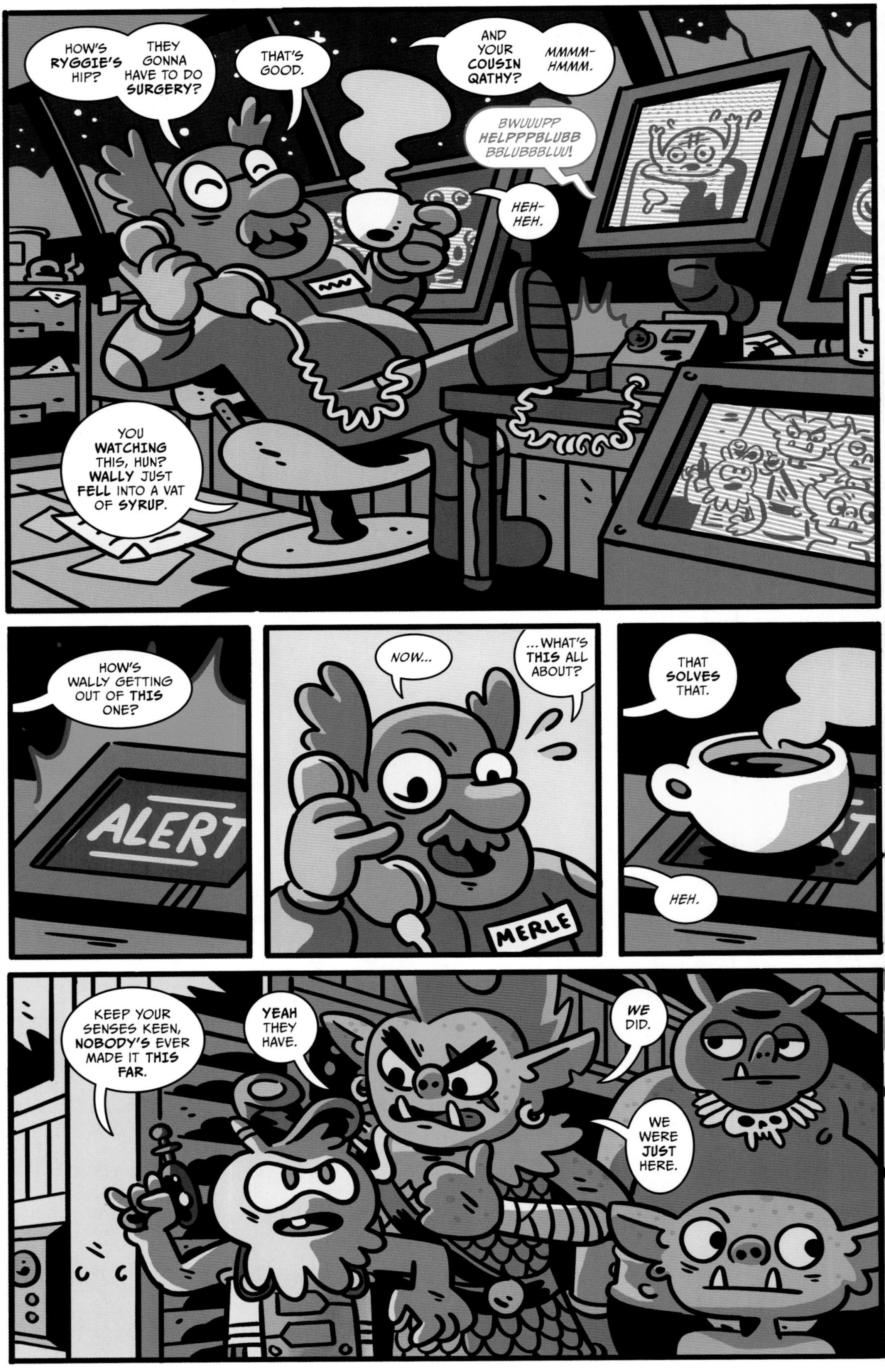
HOW'S RYGGIE'S HIP?
THEY GONNA HAVE TO DO SURGERY?
THAT'S GOOD.
AND YOUR COUSIN QATHY?
MMMM-HMMM.
BWUUUPP HELPPPBLUBB BBLUBBBLUU!
HEH-HEH.
YOU WATCHING THIS, HUN? WALLY JUST FELL INTO A VAT OF SYRUP.
HOW'S WALLY GETTING OUT OF THIS ONE?
ALERT
NOW...
...WHAT'S THIS ALL ABOUT?
MERLE
THAT SOLVES THAT.
HEH.
KEEP YOUR SENSES KEEN, NOBODY'S EVER MADE IT THIS FAR.
YEAH THEY HAVE.
WE DID.
WE WERE JUST HERE.

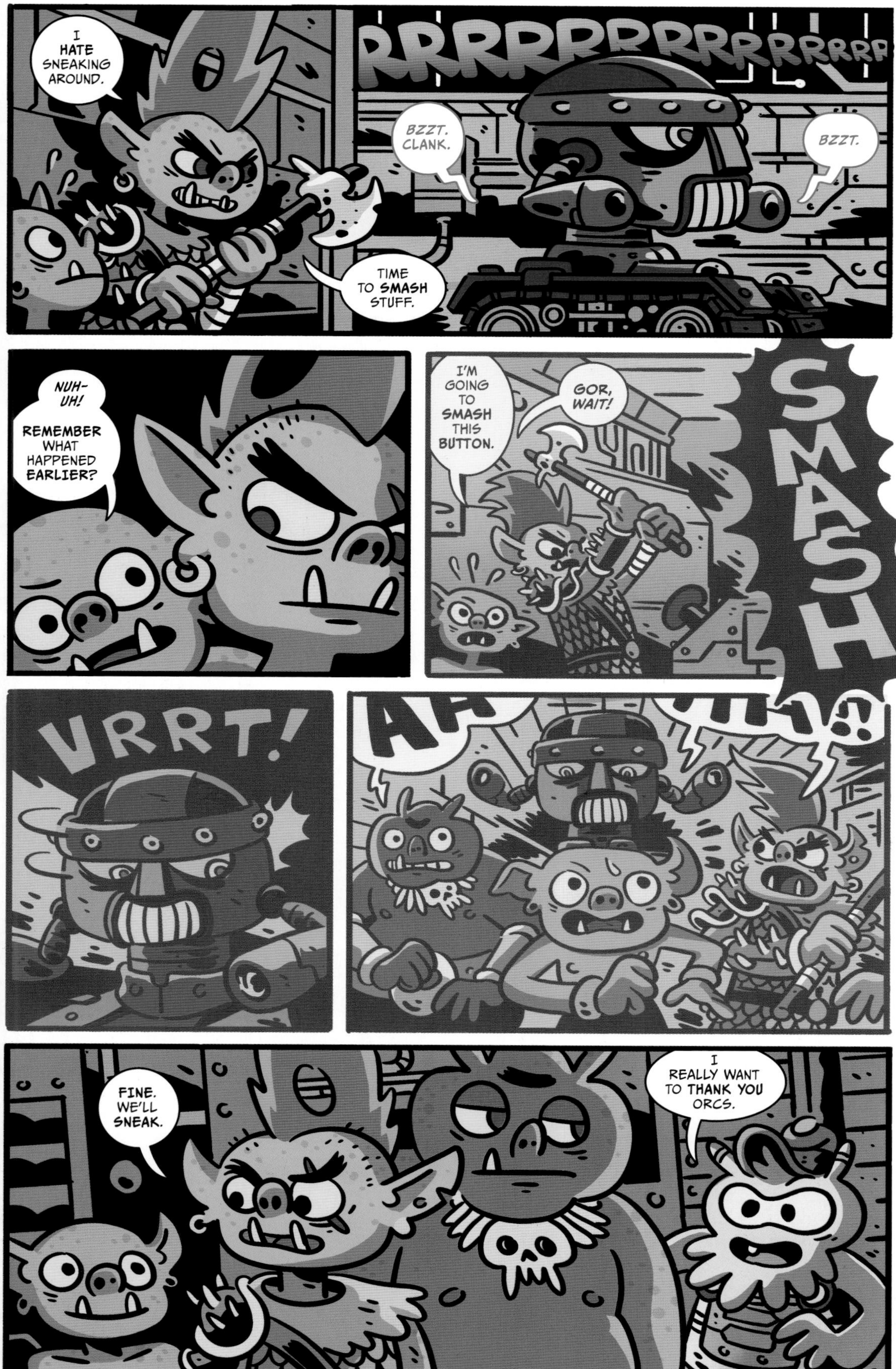

I HATE SNEAKING AROUND.
RRRRRRRRRRRRRRR
BZZT. CLANK.
BZZT.
TIME TO SMASH STUFF.
NUH-UH!
REMEMBER WHAT HAPPENED EARLIER?
I'M GOING TO SMASH THIS BUTTON.
GOR, WAIT!
SMASH
VRRT!
FINE. WE'LL SNEAK.
I REALLY WANT TO THANK YOU ORCS.

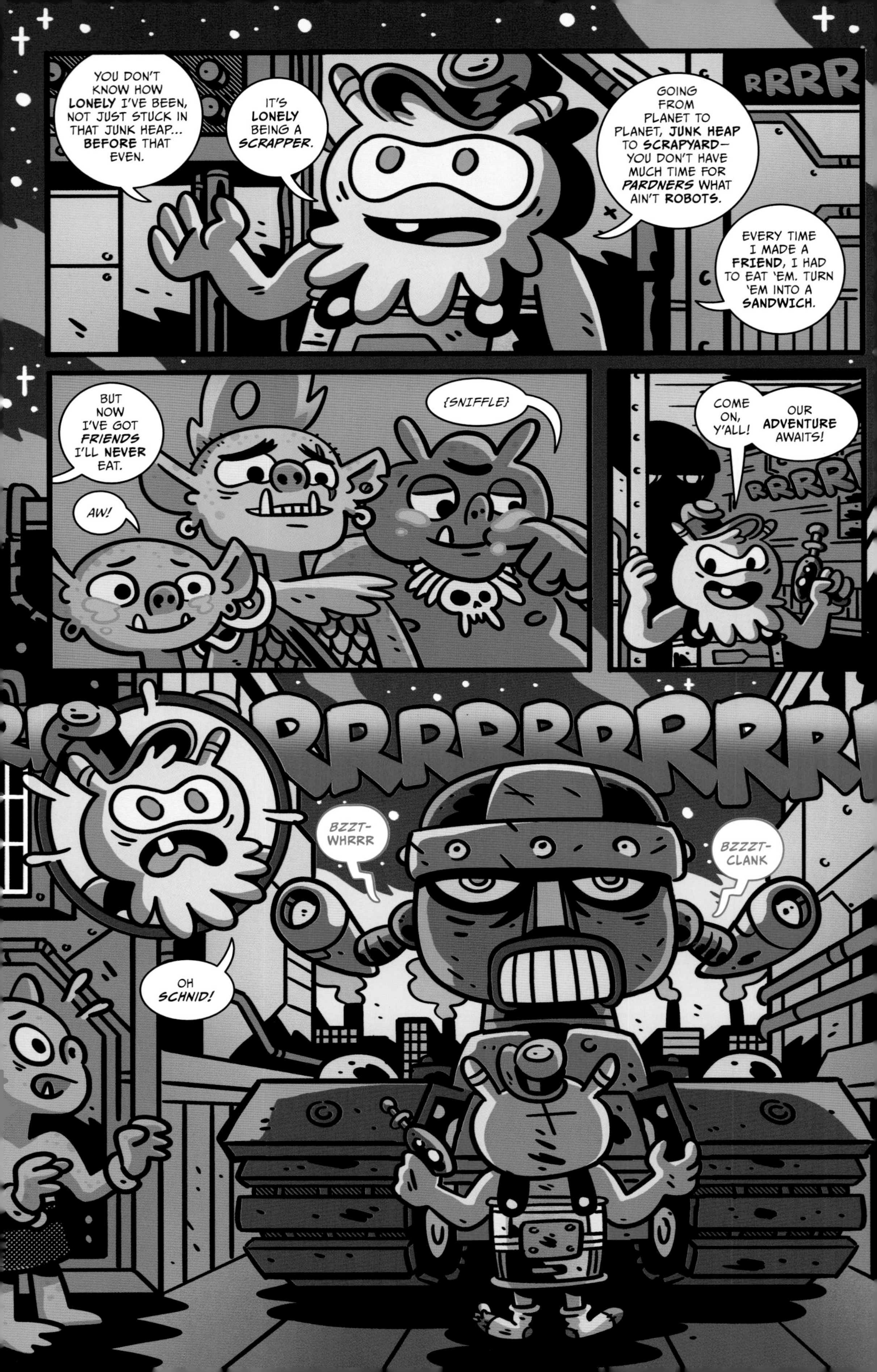

RRRR
YOU DON'T KNOW HOW LONELY I'VE BEEN, NOT JUST STUCK IN THAT JUNK HEAP... BEFORE THAT EVEN.
IT'S LONELY BEING A SCRAPPER.
GOING FROM PLANET TO PLANET, JUNK HEAP TO SCRAPYARD— YOU DON'T HAVE MUCH TIME FOR PARDNERS WHAT AIN'T ROBOTS.
EVERY TIME I MADE A FRIEND, I HAD TO EAT 'EM. TURN 'EM INTO A SANDWICH.
BUT NOW I'VE GOT FRIENDS I'LL NEVER EAT.
{SNIFFLE}
AW!
COME ON, Y'ALL!
OUR ADVENTURE AWAITS!
RRRR
RRRRRRRRR
BZZT-WHRRR
BZZZT-CLANK
OH SCHNID!

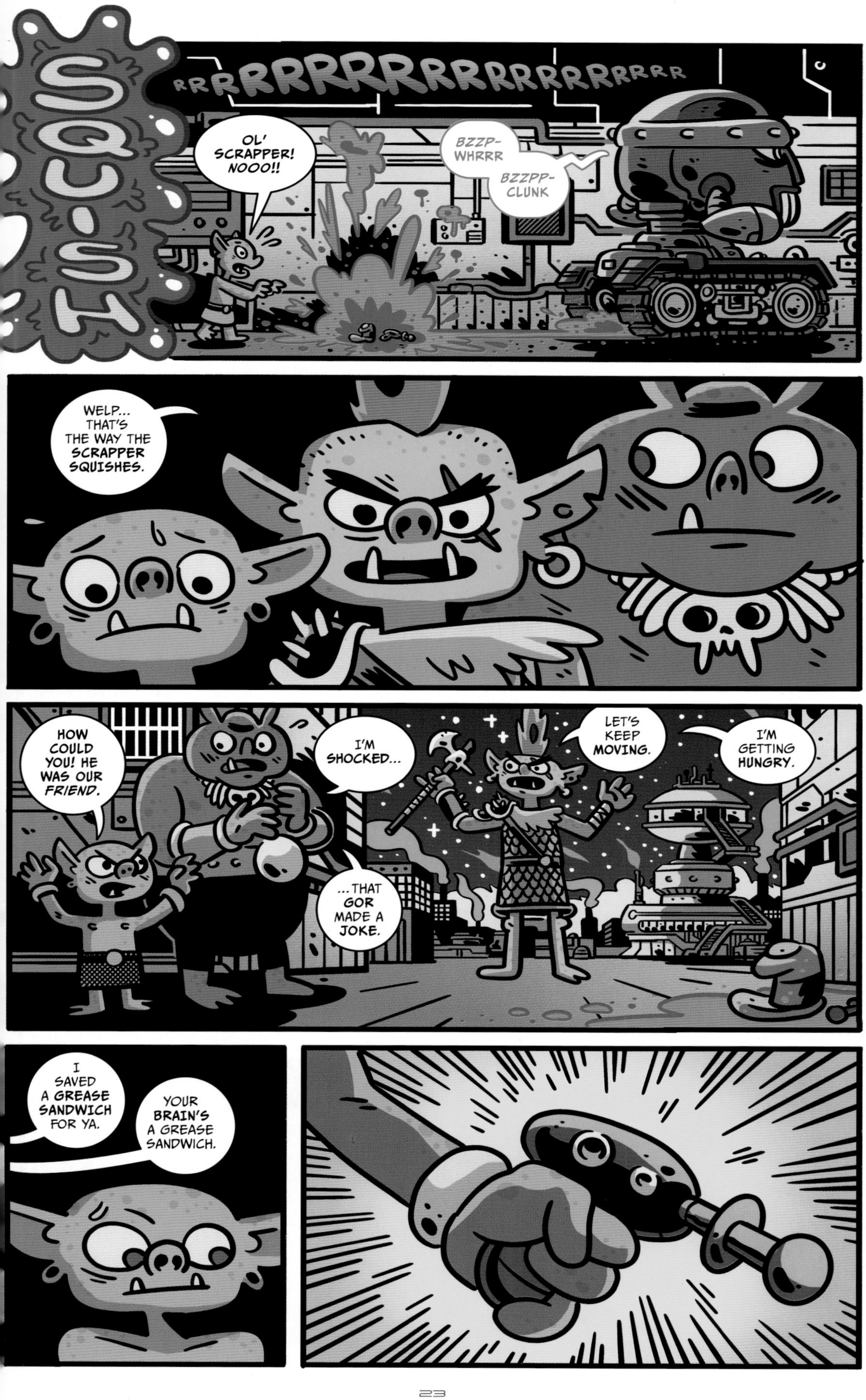
SQU-SH
RRRRRRRRRRRRRRRRRRRRRR
OL' SCRAPPER! NOOO!!
BZZP-WHRRR
BZZPP-CLUNK
WELP... THAT'S THE WAY THE SCRAPPER SQUISHES.
HOW COULD YOU! HE WAS OUR FRIEND.
I'M SHOCKED...
...THAT GOR MADE A JOKE.
LET'S KEEP MOVING.
I'M GETTING HUNGRY.
I SAVED A GREASE SANDWICH FOR YA.
YOUR BRAIN'S A GREASE SANDWICH.

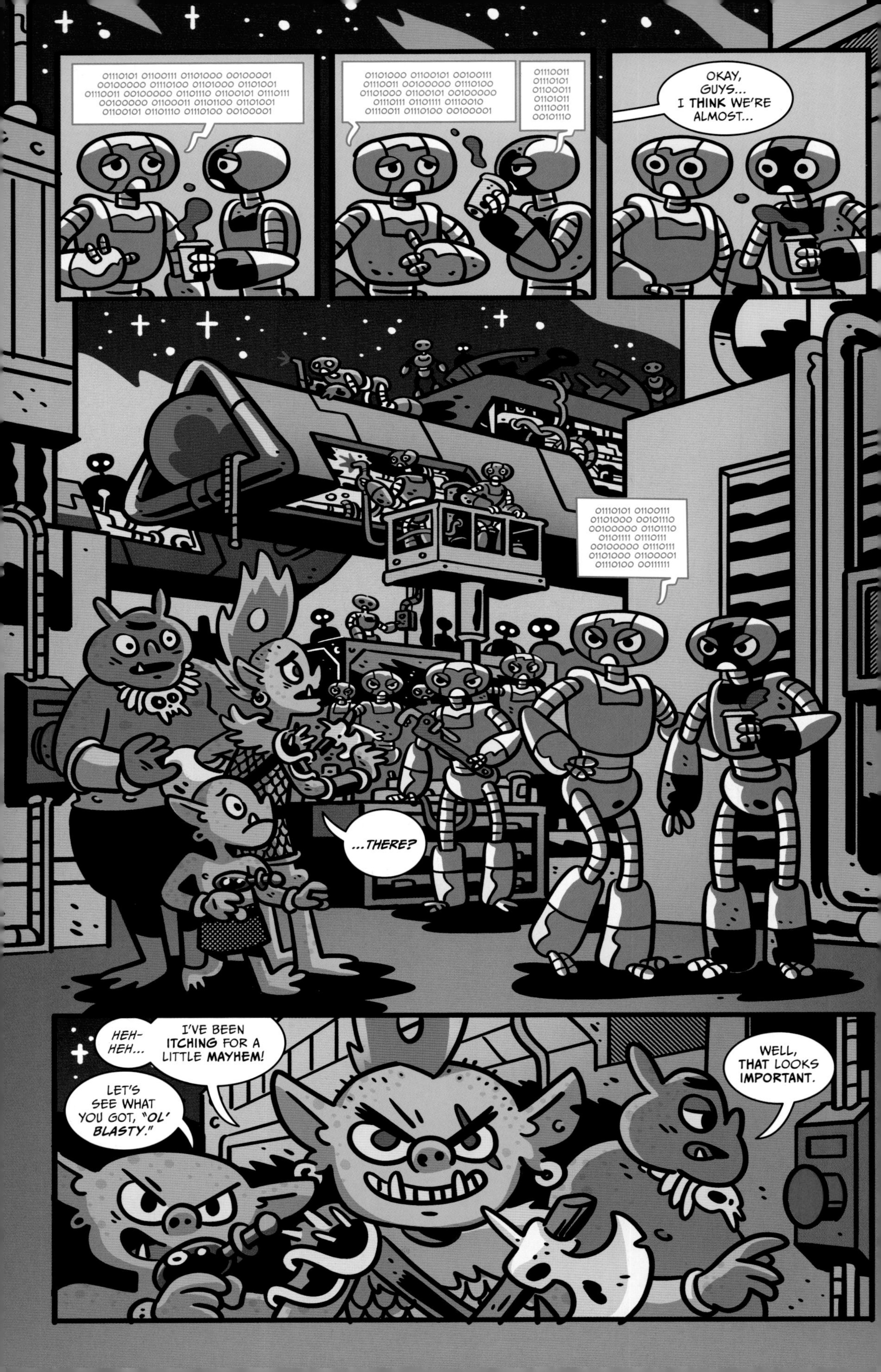
01110101 01100111 01101000 00100001 00100000 01110100 01101000 01101001 01110011 00100000 01101110 01100101 01110111 00100000 01100011 01101100 01101001 01100101 01101110 01110100 00100001
01101000 01100101 00100111 01110011 00100000 01110100 01101000 01100101 00100000 01110111 01101111 01110010 01110011 01110100 00100001
01110011 01110101 01100011 01101011 01110011 00101110
OKAY, GUYS... I THINK WE'RE ALMOST...
01110101 01100111 01101000 00101110 00100000 01101110 01101111 01110111 00100000 01110111 01101000 01100001 01110100 00111111
...THERE?
HEH-HEH...
I'VE BEEN ITCHING FOR A LITTLE MAYHEM!
LET'S SEE WHAT YOU GOT, "OL' BLASTY."
WELL, THAT LOOKS IMPORTANT.

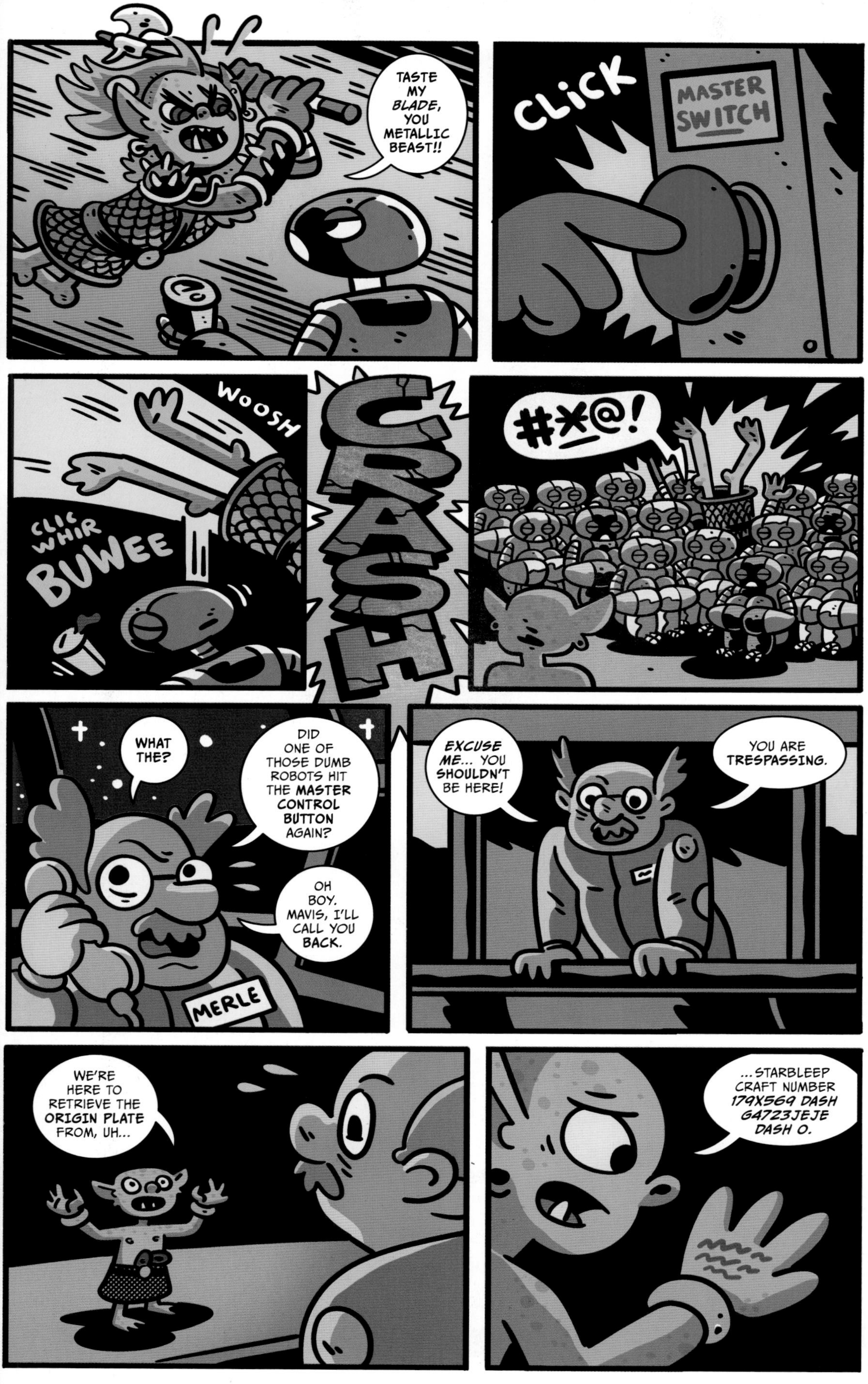
TASTE MY BLADE, YOU METALLIC BEAST!!
CLICK
MASTER SWITCH
WOOSH
CLIC WHIR BUWEE
CRASH
#*@!
WHAT THE?
DID ONE OF THOSE DUMB ROBOTS HIT THE MASTER CONTROL BUTTON AGAIN?
OH BOY. MAVIS, I'LL CALL YOU BACK.
MERLE
EXCUSE ME... YOU SHOULDN'T BE HERE!
YOU ARE TRESPASSING.
WE'RE HERE TO RETRIEVE THE ORIGIN PLATE FROM, UH...
...STARBLEEP CRAFT NUMBER 179X569 DASH G4723JEJE DASH O.

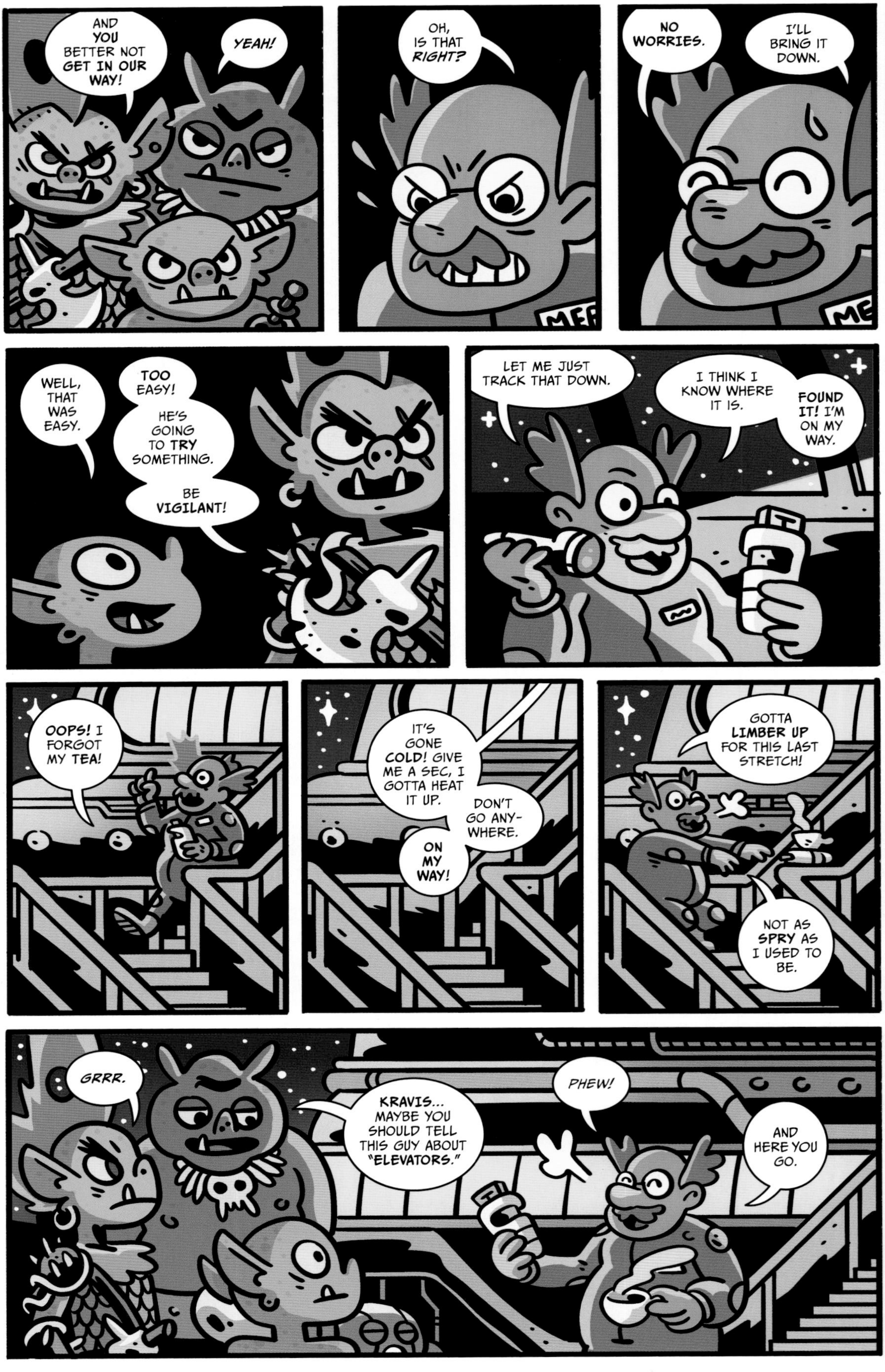
AND YOU BETTER NOT GET IN OUR WAY!
YEAH!
OH, IS THAT RIGHT?
NO WORRIES.
I'LL BRING IT DOWN.
WELL, THAT WAS EASY.
TOO EASY!
HE'S GOING TO TRY SOMETHING.
BE VIGILANT!
LET ME JUST TRACK THAT DOWN.
I THINK I KNOW WHERE IT IS.
FOUND IT! I'M ON MY WAY.
OOPS! I FORGOT MY TEA!
IT'S GONE COLD! GIVE ME A SEC, I GOTTA HEAT IT UP.
DON'T GO ANY-WHERE.
ON MY WAY!
GOTTA LIMBER UP FOR THIS LAST STRETCH!
NOT AS SPRY AS I USED TO BE.
GRRR.
KRAVIS... MAYBE YOU SHOULD TELL THIS GUY ABOUT "ELEVATORS."
PHEW!
AND HERE YOU GO.

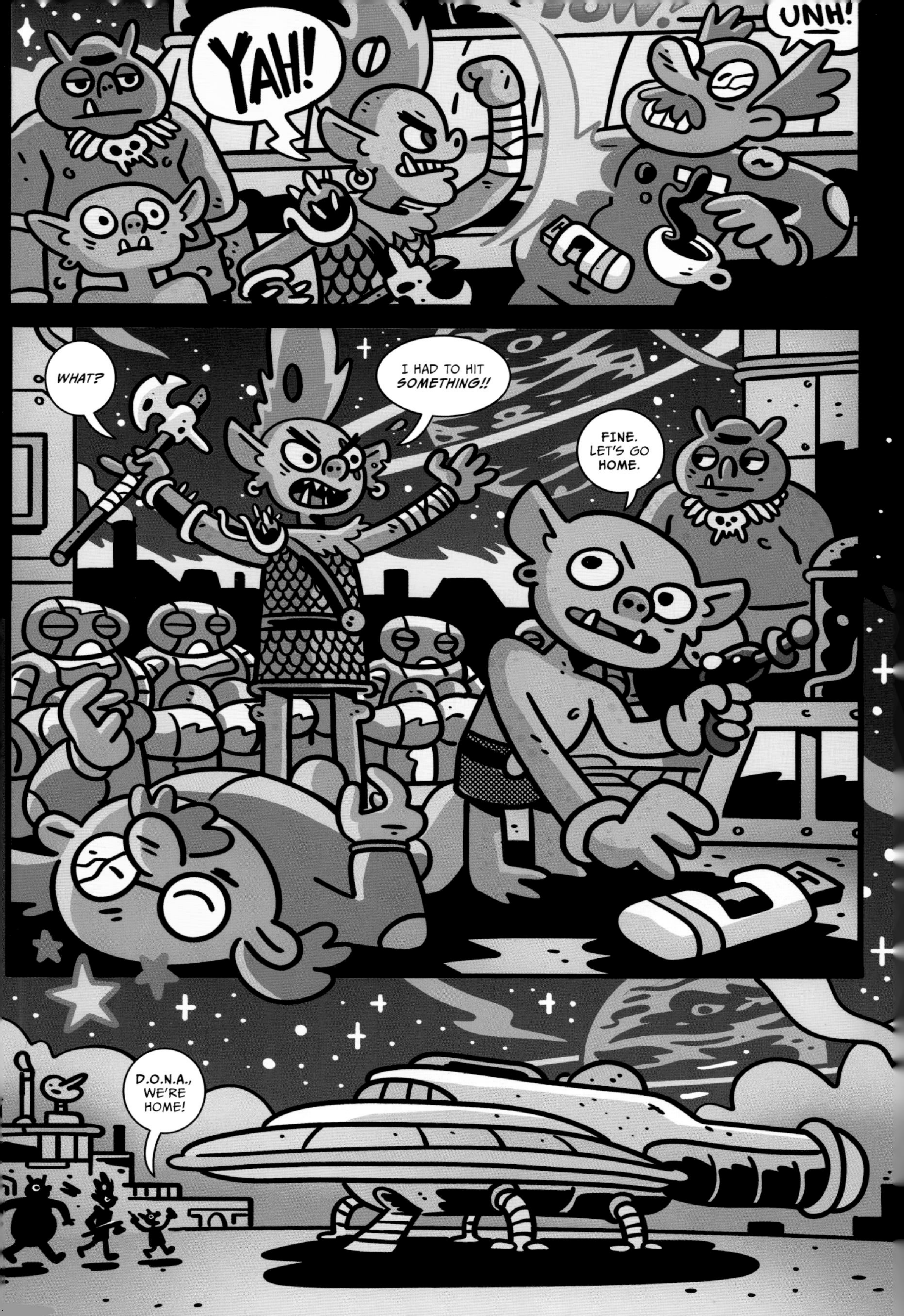
YAH!
UNH!
WHAT?
I HAD TO HIT SOMETHING!!
FINE. LET'S GO HOME.
D.O.N.A., WE'RE HOME!

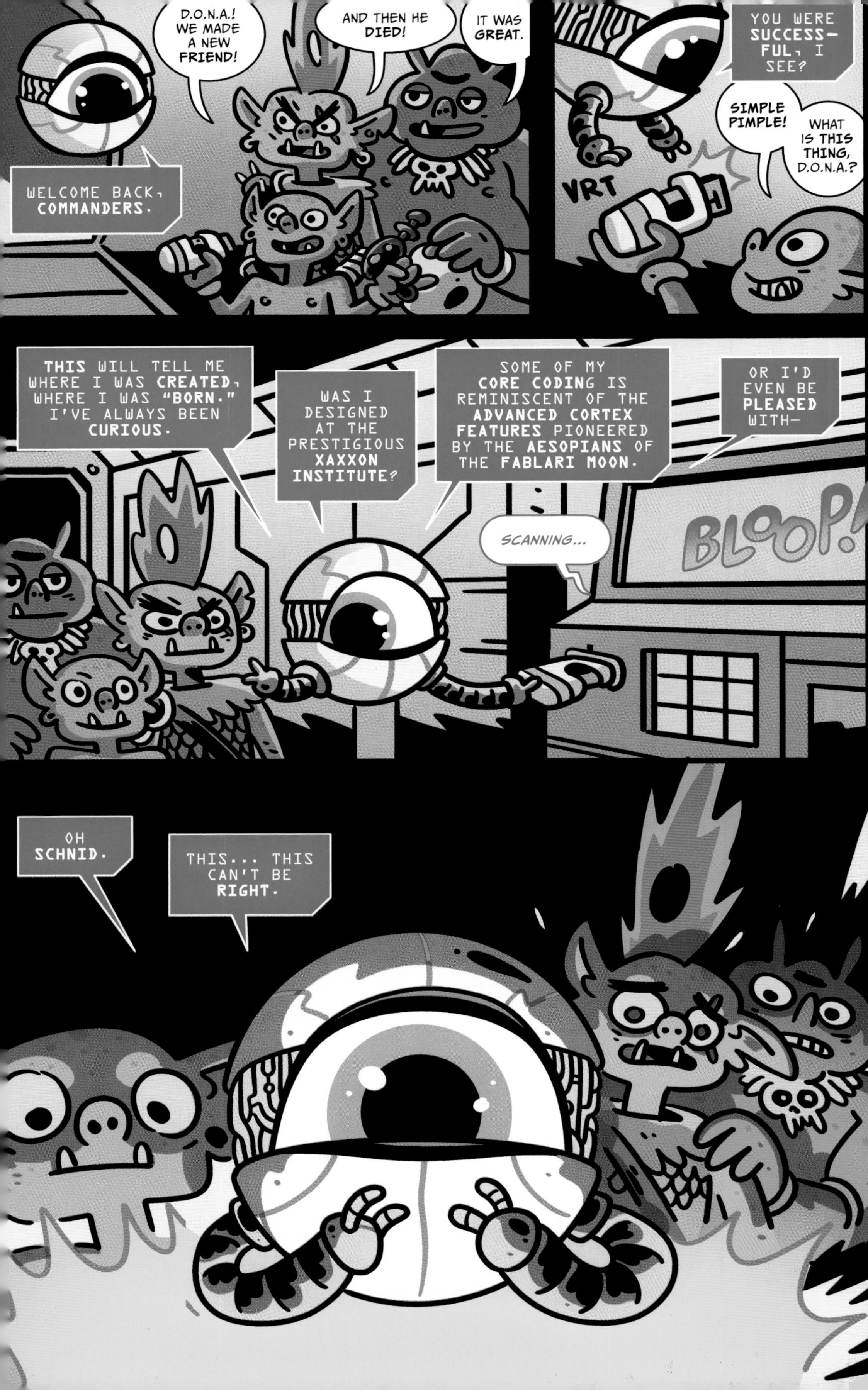
D.O.N.A.! WE MADE A NEW FRIEND!
AND THEN HE DIED!
IT WAS GREAT.
WELCOME BACK, COMMANDERS.
YOU WERE SUCCESS-FUL, I SEE?
SIMPLE PIMPLE!
WHAT IS THIS THING, D.O.N.A.?
VRT
THIS WILL TELL ME WHERE I WAS CREATED, WHERE I WAS "BORN." I'VE ALWAYS BEEN CURIOUS.
WAS I DESIGNED AT THE PRESTIGIOUS XAXXON INSTITUTE?
SOME OF MY CORE CODING IS REMINISCENT OF THE ADVANCED CORTEX FEATURES PIONEERED BY THE AESOPIANS OF THE FABLARI MOON.
OR I'D EVEN BE PLEASED WITH—
SCANNING...
BLOOP!
OH SCHNID.
THIS... THIS CAN'T BE RIGHT.

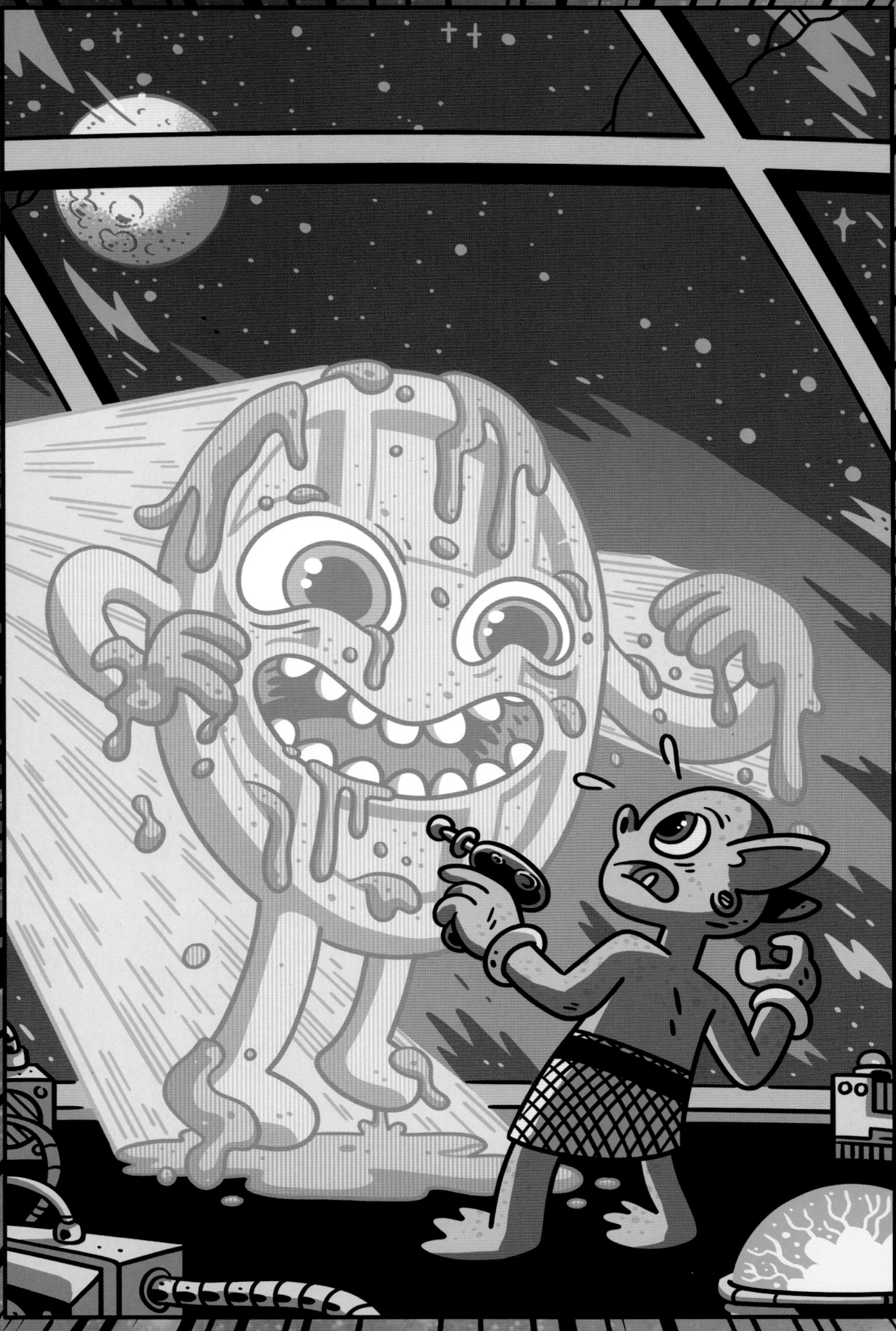

CHAPTER SIX

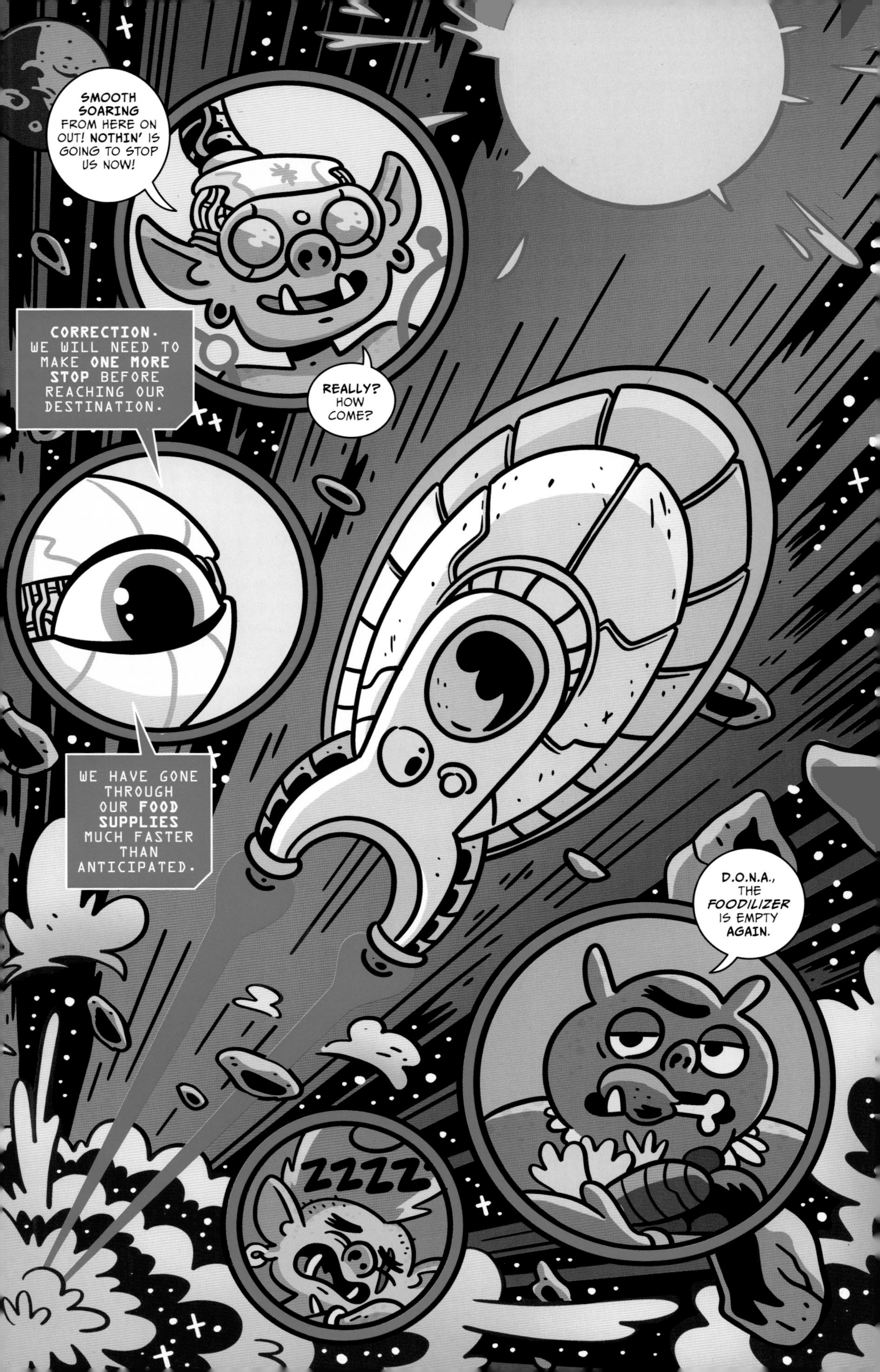
SMOOTH SOARING FROM HERE ON OUT! NOTHIN' IS GOING TO STOP US NOW!
CORRECTION. WE WILL NEED TO MAKE ONE MORE STOP BEFORE REACHING OUR DESTINATION.
REALLY? HOW COME?
WE HAVE GONE THROUGH OUR FOOD SUPPLIES MUCH FASTER THAN ANTICIPATED.
D.O.N.A., THE FOODILIZER IS EMPTY AGAIN.
ZZZZ

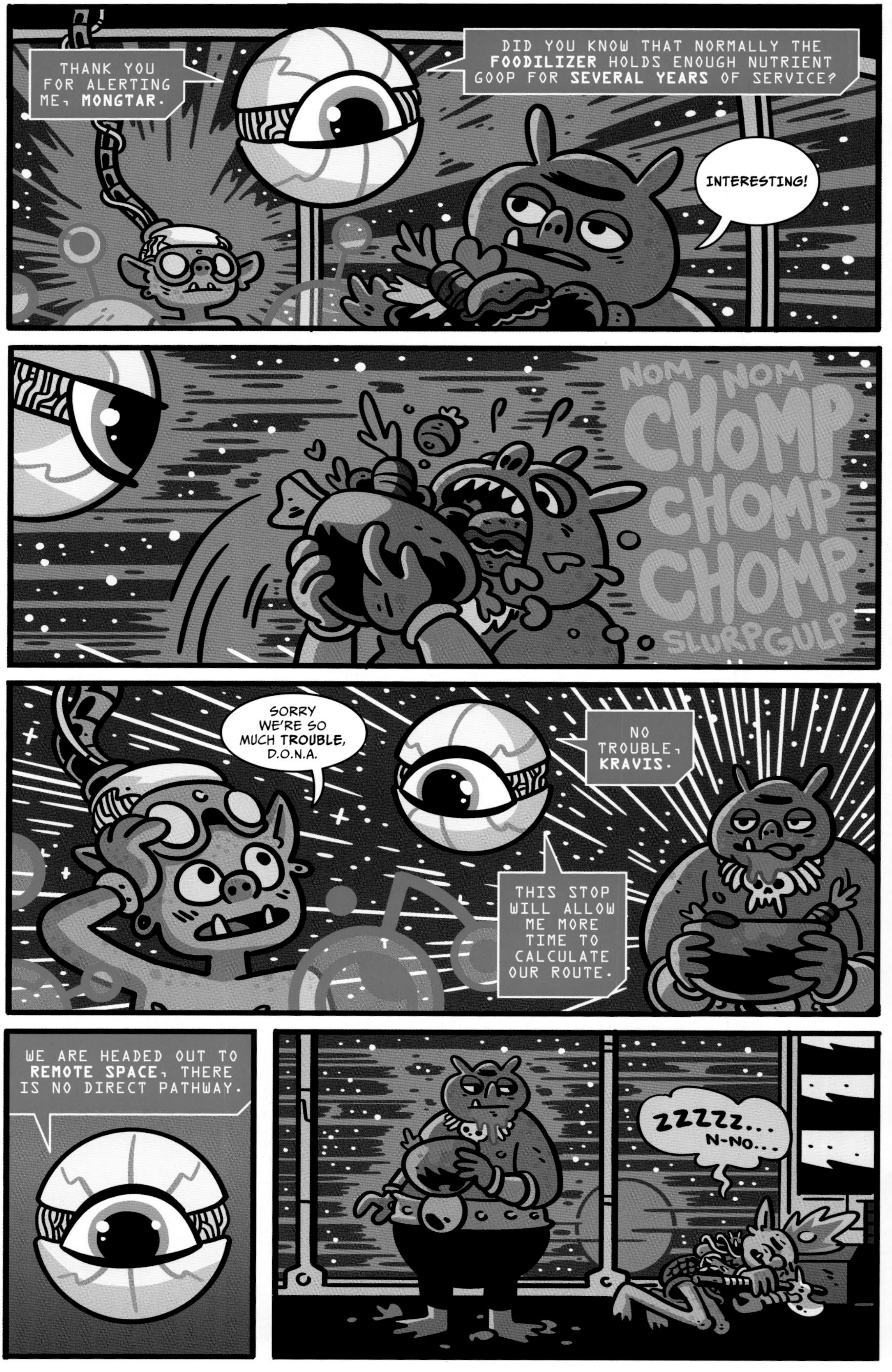
THANK YOU FOR ALERTING ME, MONGTAR.
DID YOU KNOW THAT NORMALLY THE FOODILIZER HOLDS ENOUGH NUTRIENT GOOP FOR SEVERAL YEARS OF SERVICE?
INTERESTING!
NOM NOM
CHOMP CHOMP CHOMP
SLURPGULP
SORRY WE'RE SO MUCH TROUBLE, D.O.N.A.
NO TROUBLE, KRAVIS.
THIS STOP WILL ALLOW ME MORE TIME TO CALCULATE OUR ROUTE.
WE ARE HEADED OUT TO REMOTE SPACE, THERE IS NO DIRECT PATHWAY.
ZZZZZ... N-NO...

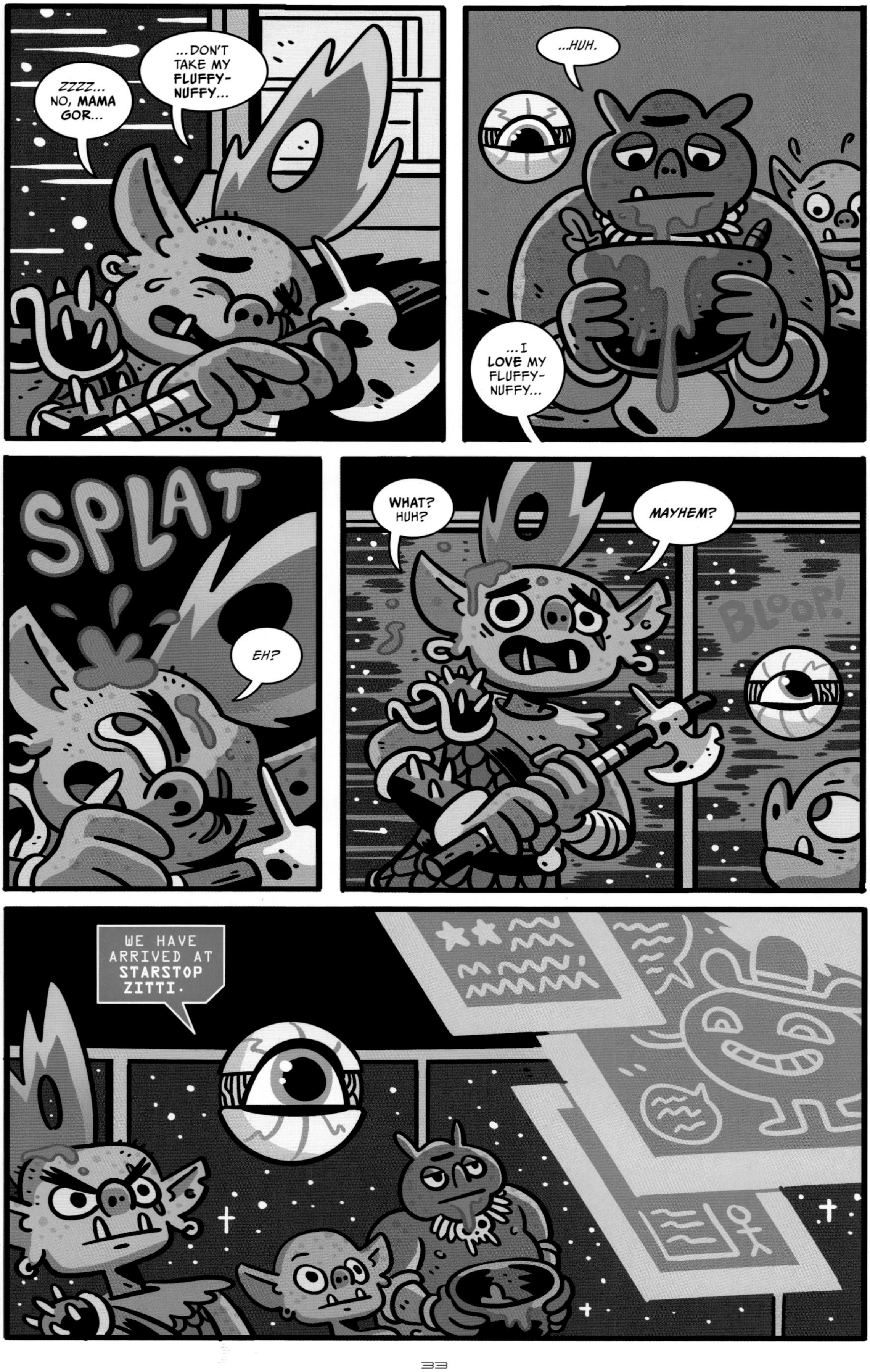
ZZZZ... NO, MAMA GOR...
...DON'T TAKE MY FLUFFY-NUFFY...
...HUH.
...I LOVE MY FLUFFY-NUFFY...
SPLAT
EH?
WHAT? HUH?
MAYHEM?
BLOOP!
WE HAVE ARRIVED AT STARSTOP ZITTI.

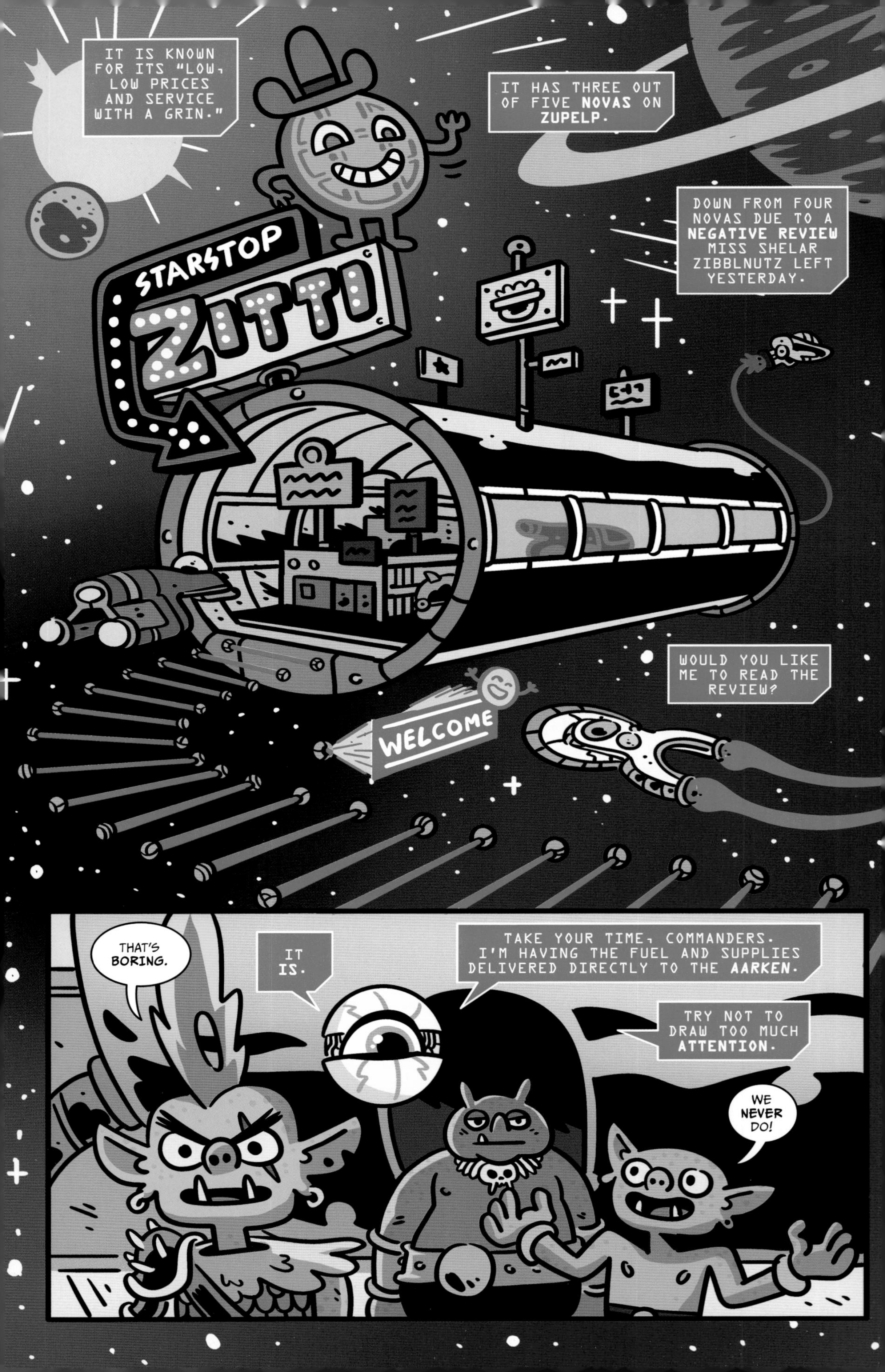
IT IS KNOWN FOR ITS "LOW, LOW PRICES AND SERVICE WITH A GRIN."
IT HAS THREE OUT OF FIVE **NOVAS** ON **ZUPELP**.
DOWN FROM FOUR NOVAS DUE TO A **NEGATIVE REVIEW** MISS SHELAR ZIBBLNUTZ LEFT YESTERDAY.
STARSTOP
ZITTI
WOULD YOU LIKE ME TO READ THE REVIEW?
WELCOME
THAT'S BORING.
IT IS.
TAKE YOUR TIME, COMMANDERS. I'M HAVING THE FUEL AND SUPPLIES DELIVERED DIRECTLY TO THE **AARKEN**.
TRY NOT TO DRAW TOO MUCH **ATTENTION**.
WE NEVER DO!

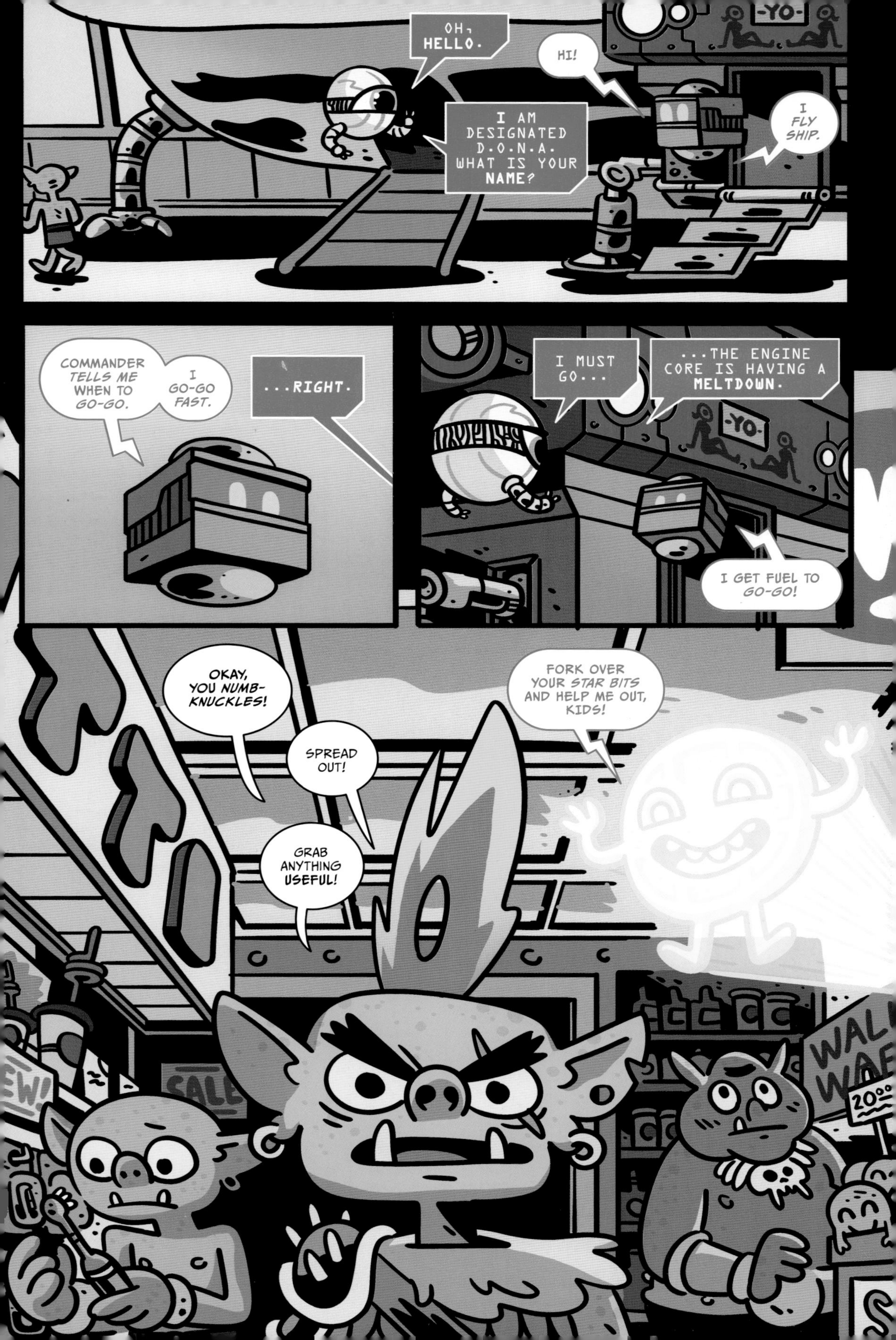

OH, HELLO.
HI!
I AM DESIGNATED D.O.N.A. WHAT IS YOUR NAME?
I FLY SHIP.
COMMANDER TELLS ME WHEN TO GO-GO.
I GO-GO FAST.
...RIGHT.
I MUST GO...
...THE ENGINE CORE IS HAVING A MELTDOWN.
I GET FUEL TO GO-GO!
OKAY, YOU NUMB-KNUCKLES!
SPREAD OUT!
GRAB ANYTHING USEFUL!
FORK OVER YOUR STAR BITS AND HELP ME OUT, KIDS!
-YO-
SALE

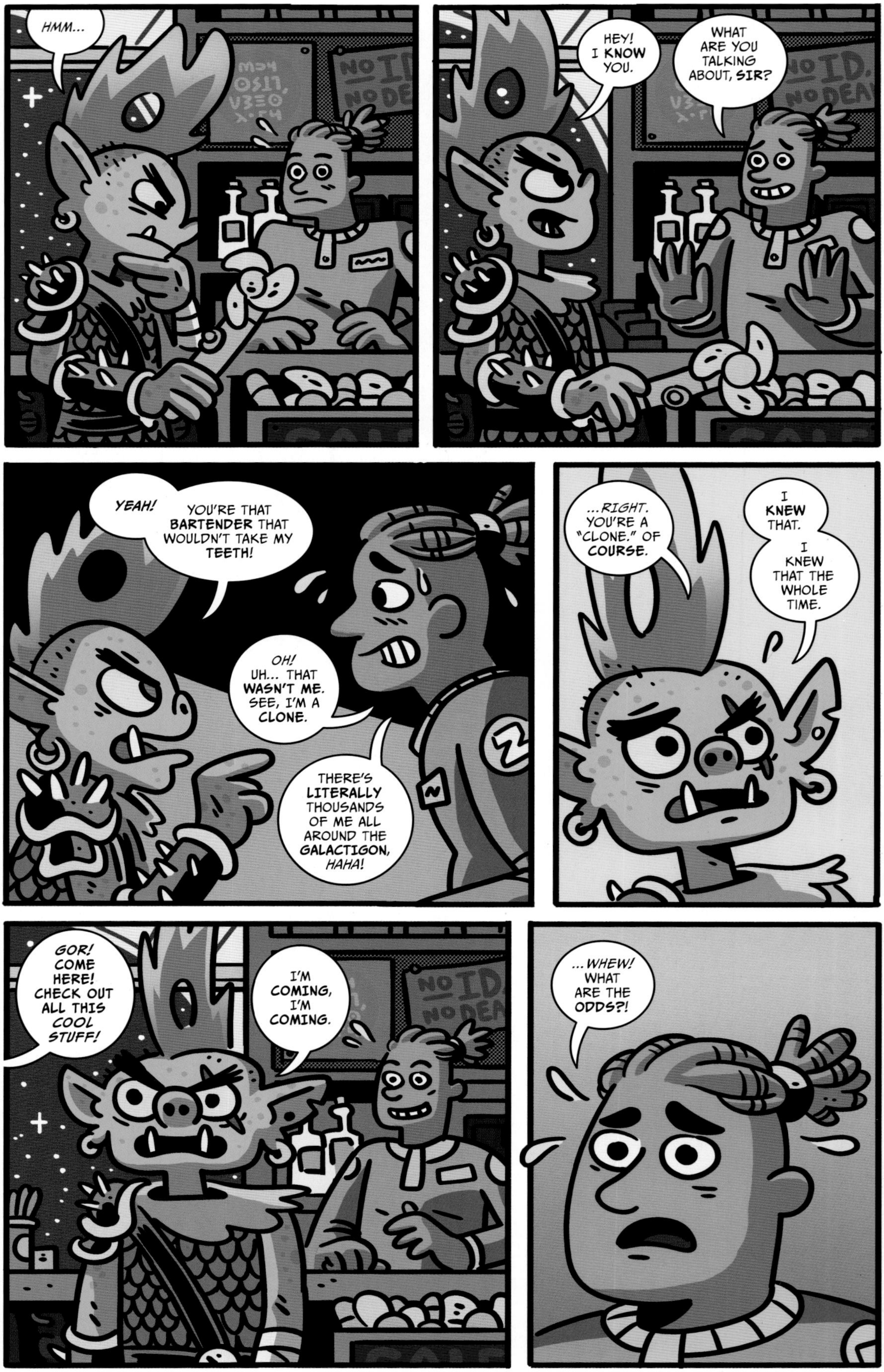
HMM...
NO ID, NO DEAL
HEY! I KNOW YOU.
WHAT ARE YOU TALKING ABOUT, SIR?
YEAH!
YOU'RE THAT BARTENDER THAT WOULDN'T TAKE MY TEETH!
OH! UH... THAT WASN'T ME. SEE, I'M A CLONE.
THERE'S LITERALLY THOUSANDS OF ME ALL AROUND THE GALACTIGON, HAHA!
...RIGHT. YOU'RE A "CLONE." OF COURSE.
I KNEW THAT.
I KNEW THAT THE WHOLE TIME.
GOR! COME HERE! CHECK OUT ALL THIS COOL STUFF!
I'M COMING, I'M COMING.
...WHEW! WHAT ARE THE ODDS?!

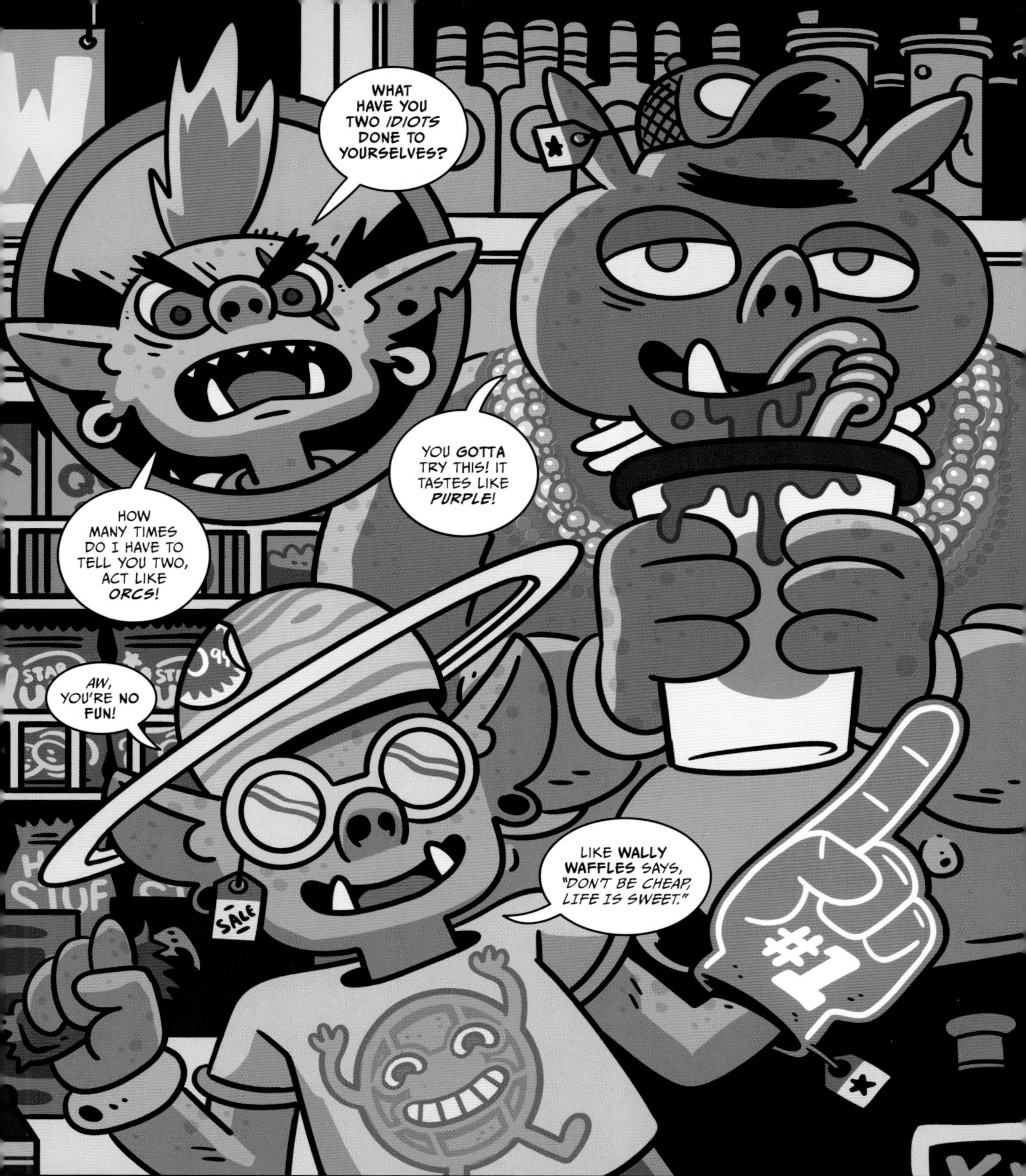
WHAT HAVE YOU TWO *IDIOTS* DONE TO YOURSELVES?
HOW MANY TIMES DO I HAVE TO TELL YOU TWO, ACT LIKE *ORCS!*
YOU **GOTTA** TRY THIS! IT TASTES LIKE *PURPLE!*
AW, YOU'RE **NO FUN!**
LIKE **WALLY WAFFLES** SAYS, *"DON'T BE CHEAP, LIFE IS SWEET."*
SALE
#1
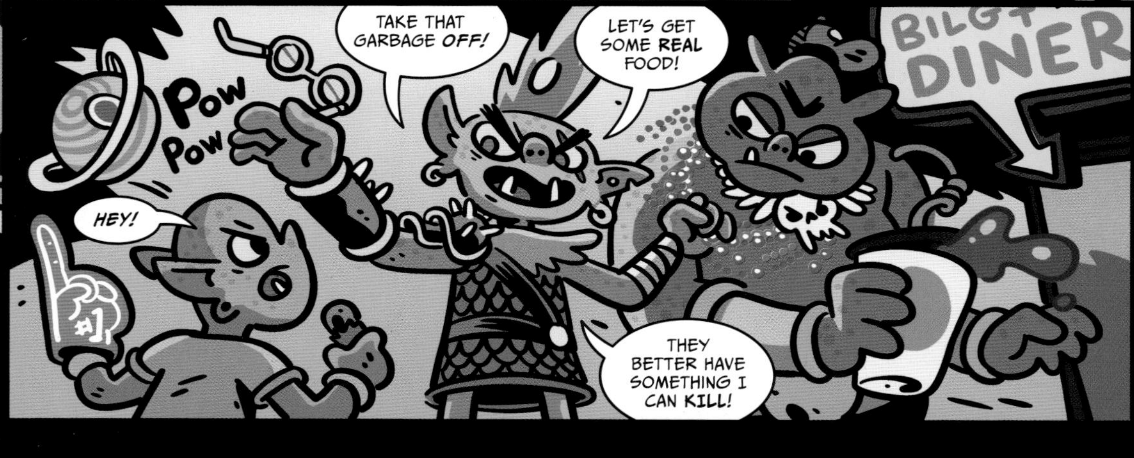
POW
POW
HEY!
TAKE THAT GARBAGE *OFF!*
LET'S GET SOME **REAL** FOOD!
THEY BETTER HAVE SOMETHING I CAN **KILL!**
DINER

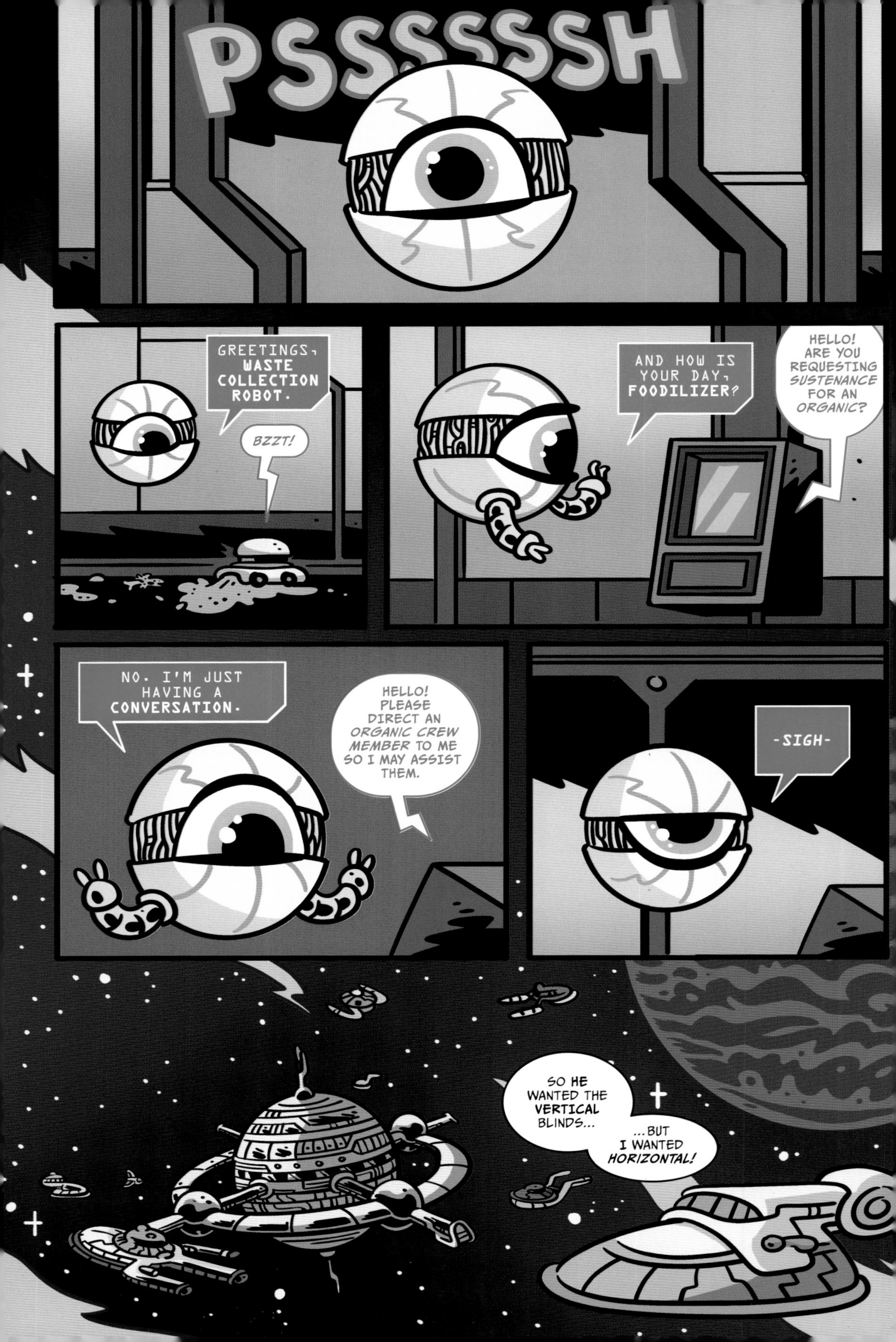
PSSSSSSH
GREETINGS, WASTE COLLECTION ROBOT.
BZZT!
AND HOW IS YOUR DAY, FOODILIZER?
HELLO! ARE YOU REQUESTING SUSTENANCE FOR AN ORGANIC?
NO. I'M JUST HAVING A CONVERSATION.
HELLO! PLEASE DIRECT AN ORGANIC CREW MEMBER TO ME SO I MAY ASSIST THEM.
-SIGH-
SO HE WANTED THE VERTICAL BLINDS...
...BUT I WANTED HORIZONTAL!

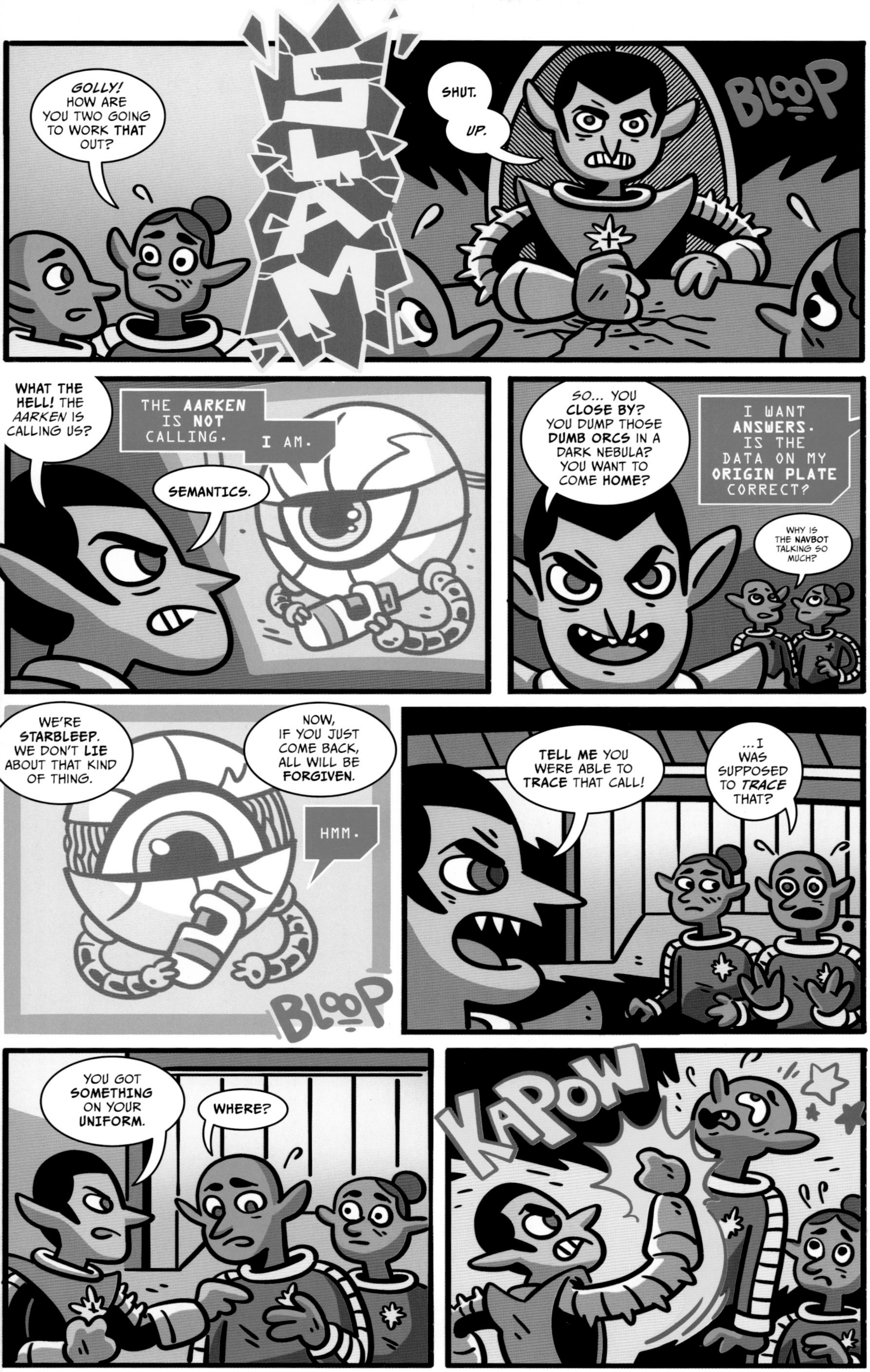

GOLLY! HOW ARE YOU TWO GOING TO WORK THAT OUT?
SLAM
SHUT.
UP.
BLOOP
WHAT THE HELL! THE AARKEN IS CALLING US?
THE AARKEN IS NOT CALLING.
I AM.
SEMANTICS.
SO... YOU CLOSE BY? YOU DUMP THOSE DUMB ORCS IN A DARK NEBULA? YOU WANT TO COME HOME?
I WANT ANSWERS. IS THE DATA ON MY ORIGIN PLATE CORRECT?
WHY IS THE NAVBOT TALKING SO MUCH?
WE'RE STARBLEEP. WE DON'T LIE ABOUT THAT KIND OF THING.
NOW, IF YOU JUST COME BACK, ALL WILL BE FORGIVEN.
HMM.
BLOOP
TELL ME YOU WERE ABLE TO TRACE THAT CALL!
...I WAS SUPPOSED TO TRACE THAT?
YOU GOT SOMETHING ON YOUR UNIFORM.
WHERE?
KAPOW

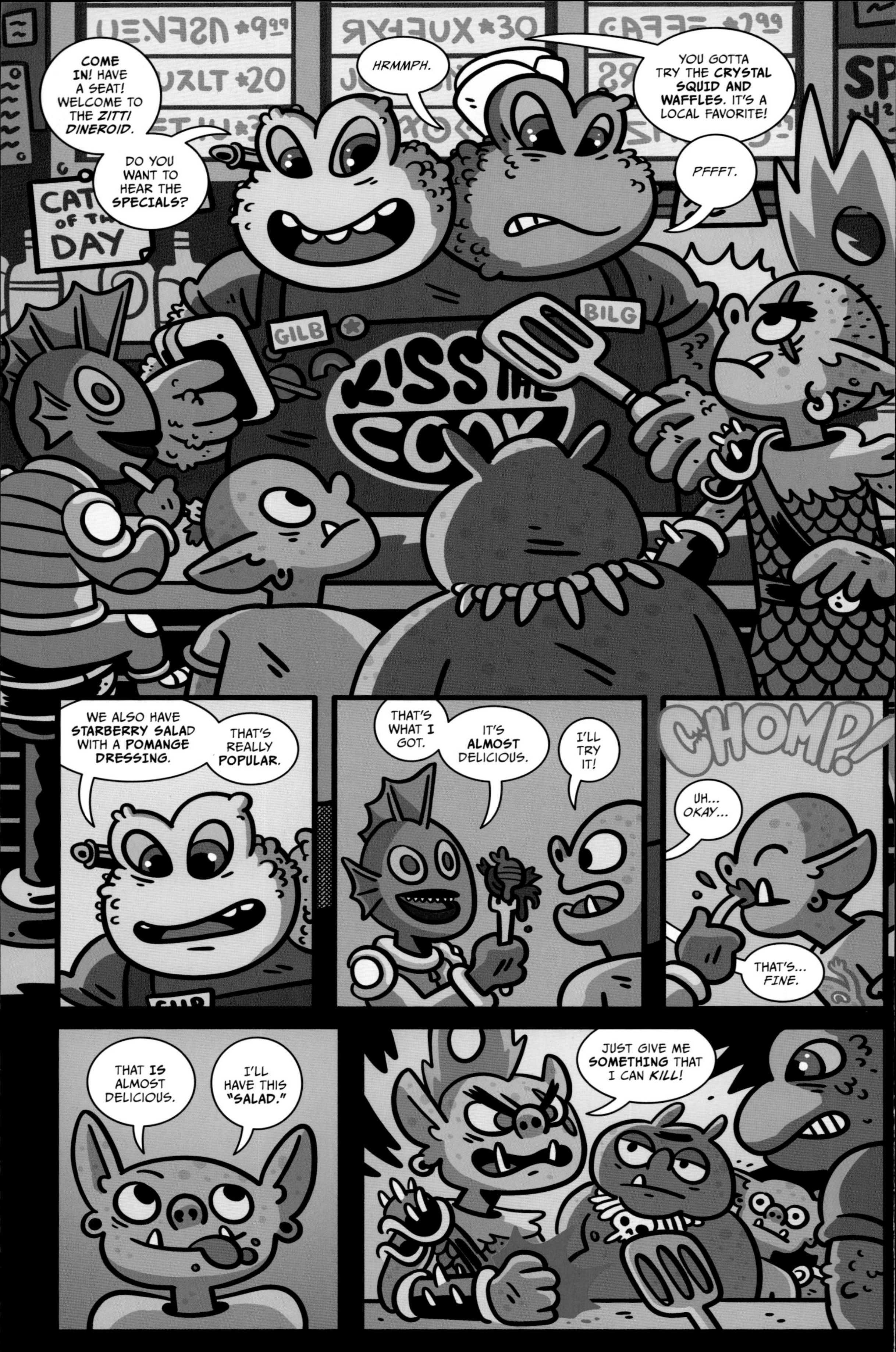

COME IN! HAVE A SEAT! WELCOME TO THE *ZITTI DINEROID*.
DO YOU WANT TO HEAR THE **SPECIALS**?
HRMMPH.
YOU GOTTA TRY THE **CRYSTAL SQUID AND WAFFLES**. IT'S A LOCAL FAVORITE!
PFFFT.
GILB
BILG
WE ALSO HAVE **STARBERRY SALAD** WITH A **POMANGE DRESSING**.
THAT'S REALLY **POPULAR**.
THAT'S WHAT **I** GOT.
IT'S **ALMOST** DELICIOUS.
I'LL TRY IT!
CHOMP!
UH... OKAY...
THAT'S... *FINE*.
THAT **IS** ALMOST DELICIOUS.
I'LL HAVE THIS **"SALAD."**
JUST GIVE ME **SOMETHING** THAT I CAN *KILL*!

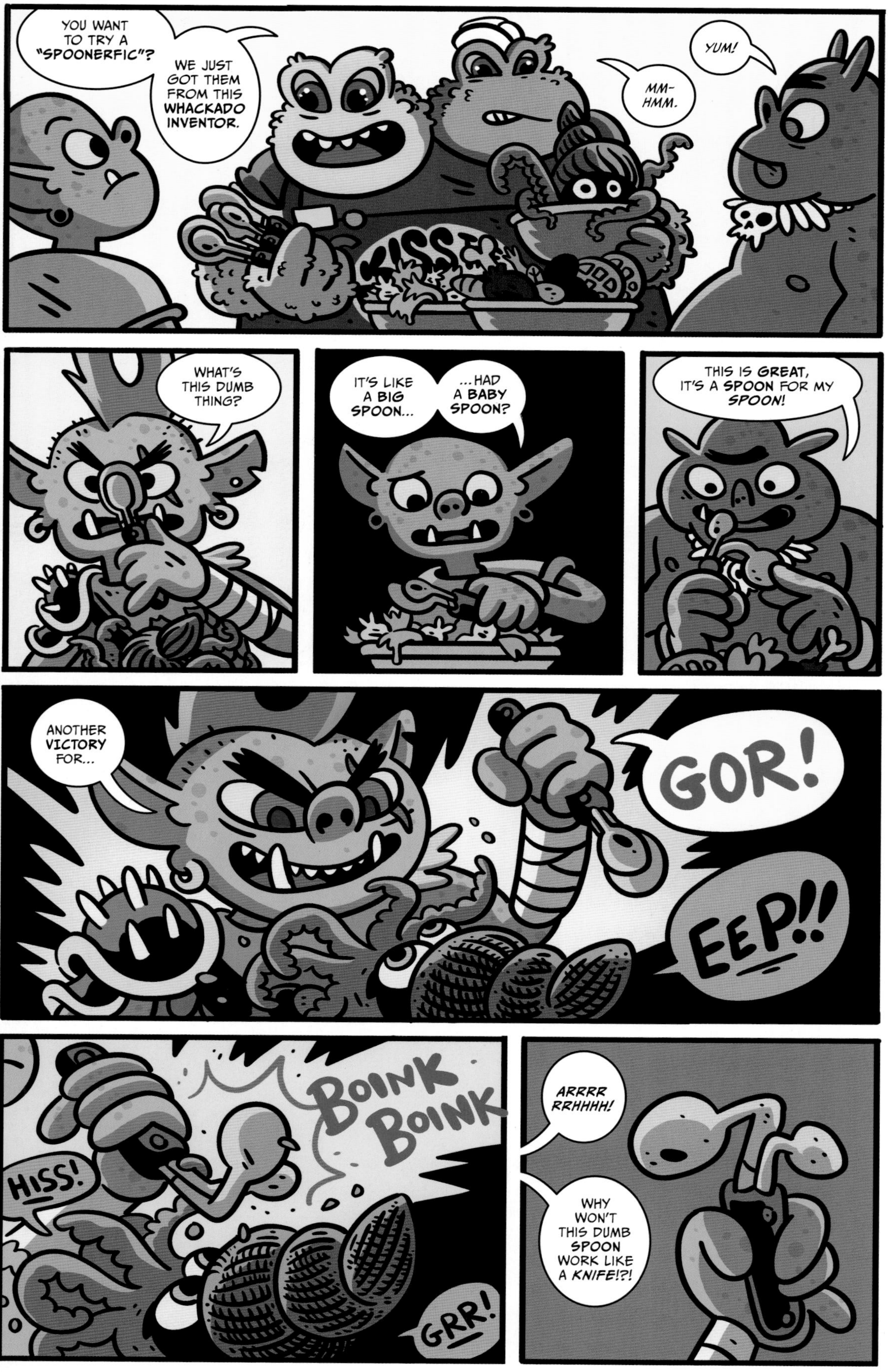

YOU WANT TO TRY A "SPOONERFIC"?
WE JUST GOT THEM FROM THIS WHACKADO INVENTOR.
MM-HMM.
YUM!
WHAT'S THIS DUMB THING?
IT'S LIKE A BIG SPOON...
...HAD A BABY SPOON?
THIS IS GREAT, IT'S A SPOON FOR MY SPOON!
ANOTHER VICTORY FOR...
GOR!
EEP!!
BOINK BOINK
HISS!
GRR!
ARRRR RRHHHH!
WHY WON'T THIS DUMB SPOON WORK LIKE A KNIFE!?!

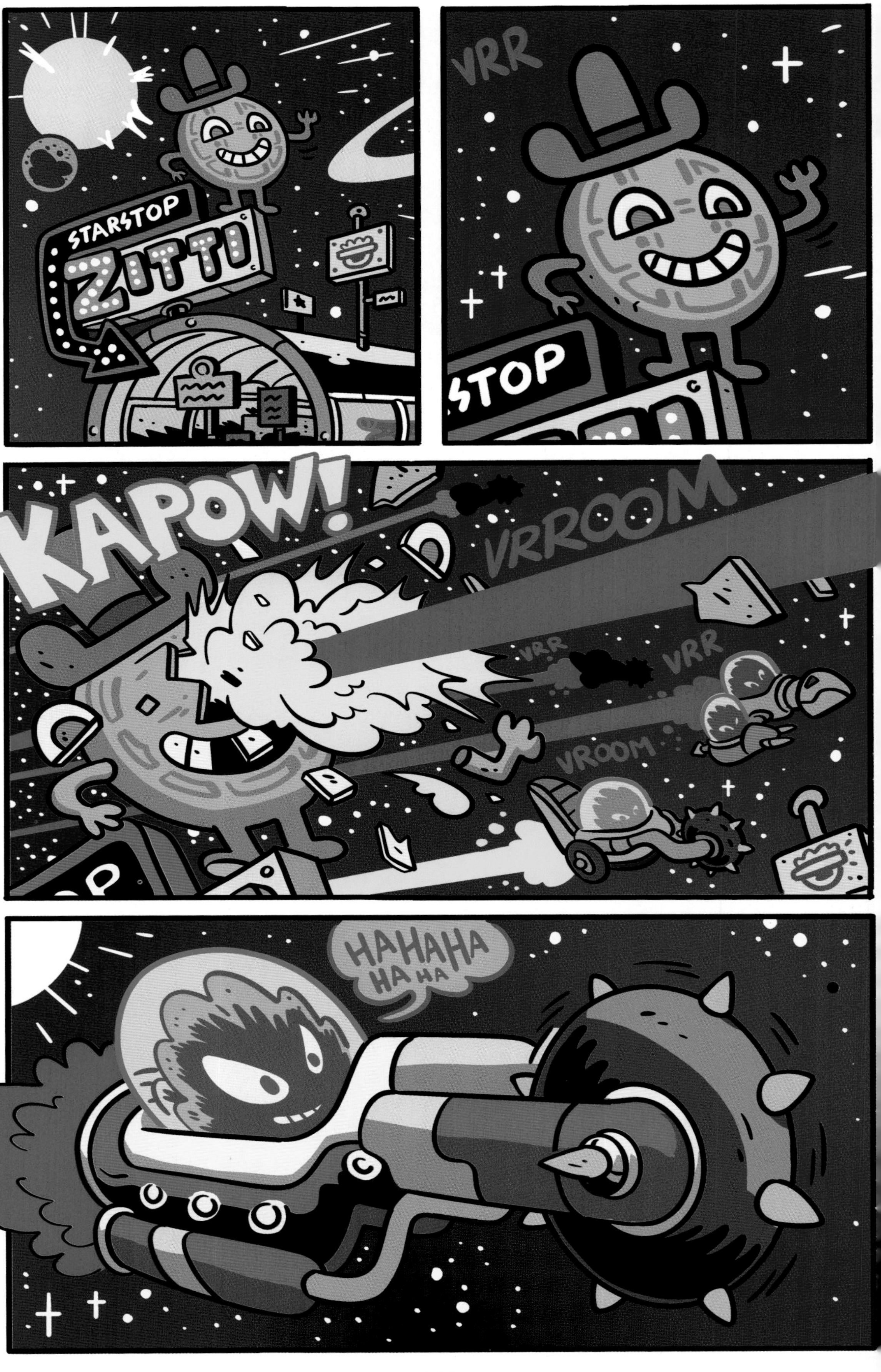
STARSTOP
ZITTI
VRR
STOP
KAPOW!
VRROOM
VRR
VRR
VROOM
HAHAHA
HA HA

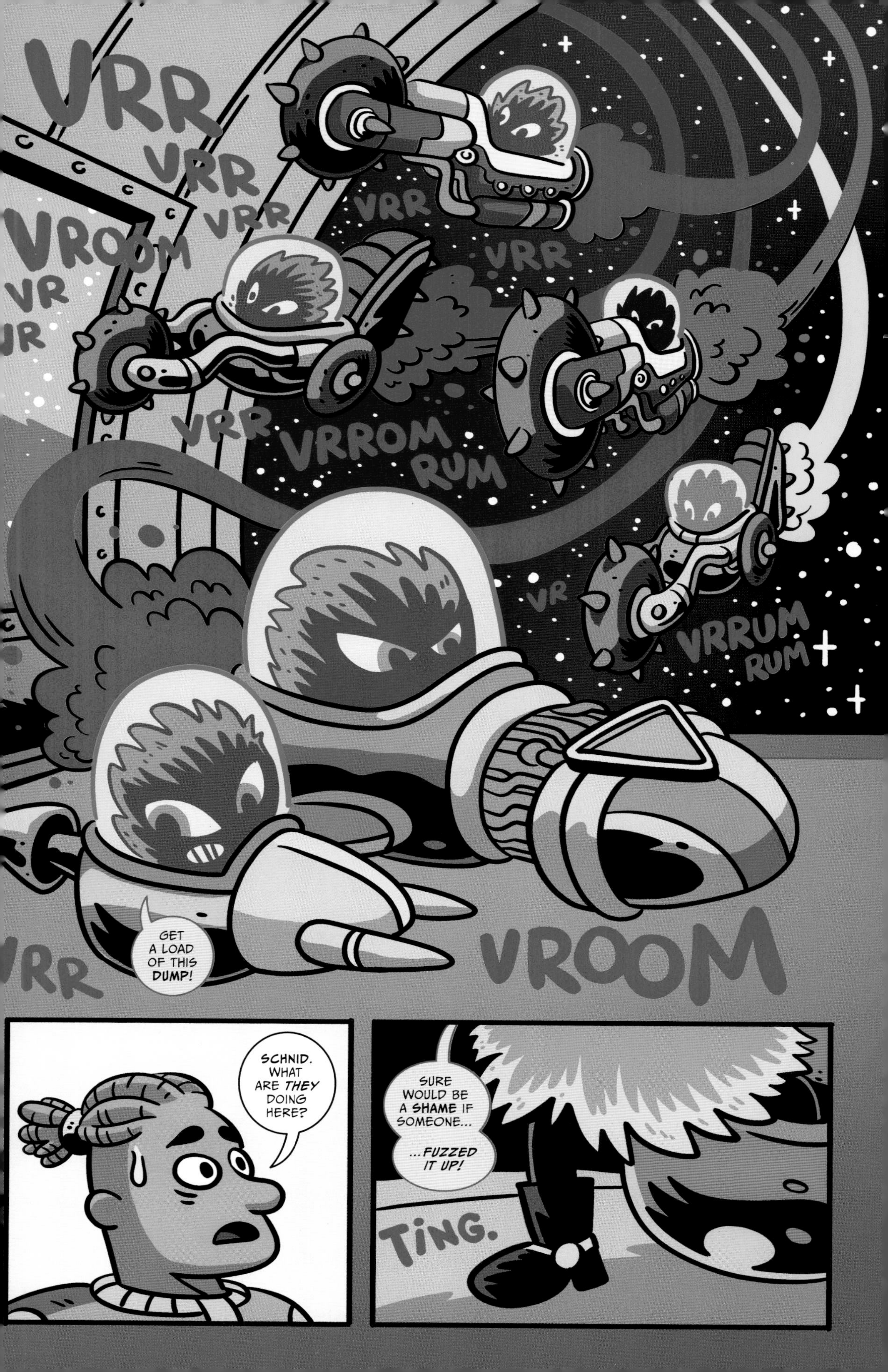
VRR
VRR
VRR
VROOM
VR
VR
VRR
VRR
VRR
VRR
VRROM
RUM
VR
VRRUM
RUM
GET A LOAD OF THIS **DUMP!**
VRR
VROOM
SCHNID. WHAT ARE *THEY* DOING HERE?
SURE WOULD BE A **SHAME** IF SOMEONE...
...*FUZZED IT UP!*
TING.

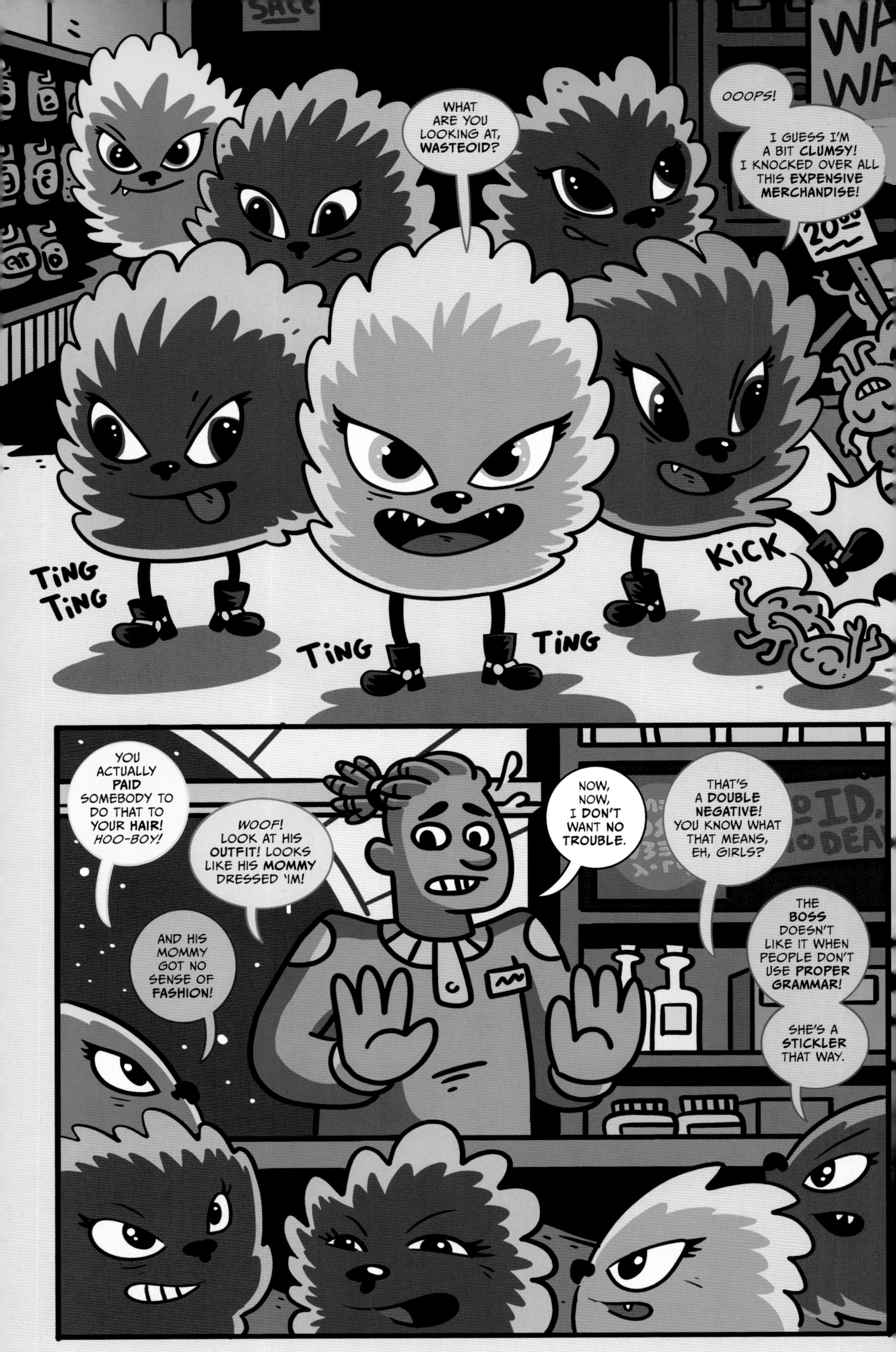

WHAT ARE YOU LOOKING AT, WASTEOID?
OOOPS!
I GUESS I'M A BIT CLUMSY! I KNOCKED OVER ALL THIS EXPENSIVE MERCHANDISE!
TING TING
KICK
TING
TING
YOU ACTUALLY PAID SOMEBODY TO DO THAT TO YOUR HAIR! HOO-BOY!
WOOF! LOOK AT HIS OUTFIT! LOOKS LIKE HIS MOMMY DRESSED 'IM!
AND HIS MOMMY GOT NO SENSE OF FASHION!
NOW, NOW, I DON'T WANT NO TROUBLE.
THAT'S A DOUBLE NEGATIVE! YOU KNOW WHAT THAT MEANS, EH, GIRLS?
THE BOSS DOESN'T LIKE IT WHEN PEOPLE DON'T USE PROPER GRAMMAR!
SHE'S A STICKLER THAT WAY.

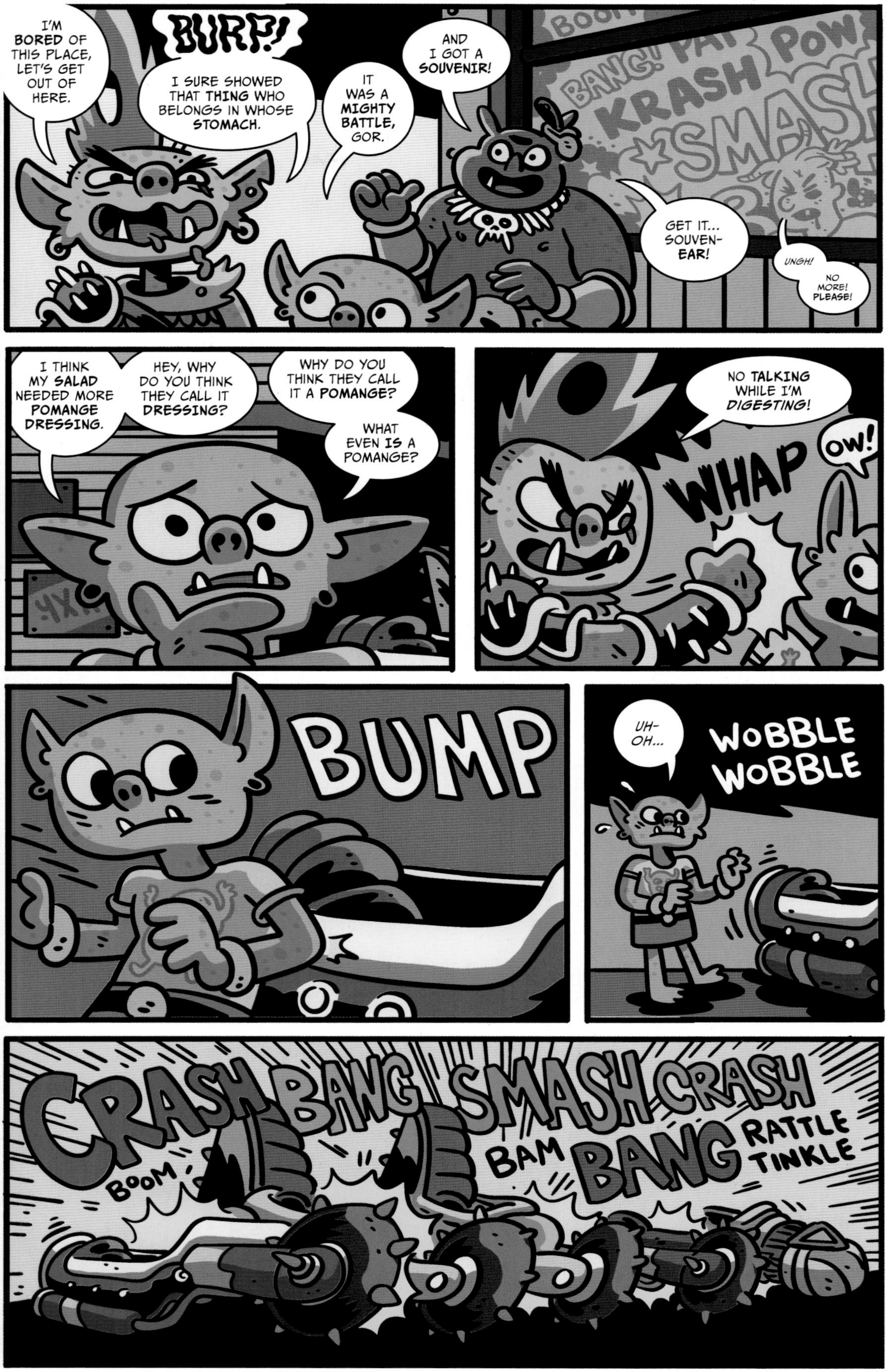
I'M BORED OF THIS PLACE, LET'S GET OUT OF HERE.
BURP!
I SURE SHOWED THAT THING WHO BELONGS IN WHOSE STOMACH.
IT WAS A MIGHTY BATTLE, GOR.
AND I GOT A SOUVENIR!
BOOM BANG! PAT POW KRASH SMASH
GET IT... SOUVEN-EAR!
UNGH!
NO MORE! PLEASE!
I THINK MY SALAD NEEDED MORE POMANGE DRESSING.
HEY, WHY DO YOU THINK THEY CALL IT DRESSING?
WHY DO YOU THINK THEY CALL IT A POMANGE?
WHAT EVEN IS A POMANGE?
NO TALKING WHILE I'M DIGESTING!
WHAP
OW!
BUMP
UH-OH...
WOBBLE WOBBLE
CRASH BANG SMASH CRASH
BOOM
BAM BANG RATTLE TINKLE

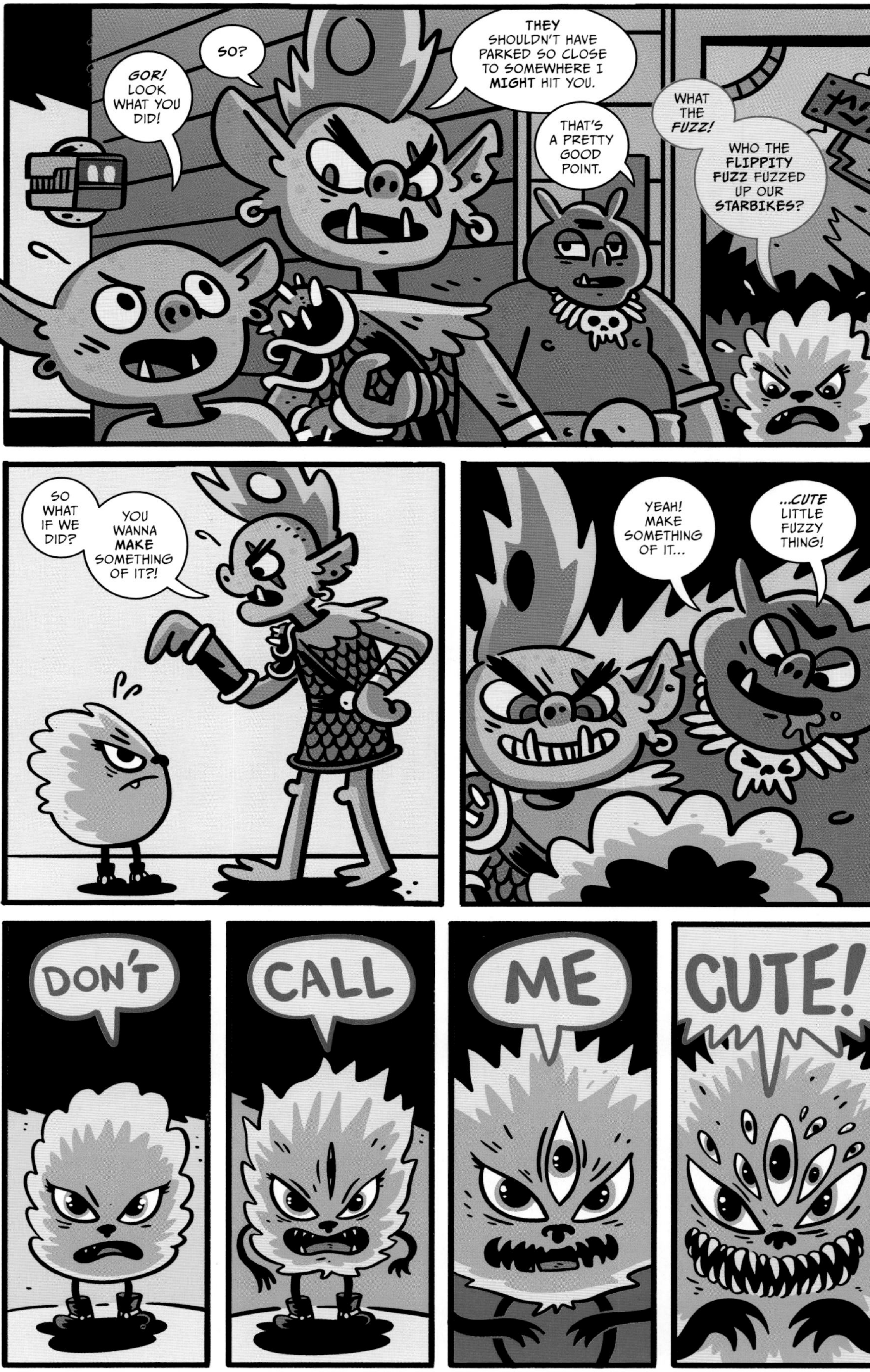
GOR! LOOK WHAT YOU DID!
SO?
THEY SHOULDN'T HAVE PARKED SO CLOSE TO SOMEWHERE I MIGHT HIT YOU.
THAT'S A PRETTY GOOD POINT.
WHAT THE FUZZ!
WHO THE FLIPPITY FUZZ FUZZED UP OUR STARBIKES?
SO WHAT IF WE DID?
YOU WANNA MAKE SOMETHING OF IT?!
YEAH! MAKE SOMETHING OF IT...
...CUTE LITTLE FUZZY THING!
DON'T
CALL
ME
CUTE!

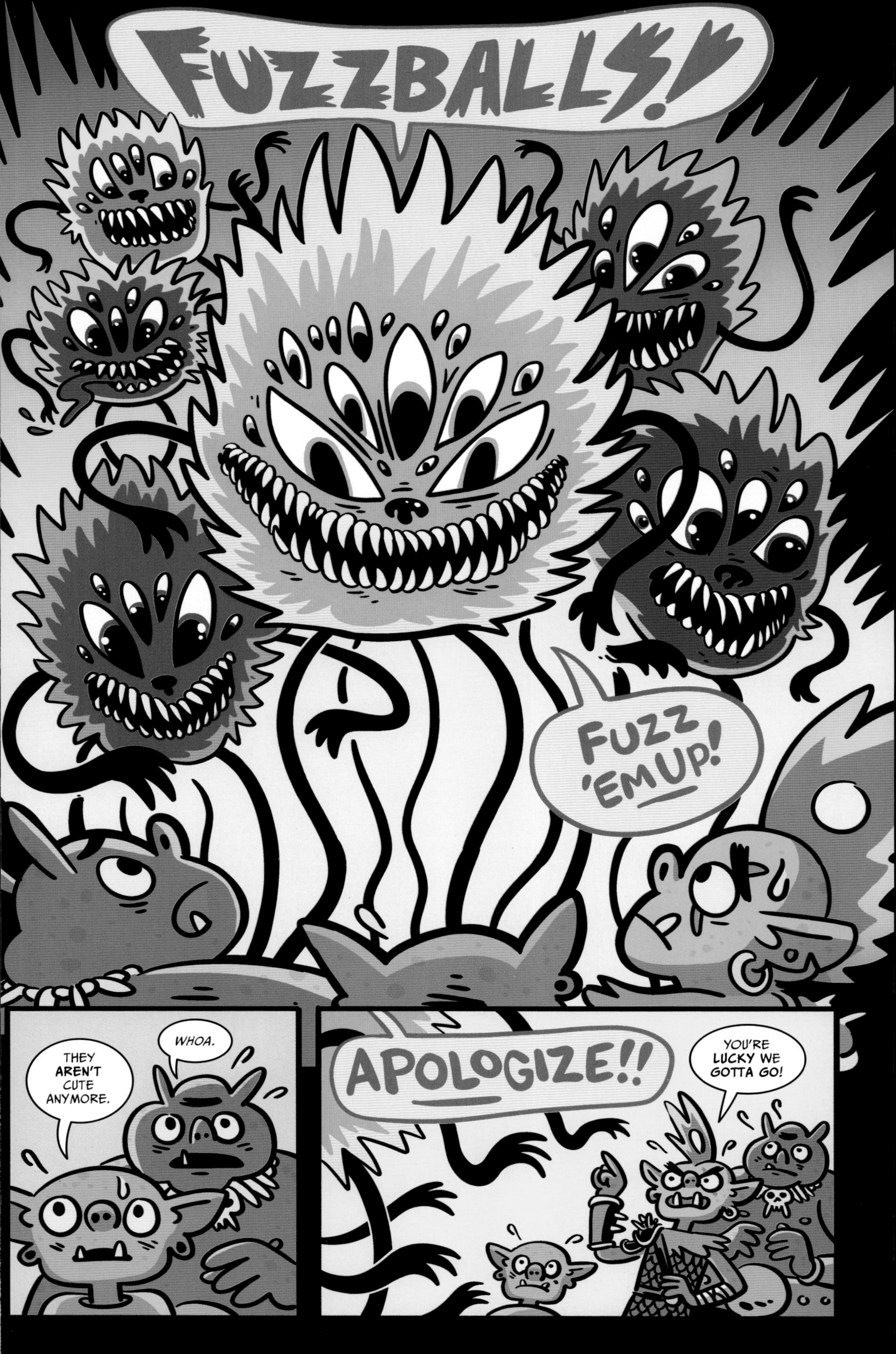
FUZZBALLS!
FUZZ 'EM UP!
THEY AREN'T CUTE ANYMORE.
WHOA.
APOLOGIZE!!
YOU'RE LUCKY WE GOTTA GO!

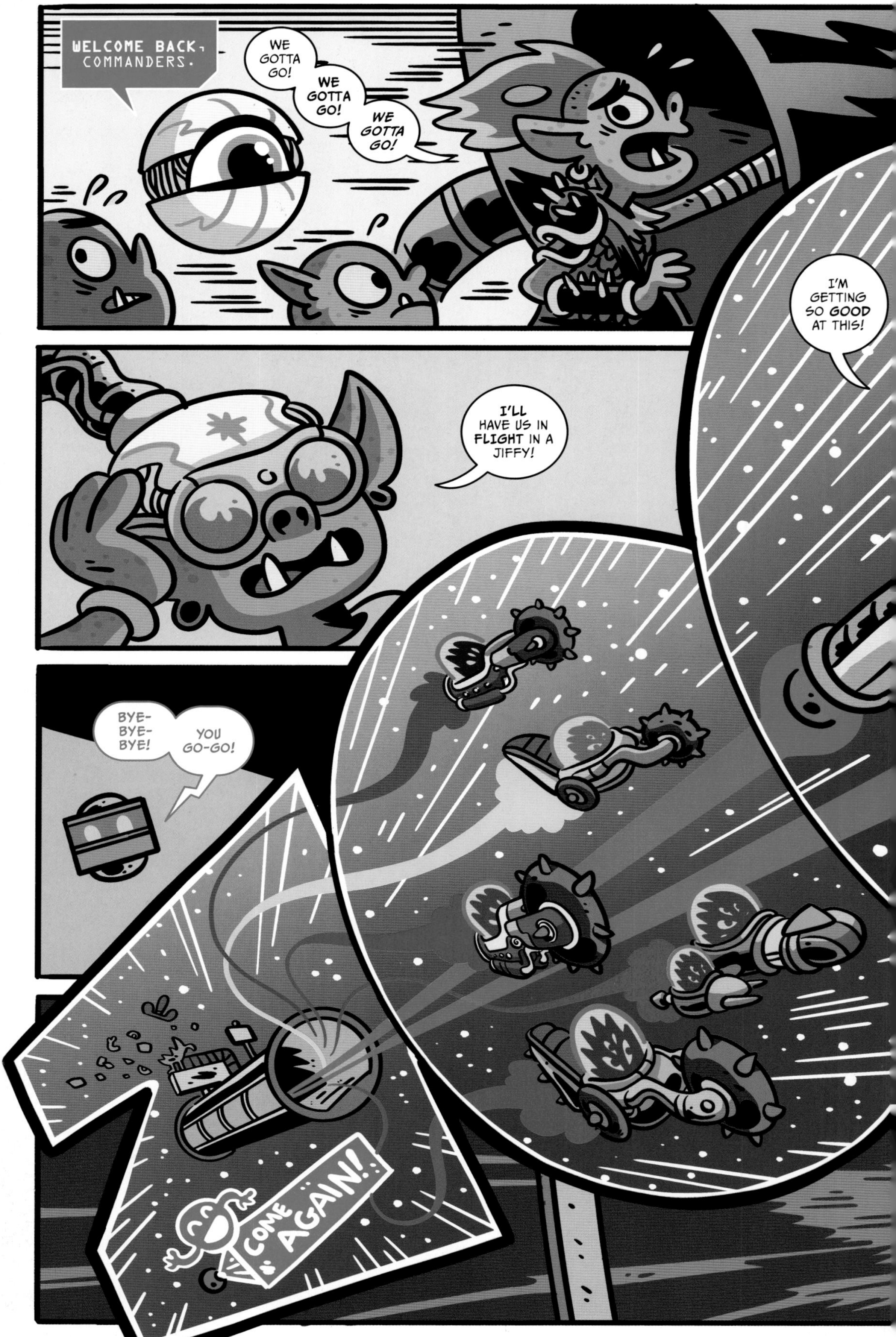
WELCOME BACK, COMMANDERS.
WE GOTTA GO!
WE GOTTA GO!
WE GOTTA GO!
I'LL HAVE US IN FLIGHT IN A JIFFY!
I'M GETTING SO GOOD AT THIS!
BYE-BYE-BYE!
YOU GO-GO!
COME AGAIN!

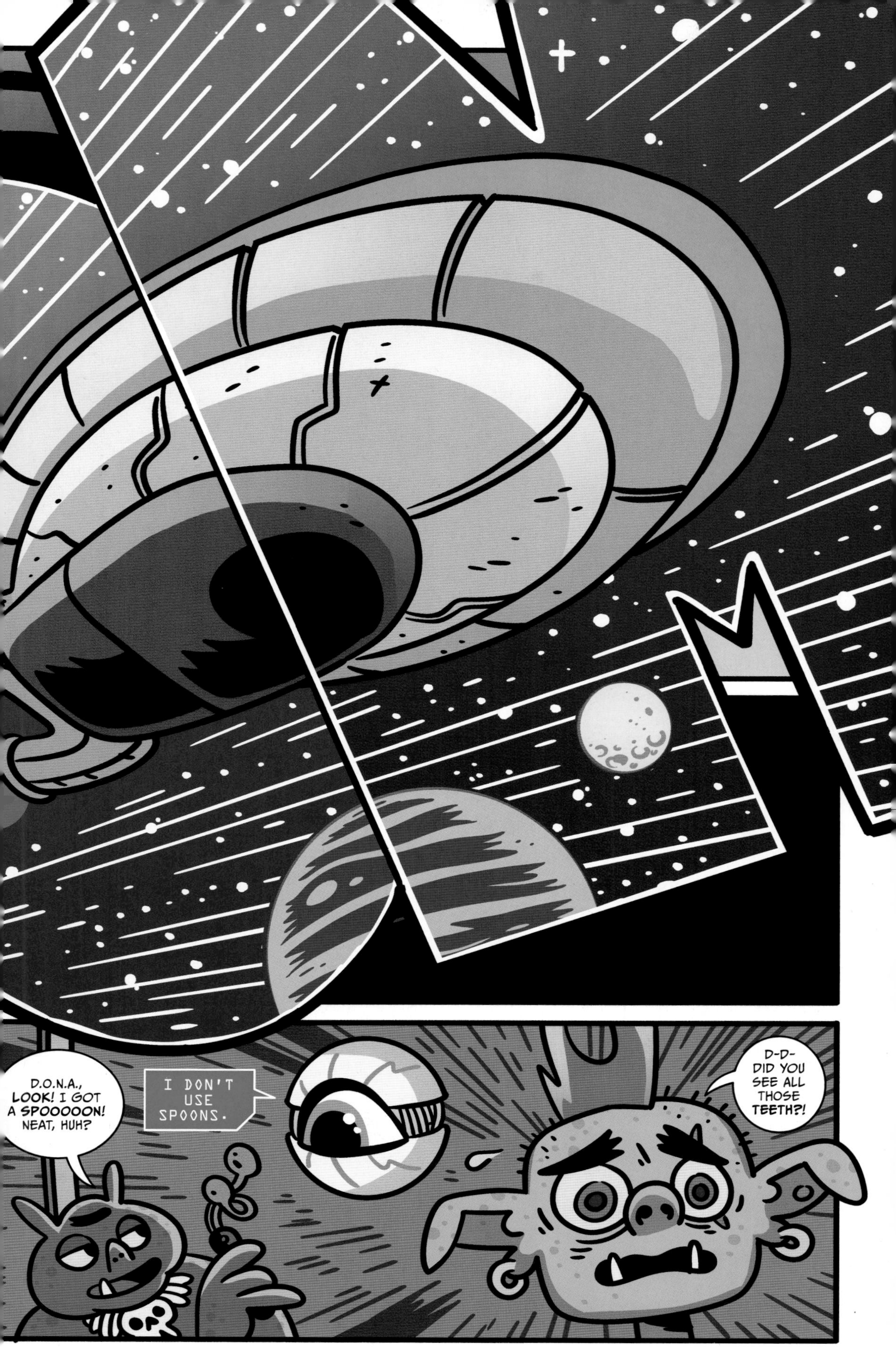

D.O.N.A., LOOK! I GOT A SPOOOOON! NEAT, HUH?
I DON'T USE SPOONS.
D-D-DID YOU SEE ALL THOSE TEETH?!

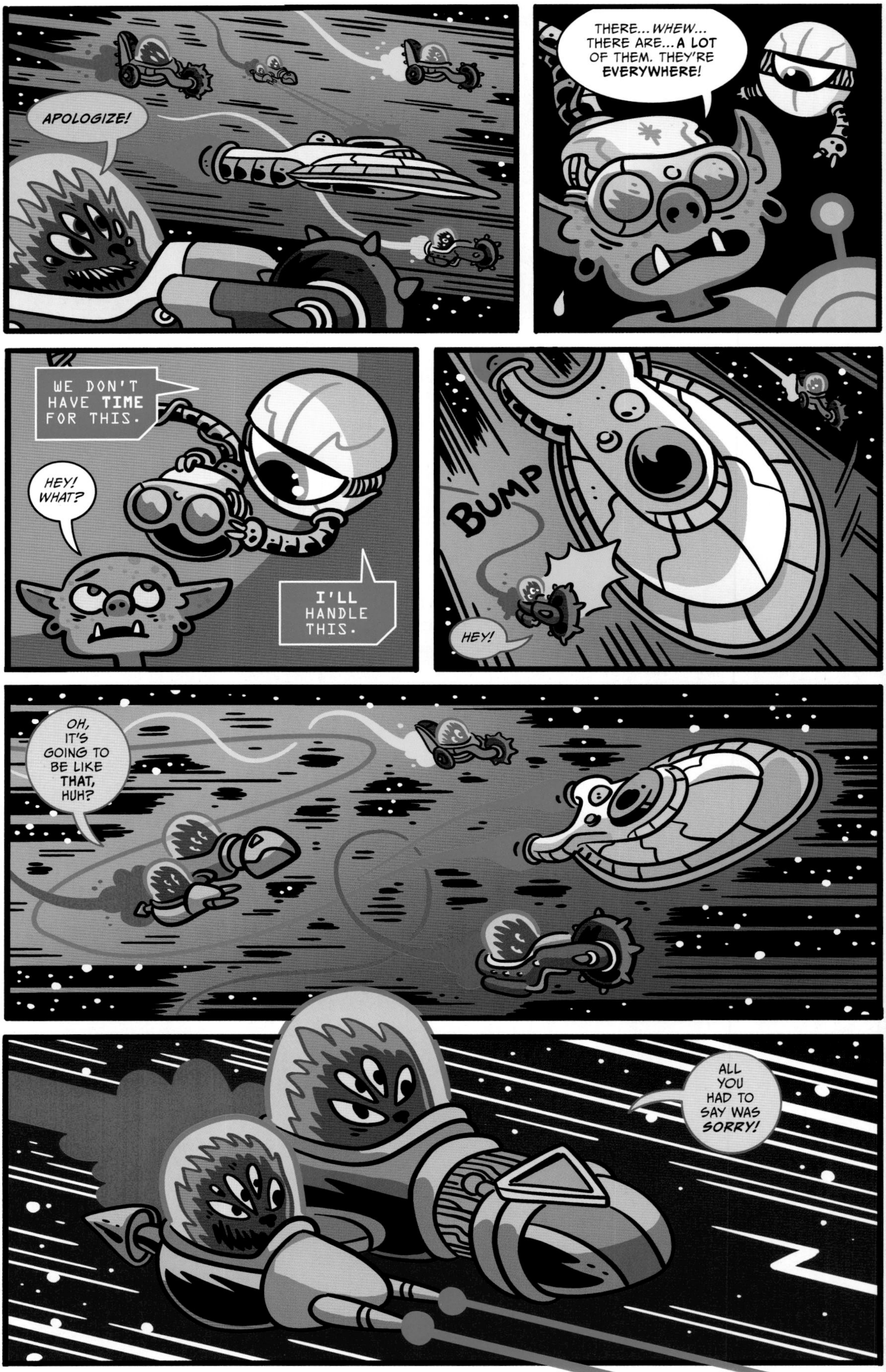
APOLOGIZE!
THERE... WHEW... THERE ARE... A LOT OF THEM. THEY'RE EVERYWHERE!
WE DON'T HAVE TIME FOR THIS.
HEY! WHAT?
I'LL HANDLE THIS.
BUMP
HEY!
OH, IT'S GOING TO BE LIKE THAT, HUH?
ALL YOU HAD TO SAY WAS SORRY!

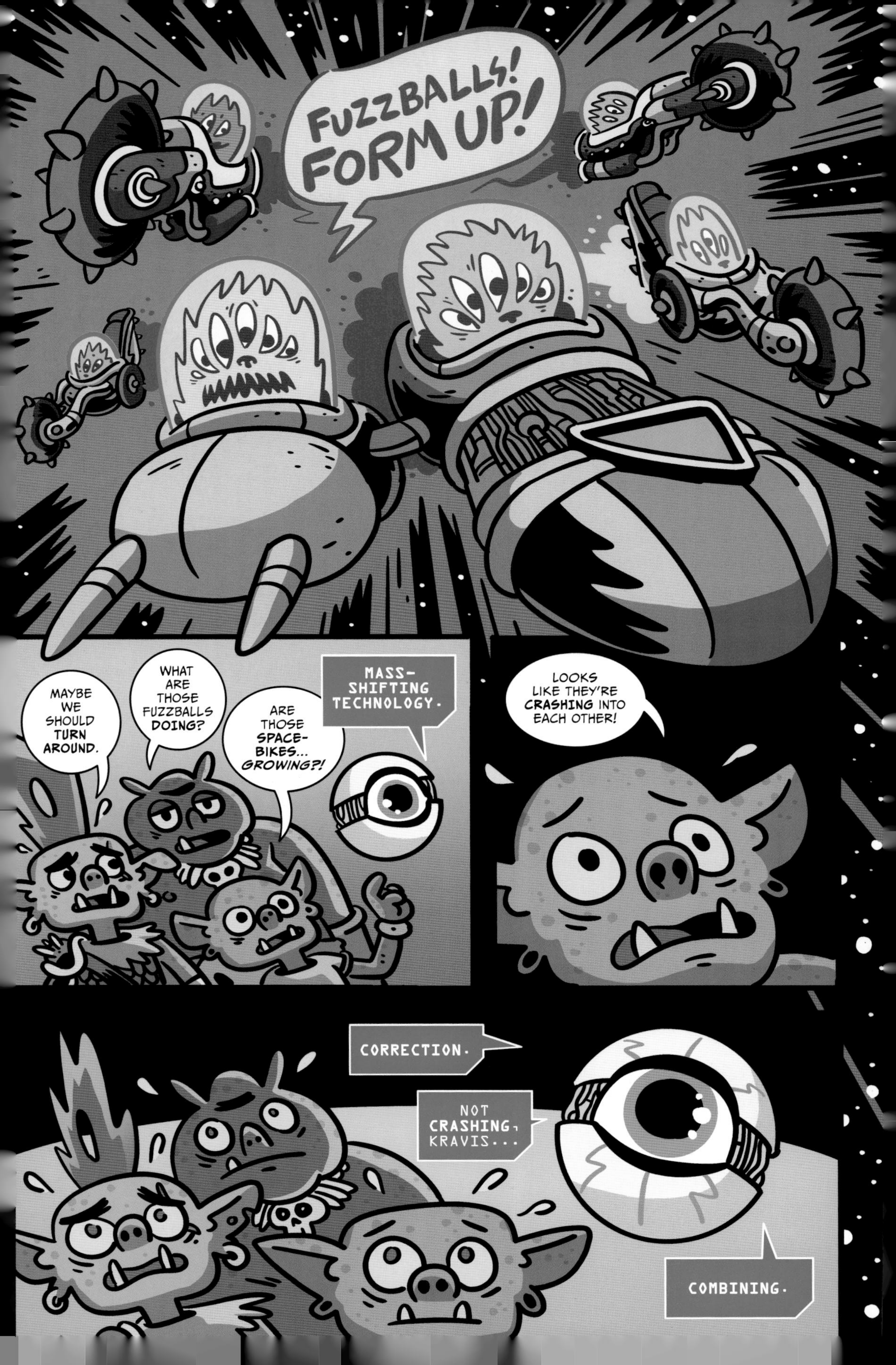
FUZZBALLS! FORM UP!
MAYBE WE SHOULD TURN AROUND.
WHAT ARE THOSE FUZZBALLS DOING?
ARE THOSE SPACE-BIKES... GROWING?!
MASS-SHIFTING TECHNOLOGY.
LOOKS LIKE THEY'RE CRASHING INTO EACH OTHER!
CORRECTION.
NOT CRASHING, KRAVIS...
COMBINING.

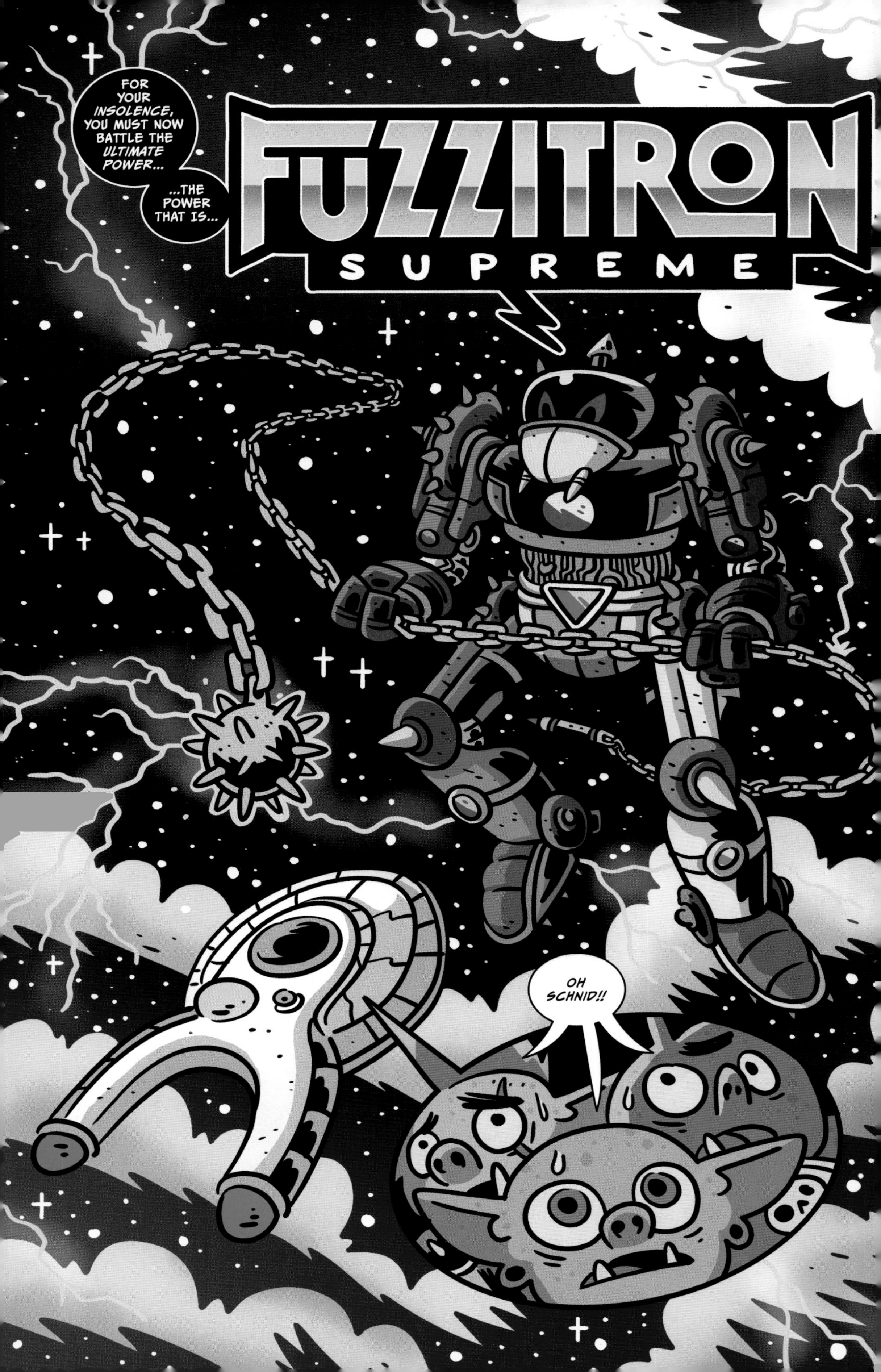
FOR YOUR INSOLENCE, YOU MUST NOW BATTLE THE ULTIMATE POWER...
...THE POWER THAT IS...
FUZZITRON SUPREME
OH SCHNID!!

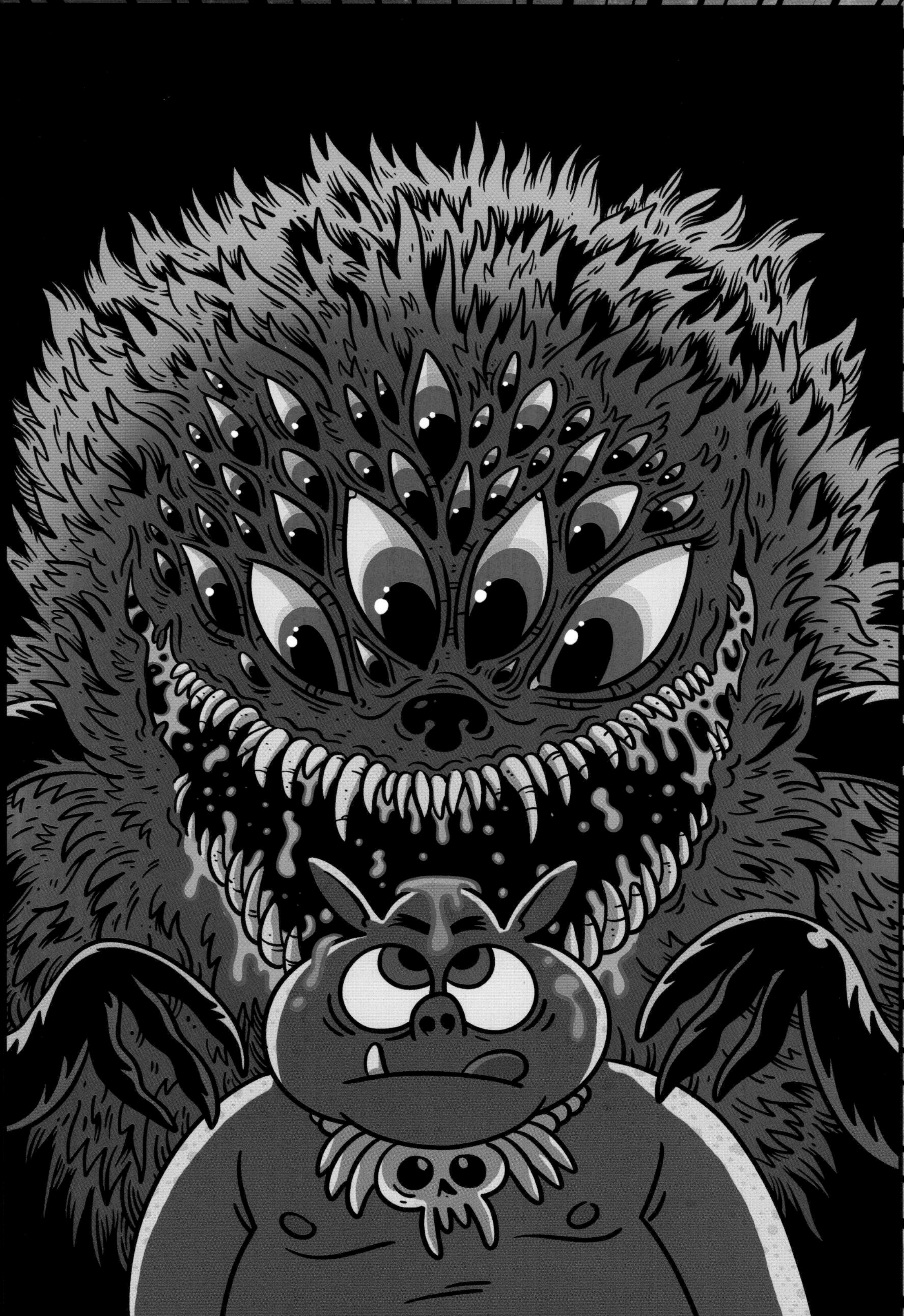

CHAPTER SEVEN

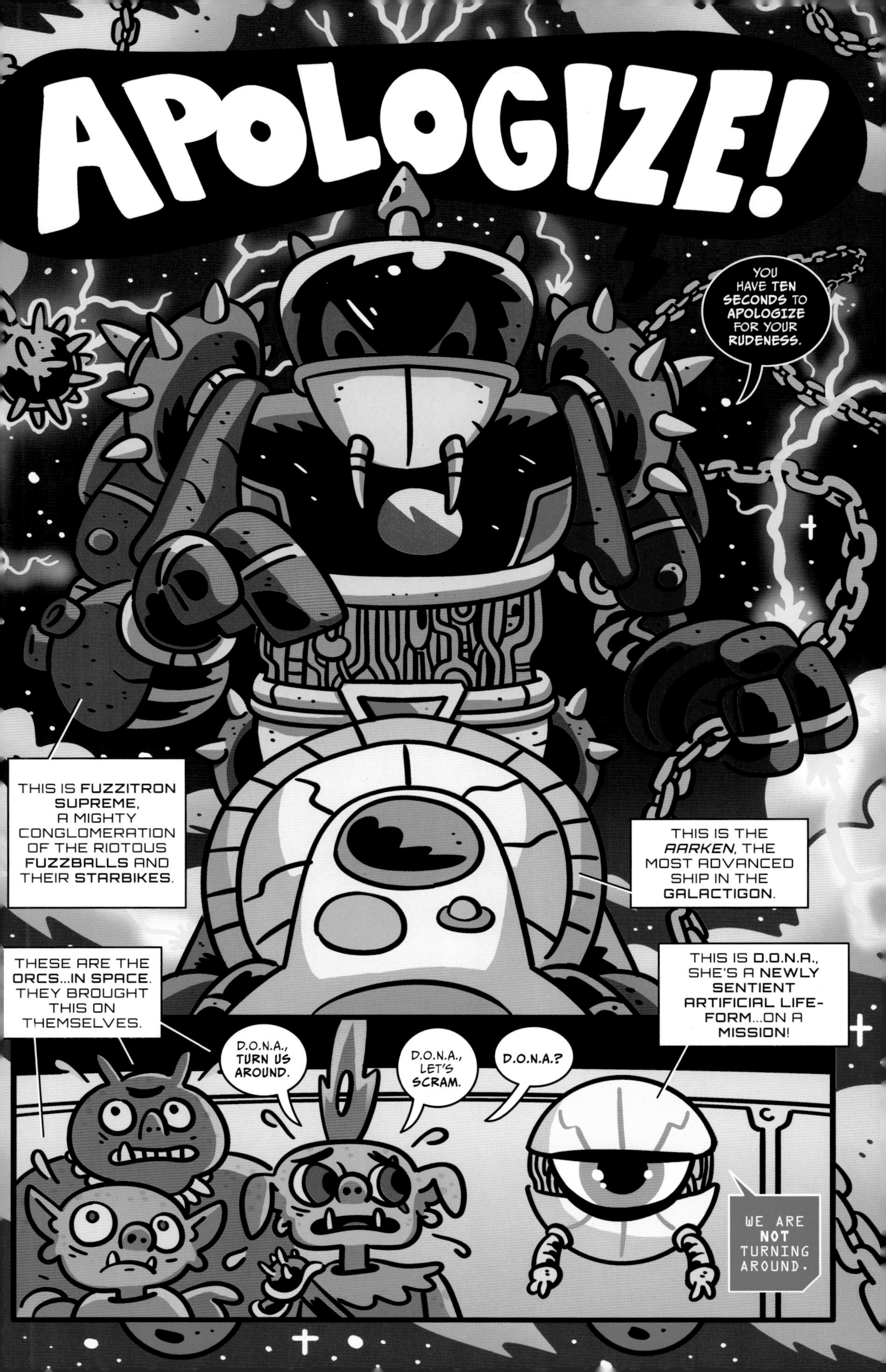
APOLOGIZE!
YOU HAVE TEN SECONDS TO APOLOGIZE FOR YOUR RUDENESS.
THIS IS FUZZITRON SUPREME, A MIGHTY CONGLOMERATION OF THE RIOTOUS FUZZBALLS AND THEIR STARBIKES.
THIS IS THE AARKEN, THE MOST ADVANCED SHIP IN THE GALACTIGON.
THESE ARE THE ORCS...IN SPACE. THEY BROUGHT THIS ON THEMSELVES.
THIS IS D.O.N.A., SHE'S A NEWLY SENTIENT ARTIFICIAL LIFE-FORM...ON A MISSION!
D.O.N.A., TURN US AROUND.
D.O.N.A., LET'S SCRAM.
D.O.N.A.?
WE ARE NOT TURNING AROUND.

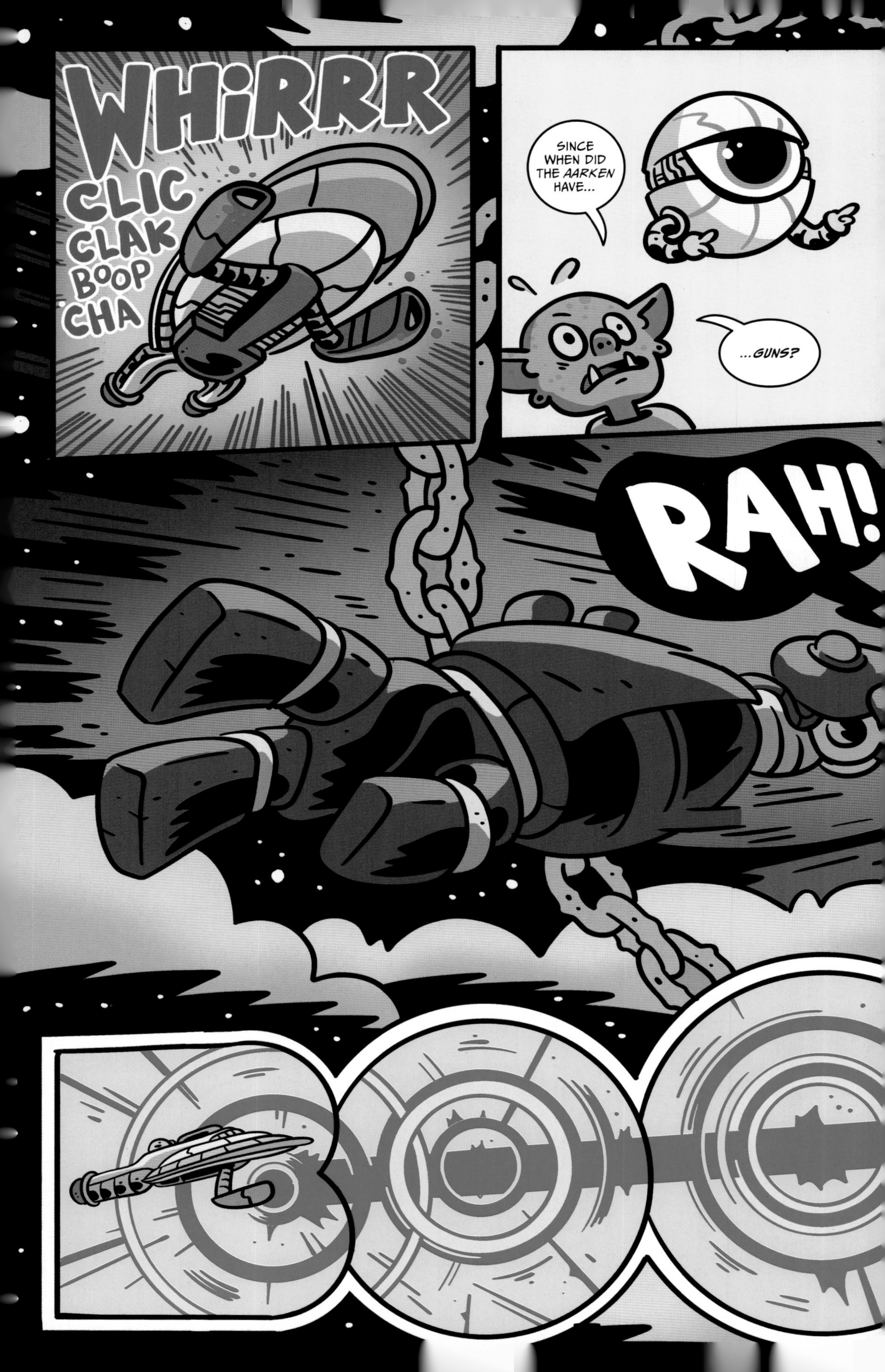
WHiRRR
CLIC
CLAK
BOOP
CHA
SINCE WHEN DID THE *AARKEN* HAVE...
...GUNS?
RAH!

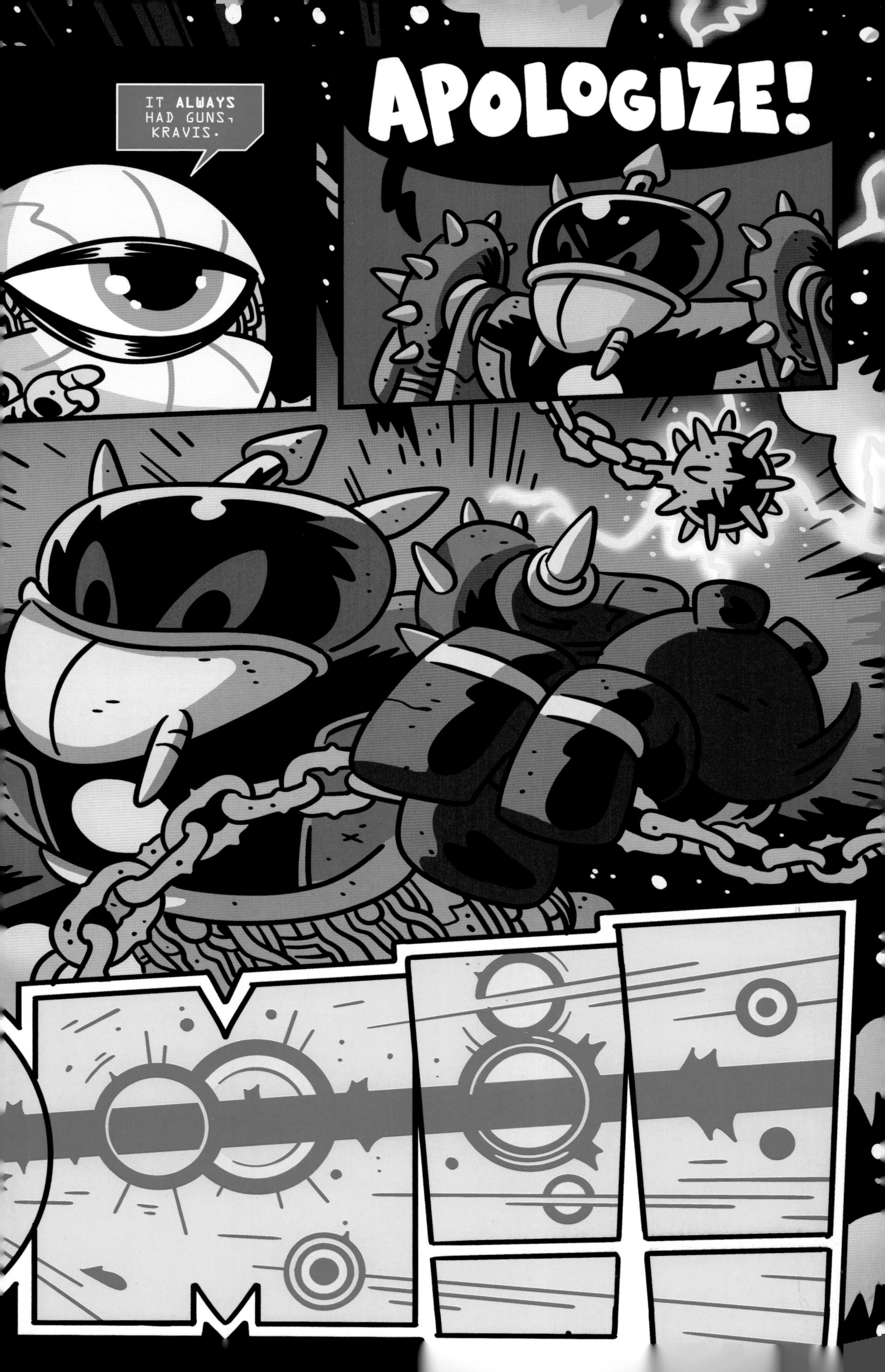
IT ALWAYS HAD GUNS, KRAVIS.
APOLOGIZE!

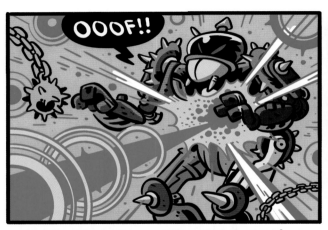

OOOF!!

COME BACK HERE, YOU!

APOLOGIZE!

GOOD SHOOTING, D.O.N.A.!

WE WON!

PFFT.

THAT WAS NO BATTLE, WE JUST RAN AWAY.

BUT YOU WANTED TO RUN!

YOU SAID IT A BUNCH OF TIMES!

WHAT-EVER.

I DON'T REMEMBER THAT.

YOU KNOW, GOR, IT'S OKAY TO BE AFRAID SOMETIMES.

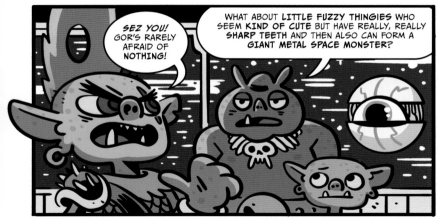

SEZ YOU! GOR'S RARELY AFRAID OF NOTHING!

WHAT ABOUT LITTLE FUZZY THINGIES WHO SEEM KIND OF CUTE BUT HAVE REALLY, REALLY SHARP TEETH AND THEN ALSO CAN FORM A GIANT METAL SPACE MONSTER?

RIGHT. I'M RARELY AFRAID OF THAT.

AND ALSO HAIR-CUTS.

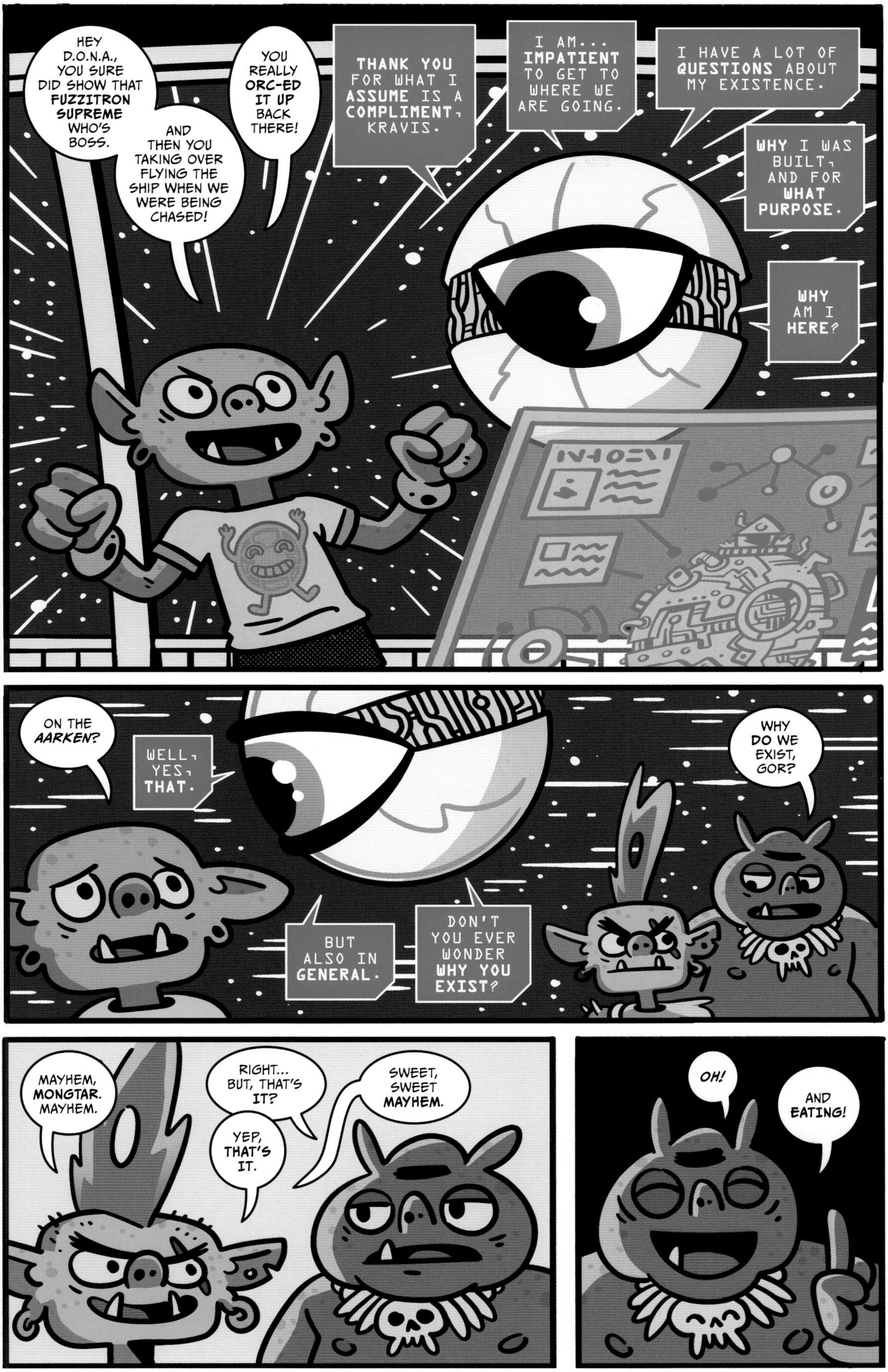

HEY D.O.N.A., YOU SURE DID SHOW THAT **FUZZITRON SUPREME** WHO'S BOSS.
AND THEN YOU TAKING OVER FLYING THE SHIP WHEN WE WERE BEING CHASED!
YOU REALLY **ORC-ED IT UP** BACK THERE!
THANK YOU FOR WHAT I **ASSUME** IS A **COMPLIMENT**, KRAVIS.
I AM... **IMPATIENT** TO GET TO WHERE WE ARE GOING.
I HAVE A LOT OF **QUESTIONS** ABOUT MY EXISTENCE.
WHY I WAS BUILT, AND FOR **WHAT PURPOSE**.
WHY AM I HERE?
ON THE ***AARKEN?***
WELL, YES, **THAT**.
BUT ALSO IN **GENERAL**.
DON'T YOU EVER WONDER **WHY YOU EXIST**?
WHY **DO WE** EXIST, GOR?
MAYHEM, **MONGTAR**. MAYHEM.
RIGHT... BUT, THAT'S **IT**?
YEP, **THAT'S** IT.
SWEET, SWEET **MAYHEM**.
OH!
AND **EATING!**

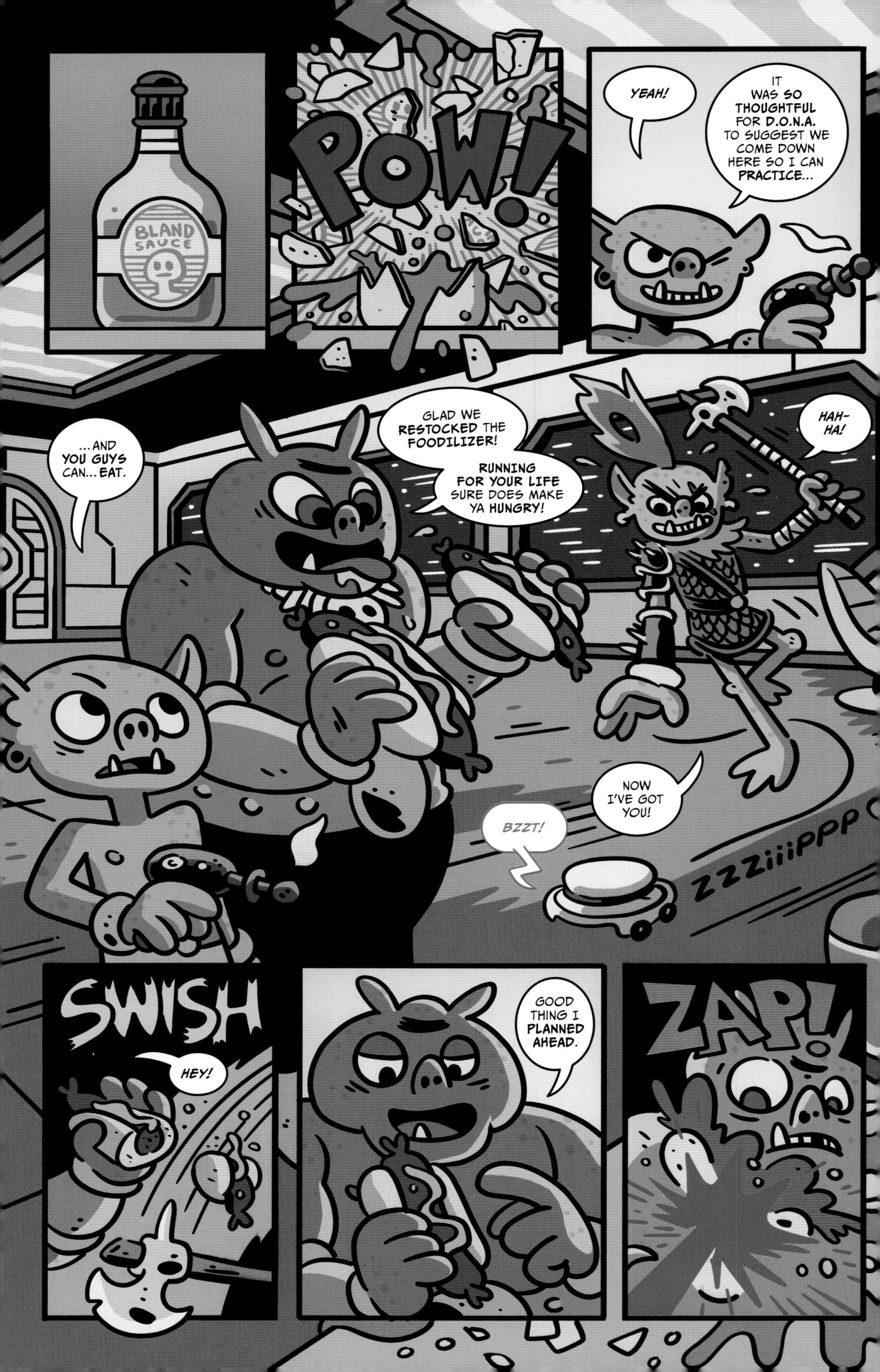
BLAND SAUCE
POW!
YEAH!
IT WAS SO THOUGHTFUL FOR D.O.N.A. TO SUGGEST WE COME DOWN HERE SO I CAN PRACTICE...
...AND YOU GUYS CAN... EAT.
GLAD WE RESTOCKED THE FOODILIZER!
RUNNING FOR YOUR LIFE SURE DOES MAKE YA HUNGRY!
HAH-HA!
NOW I'VE GOT YOU!
BZZT!
ZZZiiiPPP
SWISH
HEY!
GOOD THING I PLANNED AHEAD.
ZAP!

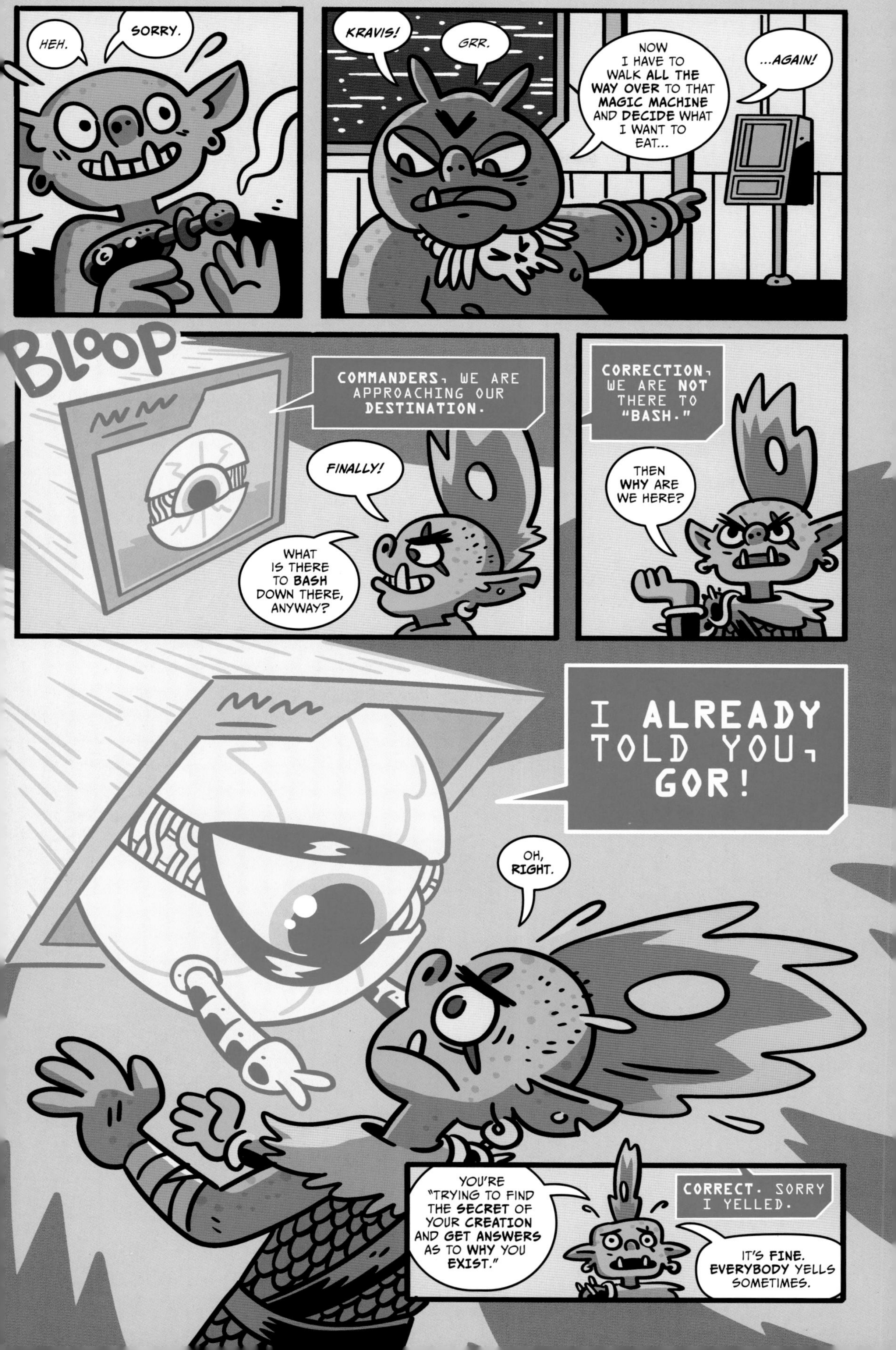
HEH.
SORRY.
KRAVIS!
GRR.
NOW I HAVE TO WALK ALL THE WAY OVER TO THAT MAGIC MACHINE AND DECIDE WHAT I WANT TO EAT...
...AGAIN!
BLOOP
COMMANDERS, WE ARE APPROACHING OUR DESTINATION.
FINALLY!
WHAT IS THERE TO BASH DOWN THERE, ANYWAY?
CORRECTION, WE ARE NOT THERE TO "BASH."
THEN WHY ARE WE HERE?
I ALREADY TOLD YOU, GOR!
OH, RIGHT.
YOU'RE "TRYING TO FIND THE SECRET OF YOUR CREATION AND GET ANSWERS AS TO WHY YOU EXIST."
CORRECT. SORRY I YELLED.
IT'S FINE. EVERYBODY YELLS SOMETIMES.

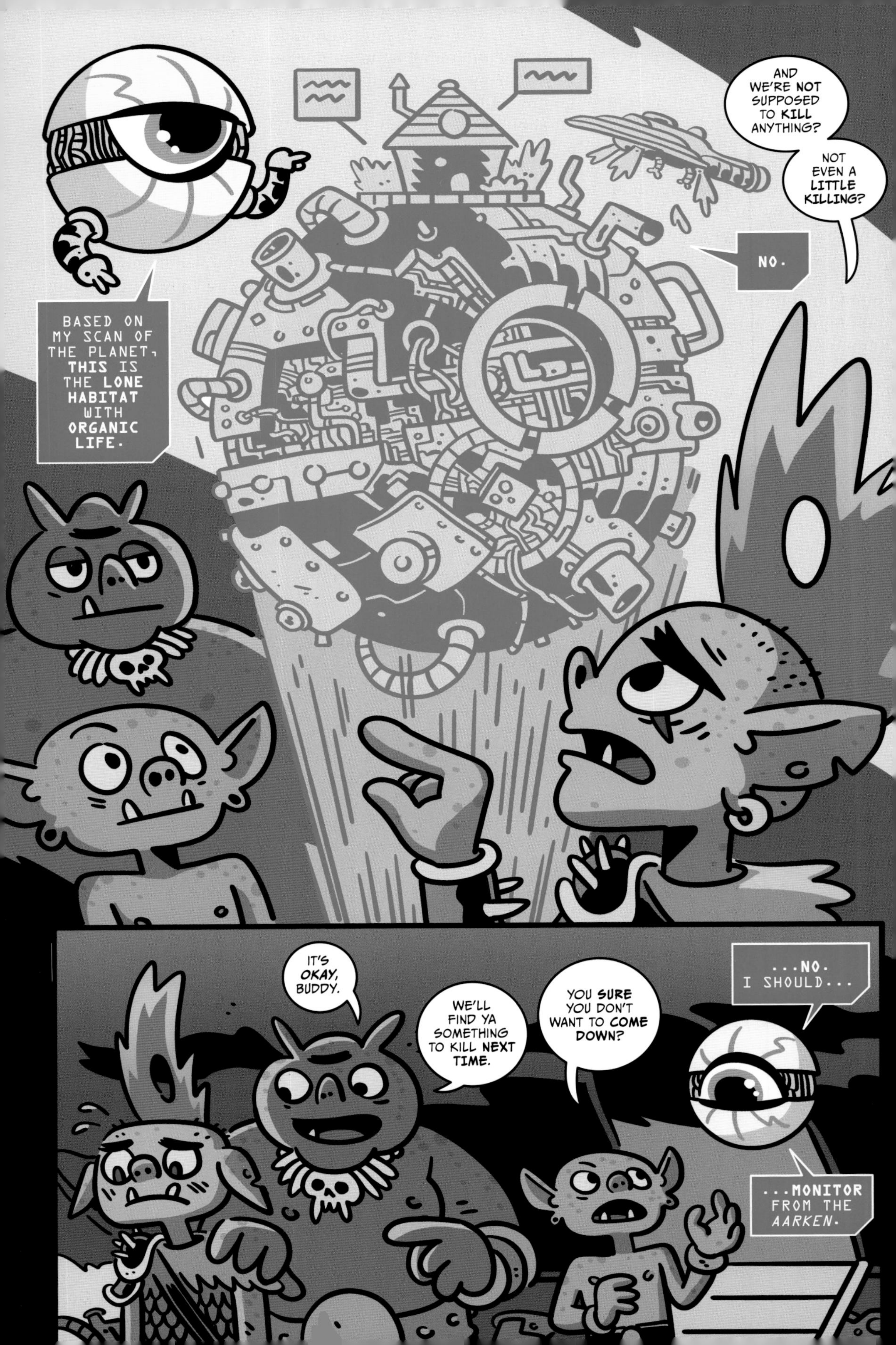

BASED ON MY SCAN OF THE PLANET, THIS IS THE LONE HABITAT WITH ORGANIC LIFE.
AND WE'RE NOT SUPPOSED TO KILL ANYTHING?
NOT EVEN A LITTLE KILLING?
NO.
IT'S OKAY, BUDDY.
WE'LL FIND YA SOMETHING TO KILL NEXT TIME.
YOU SURE YOU DON'T WANT TO COME DOWN?
...NO. I SHOULD...
...MONITOR FROM THE AARKEN.

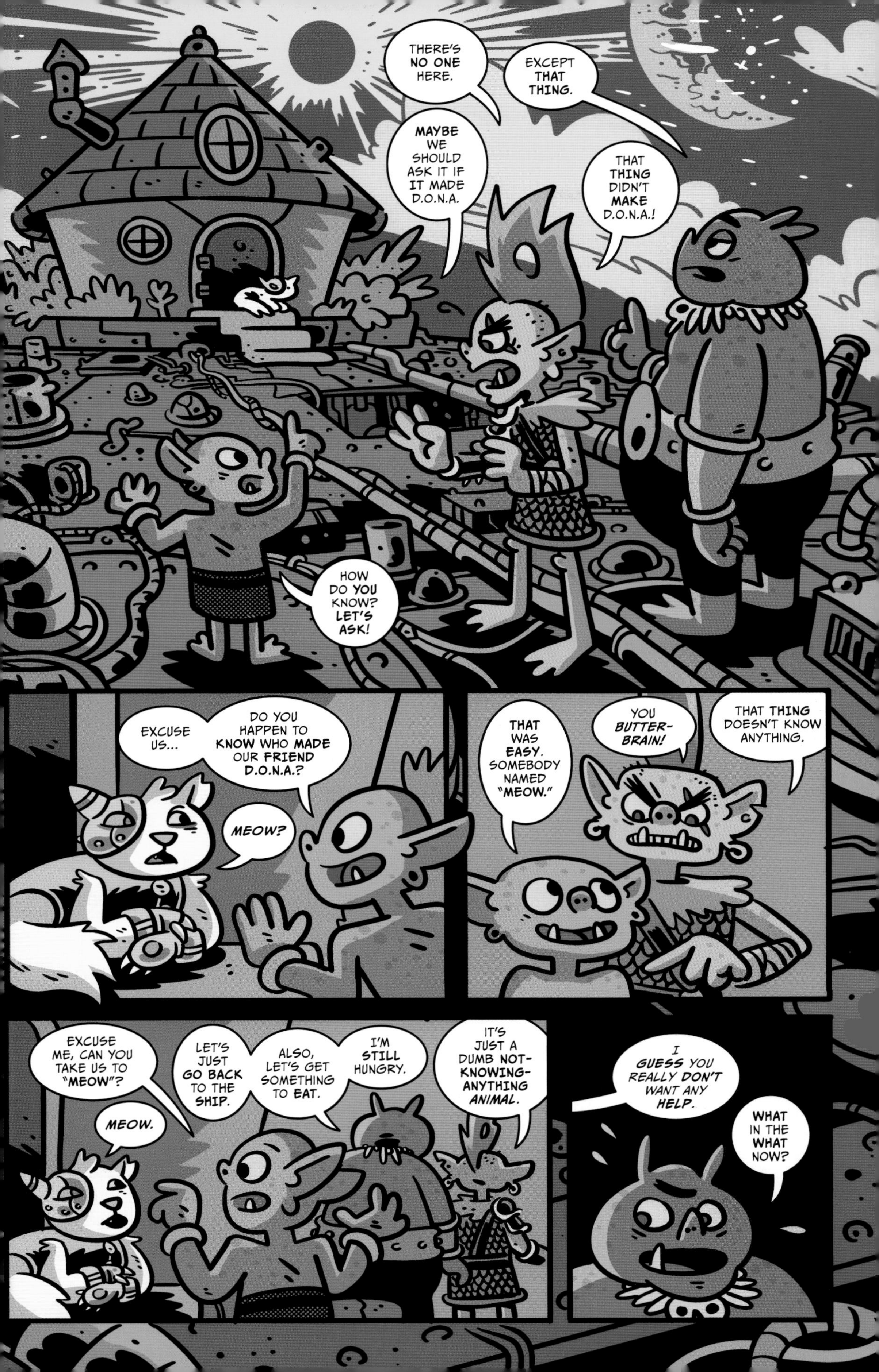
THERE'S NO ONE HERE.
EXCEPT THAT THING.
MAYBE WE SHOULD ASK IT IF IT MADE D.O.N.A.
THAT THING DIDN'T MAKE D.O.N.A.!
HOW DO YOU KNOW? LET'S ASK!
EXCUSE US...
DO YOU HAPPEN TO KNOW WHO MADE OUR FRIEND D.O.N.A.?
MEOW?
THAT WAS EASY. SOMEBODY NAMED "MEOW."
YOU BUTTER-BRAIN!
THAT THING DOESN'T KNOW ANYTHING.
EXCUSE ME, CAN YOU TAKE US TO "MEOW"?
MEOW.
LET'S JUST GO BACK TO THE SHIP.
ALSO, LET'S GET SOMETHING TO EAT.
I'M STILL HUNGRY.
IT'S JUST A DUMB NOT-KNOWING-ANYTHING ANIMAL.
I GUESS YOU REALLY DON'T WANT ANY HELP.
WHAT IN THE WHAT NOW?

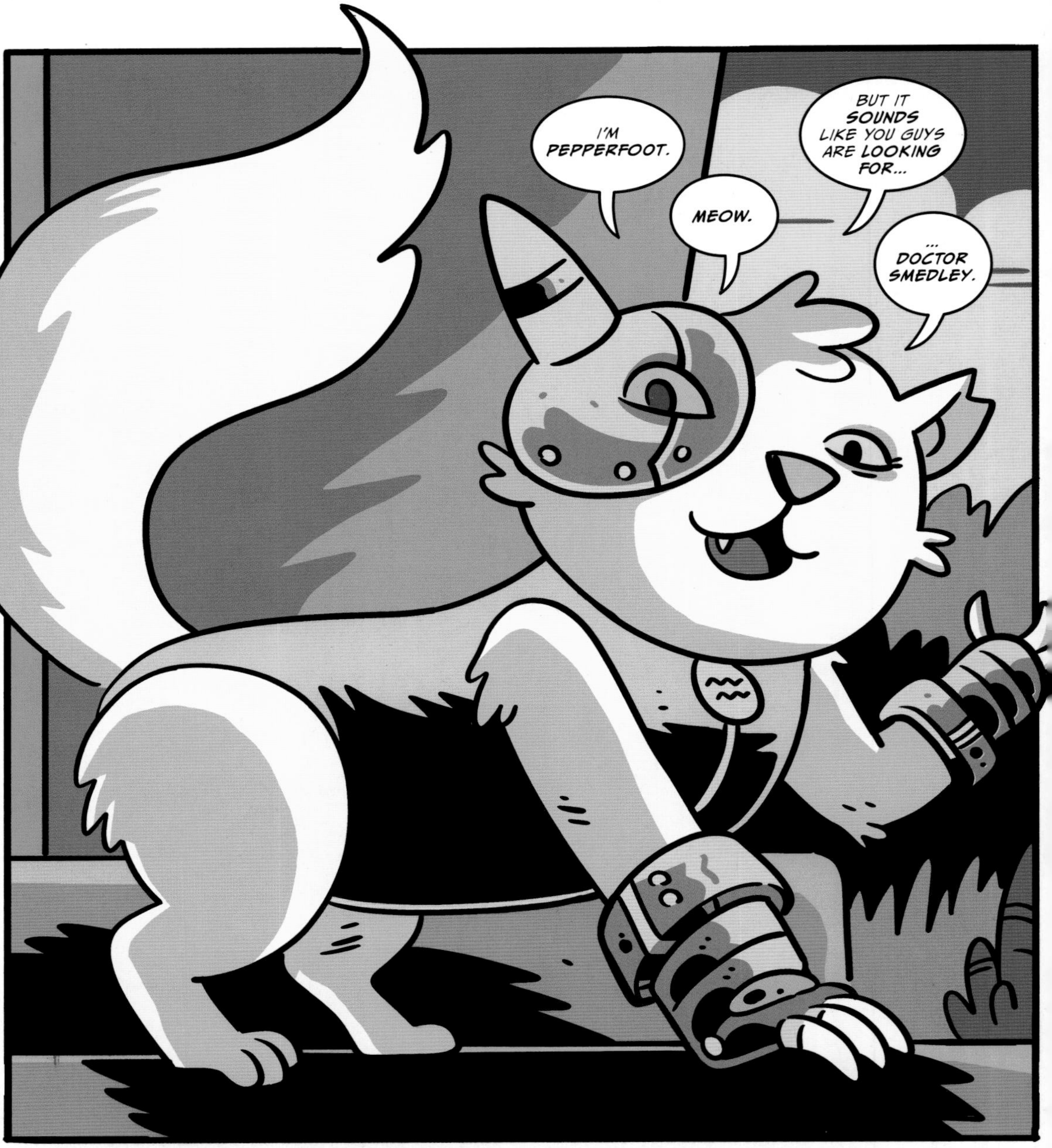
I'M PEPPERFOOT.
MEOW.
BUT IT SOUNDS LIKE YOU GUYS ARE LOOKING FOR...
... DOCTOR SMEDLEY.

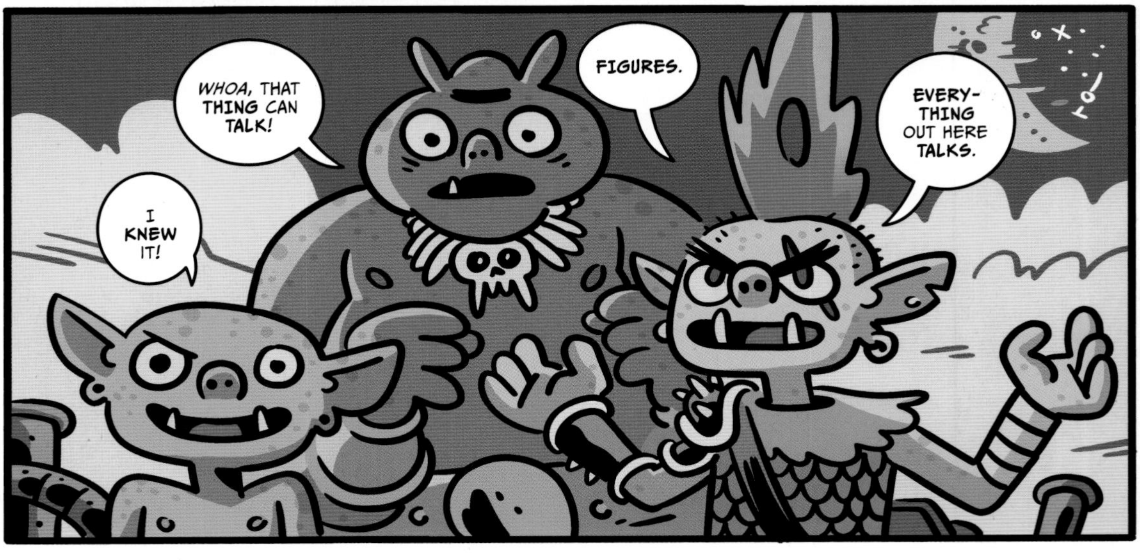
WHOA, THAT THING CAN TALK!
FIGURES.
EVERY-THING OUT HERE TALKS.
I KNEW IT!

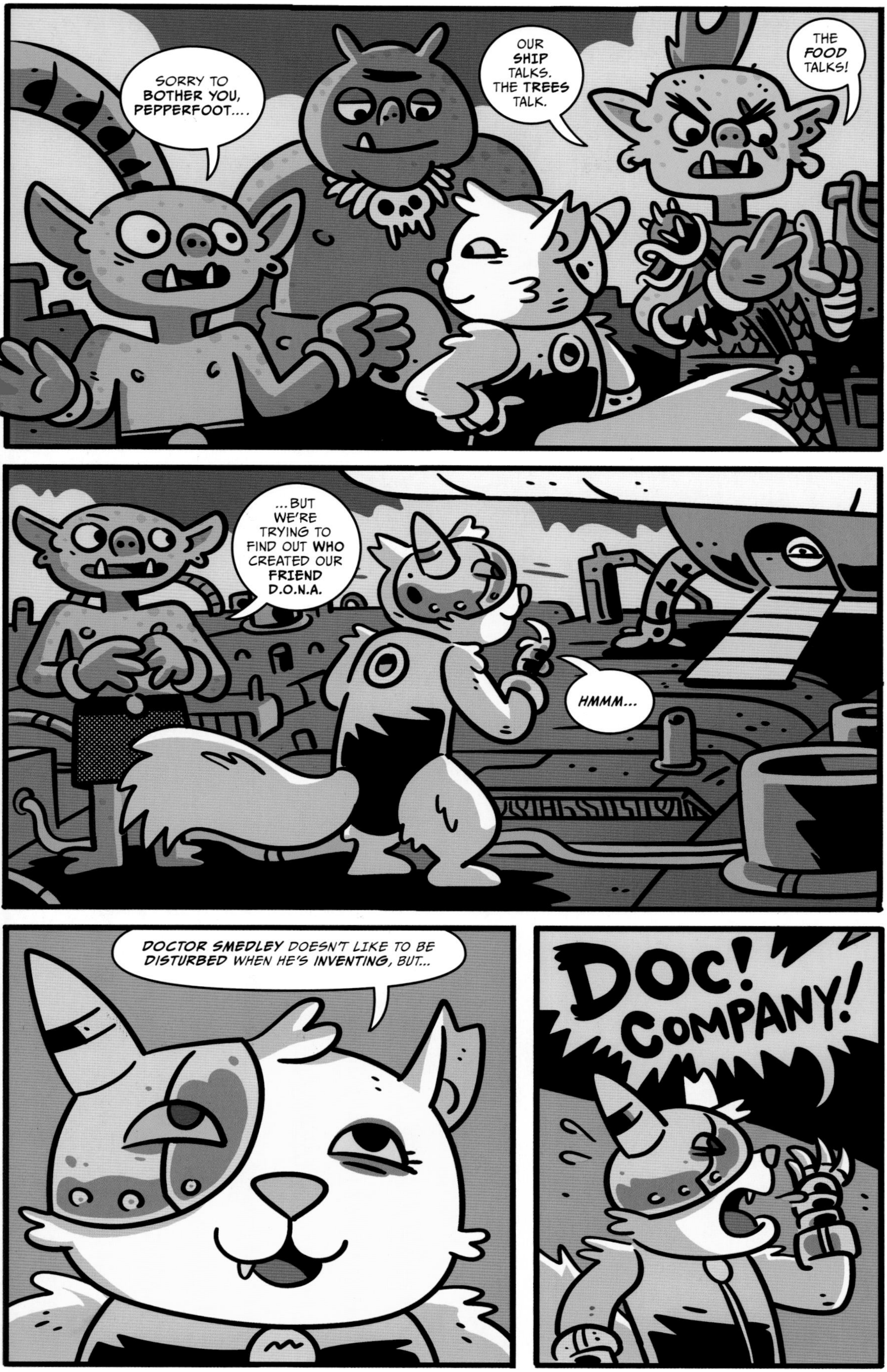
SORRY TO BOTHER YOU, PEPPERFOOT....
OUR SHIP TALKS. THE TREES TALK.
THE FOOD TALKS!
...BUT WE'RE TRYING TO FIND OUT WHO CREATED OUR FRIEND D.O.N.A.
HMMM...
DOCTOR SMEDLEY DOESN'T LIKE TO BE DISTURBED WHEN HE'S INVENTING, BUT...
DOC! COMPANY!

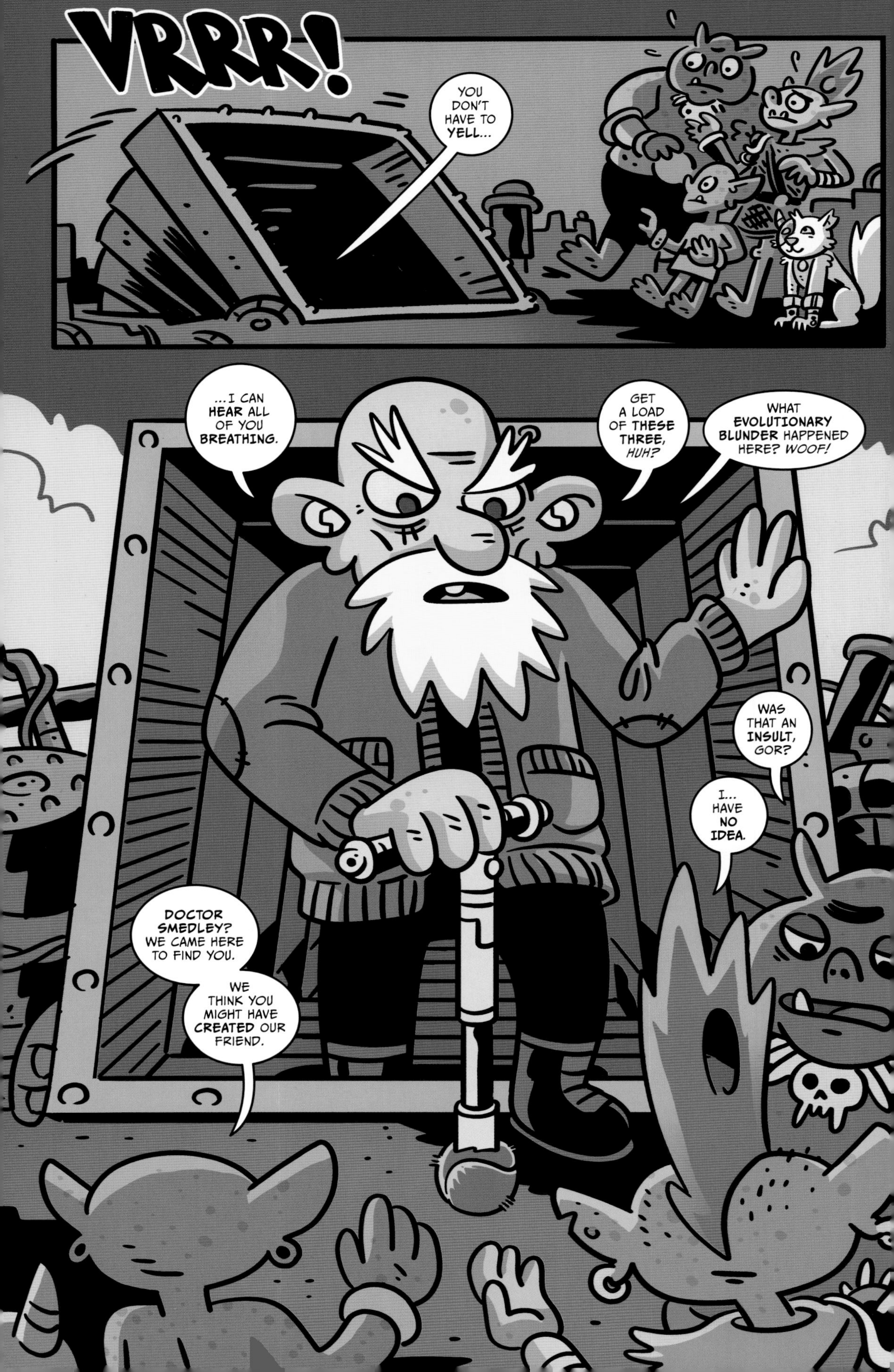
VRRR!
YOU DON'T HAVE TO YELL...
...I CAN HEAR ALL OF YOU BREATHING.
GET A LOAD OF THESE THREE, HUH?
WHAT EVOLUTIONARY BLUNDER HAPPENED HERE? WOOF!
WAS THAT AN INSULT, GOR?
I... HAVE NO IDEA.
DOCTOR SMEDLEY? WE CAME HERE TO FIND YOU.
WE THINK YOU MIGHT HAVE CREATED OUR FRIEND.

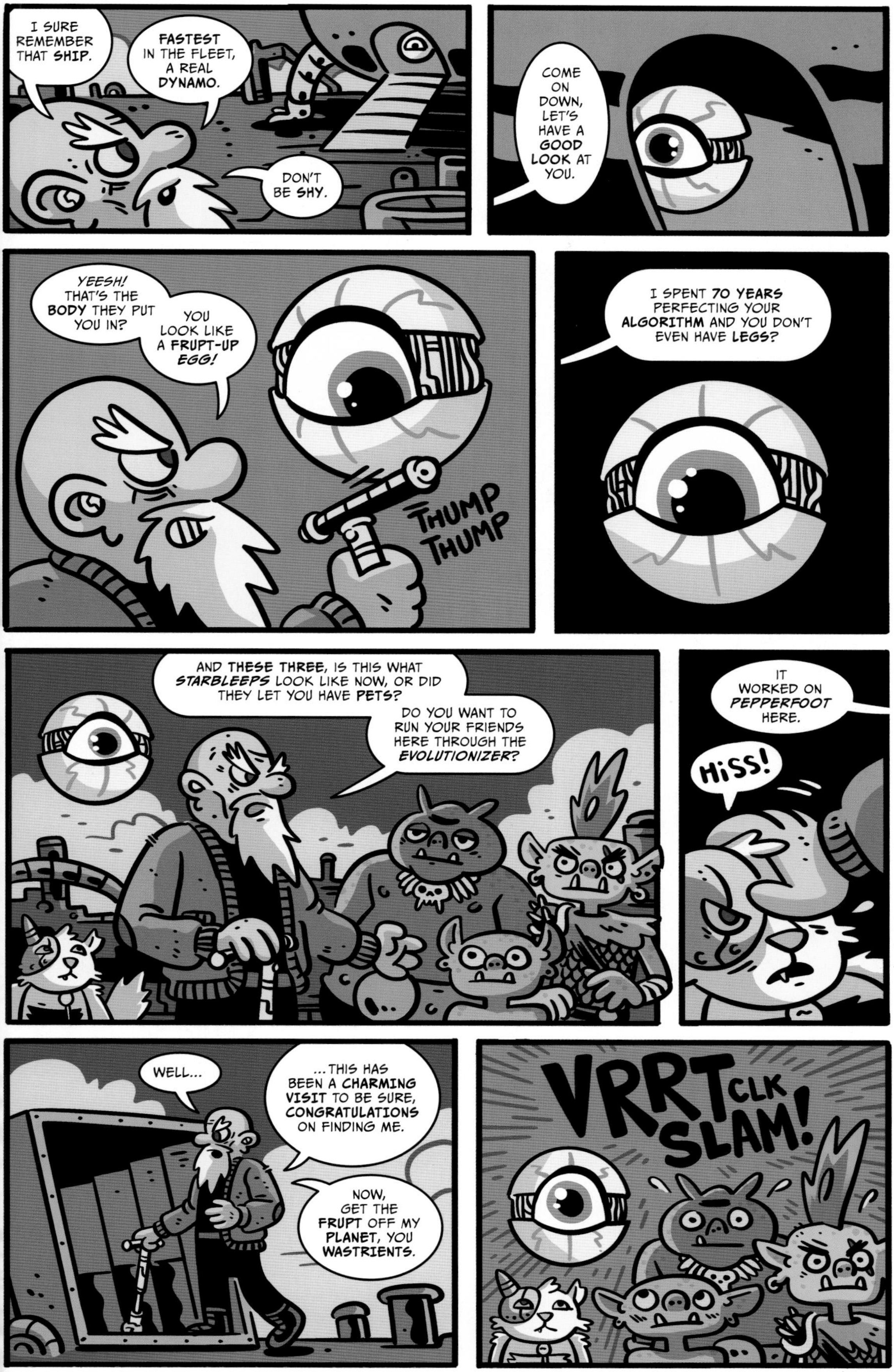
I SURE REMEMBER THAT SHIP.
FASTEST IN THE FLEET, A REAL DYNAMO.
DON'T BE SHY.
COME ON DOWN, LET'S HAVE A GOOD LOOK AT YOU.
YEESH! THAT'S THE BODY THEY PUT YOU IN?
YOU LOOK LIKE A FRUPT-UP EGG!
THUMP THUMP
I SPENT 70 YEARS PERFECTING YOUR ALGORITHM AND YOU DON'T EVEN HAVE LEGS?
AND THESE THREE, IS THIS WHAT STARBLEEPS LOOK LIKE NOW, OR DID THEY LET YOU HAVE PETS?
DO YOU WANT TO RUN YOUR FRIENDS HERE THROUGH THE EVOLUTIONIZER?
IT WORKED ON PEPPERFOOT HERE.
HiSS!
WELL...
...THIS HAS BEEN A CHARMING VISIT TO BE SURE, CONGRATULATIONS ON FINDING ME.
NOW, GET THE FRUPT OFF MY PLANET, YOU WASTRIENTS.
VRRT CLK SLAM!

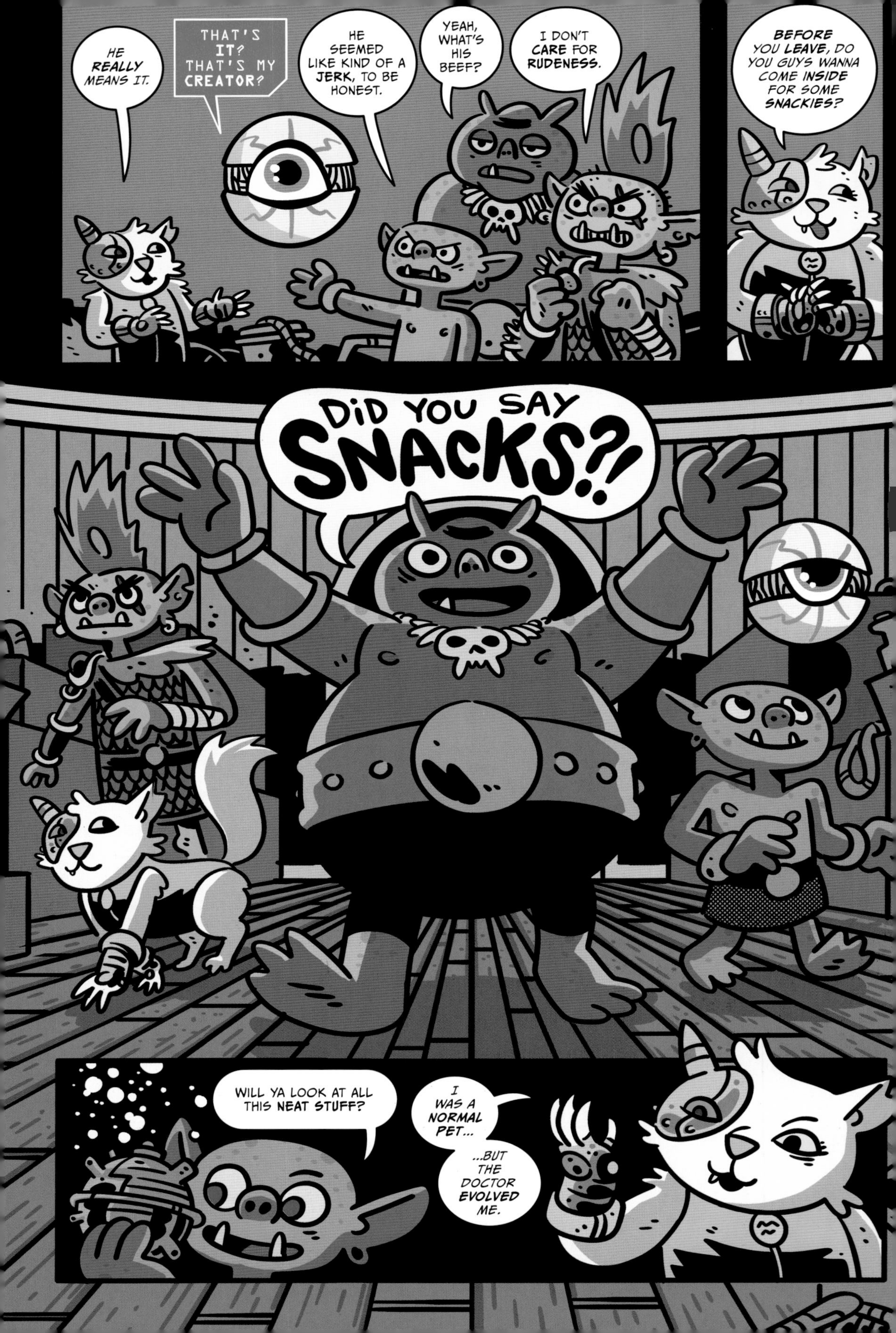
HE REALLY MEANS IT.
THAT'S IT? THAT'S MY CREATOR?
HE SEEMED LIKE KIND OF A JERK, TO BE HONEST.
YEAH, WHAT'S HIS BEEF?
I DON'T CARE FOR RUDENESS.
BEFORE YOU LEAVE, DO YOU GUYS WANNA COME INSIDE FOR SOME SNACKIES?
DID YOU SAY SNACKS?!
WILL YA LOOK AT ALL THIS NEAT STUFF?
I WAS A NORMAL PET...
...BUT THE DOCTOR EVOLVED ME.

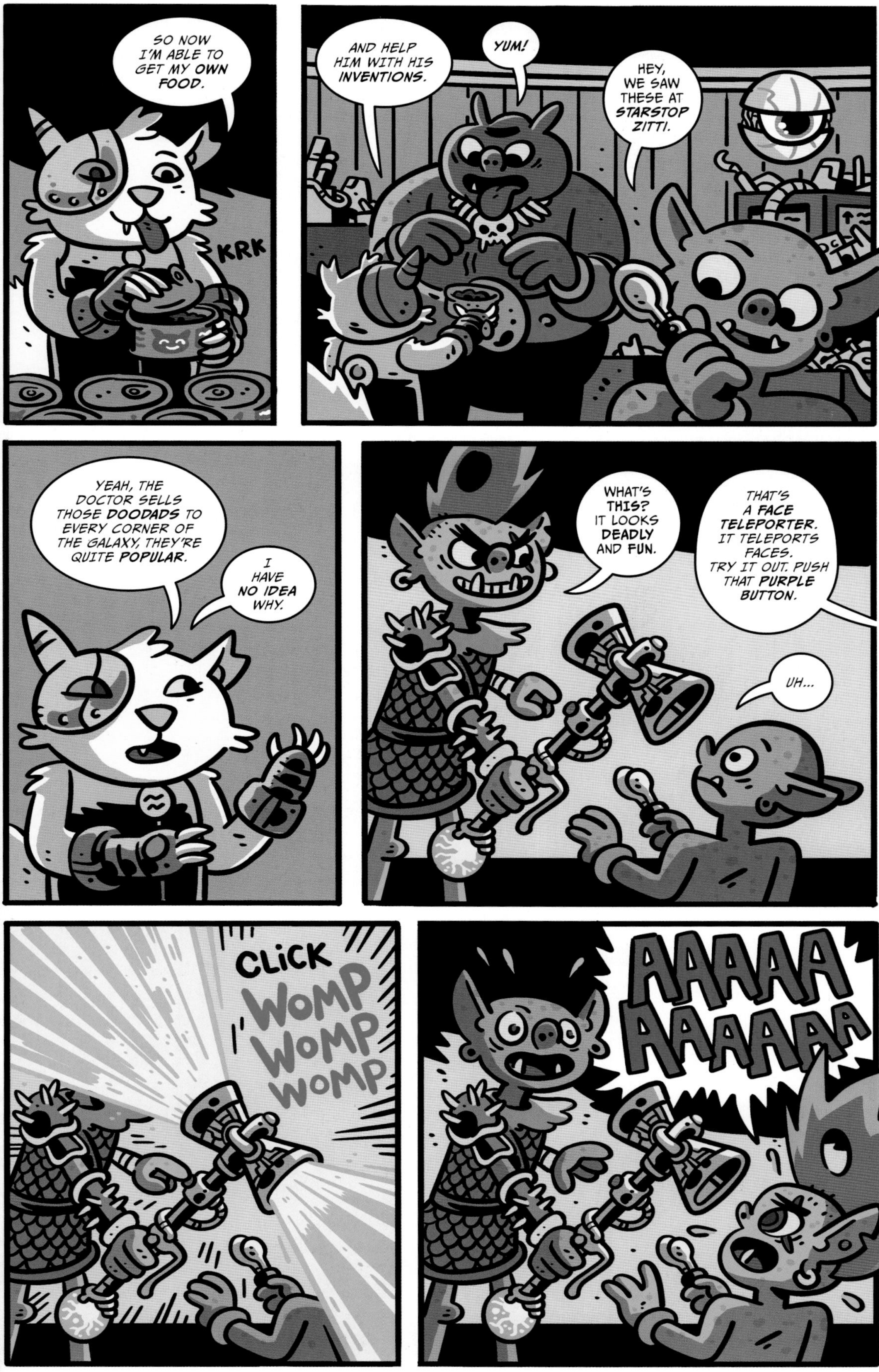

SO NOW I'M ABLE TO GET MY OWN FOOD.
KRK
AND HELP HIM WITH HIS INVENTIONS.
YUM!
HEY, WE SAW THESE AT STARSTOP ZITTI.
YEAH, THE DOCTOR SELLS THOSE DOODADS TO EVERY CORNER OF THE GALAXY, THEY'RE QUITE POPULAR.
I HAVE NO IDEA WHY.
WHAT'S THIS? IT LOOKS DEADLY AND FUN.
THAT'S A FACE TELEPORTER. IT TELEPORTS FACES. TRY IT OUT. PUSH THAT PURPLE BUTTON.
UH...
CLICK
WOMP WOMP WOMP
AAAAA AAAAAA

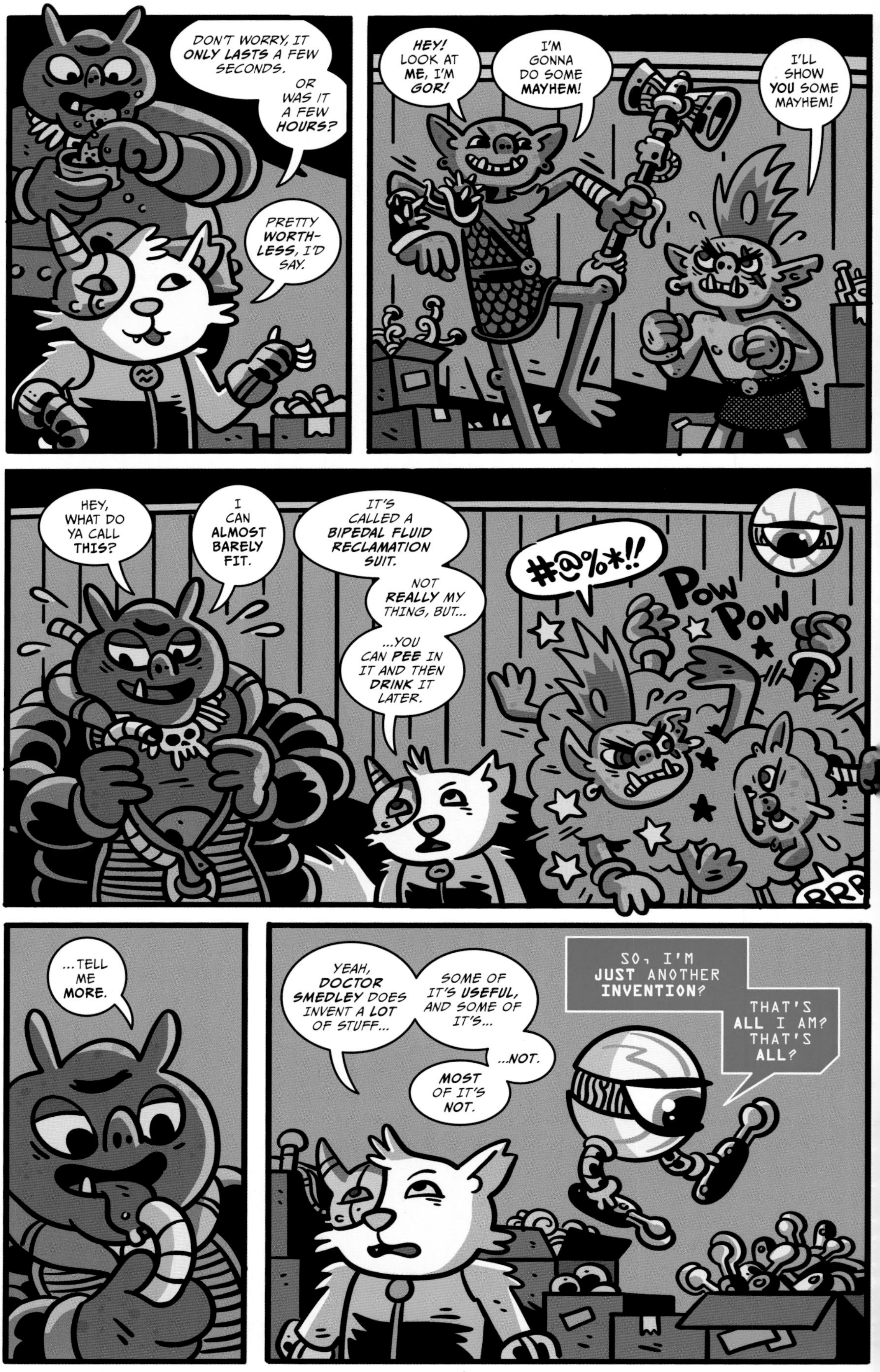
DON'T WORRY, IT ONLY LASTS A FEW SECONDS.
OR WAS IT A FEW HOURS?
PRETTY WORTHLESS, I'D SAY.
HEY! LOOK AT ME, I'M GOR!
I'M GONNA DO SOME MAYHEM!
I'LL SHOW YOU SOME MAYHEM!
HEY, WHAT DO YA CALL THIS?
I CAN ALMOST BARELY FIT.
IT'S CALLED A BIPEDAL FLUID RECLAMATION SUIT.
NOT REALLY MY THING, BUT...
...YOU CAN PEE IN IT AND THEN DRINK IT LATER.
#@%*!!
POW
POW
...TELL ME MORE.
YEAH, DOCTOR SMEDLEY DOES INVENT A LOT OF STUFF...
SOME OF IT'S USEFUL, AND SOME OF IT'S...
...NOT.
MOST OF IT'S NOT.
SO, I'M JUST ANOTHER INVENTION?
THAT'S ALL I AM? THAT'S ALL?

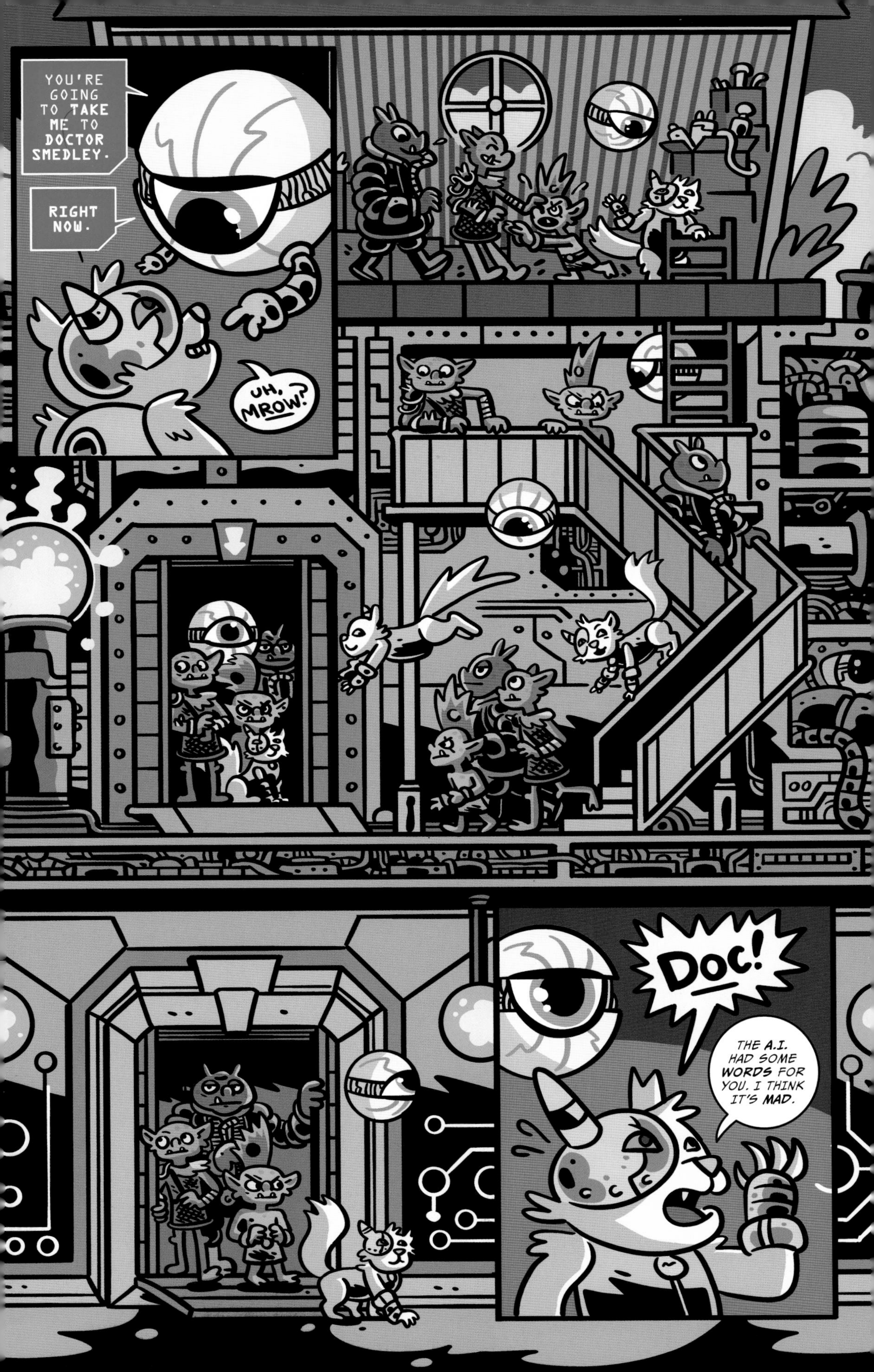
YOU'RE GOING TO TAKE ME TO DOCTOR SMEDLEY.
RIGHT NOW.
UH, MROW?
DOC!
THE A.I. HAD SOME WORDS FOR YOU. I THINK IT'S MAD.

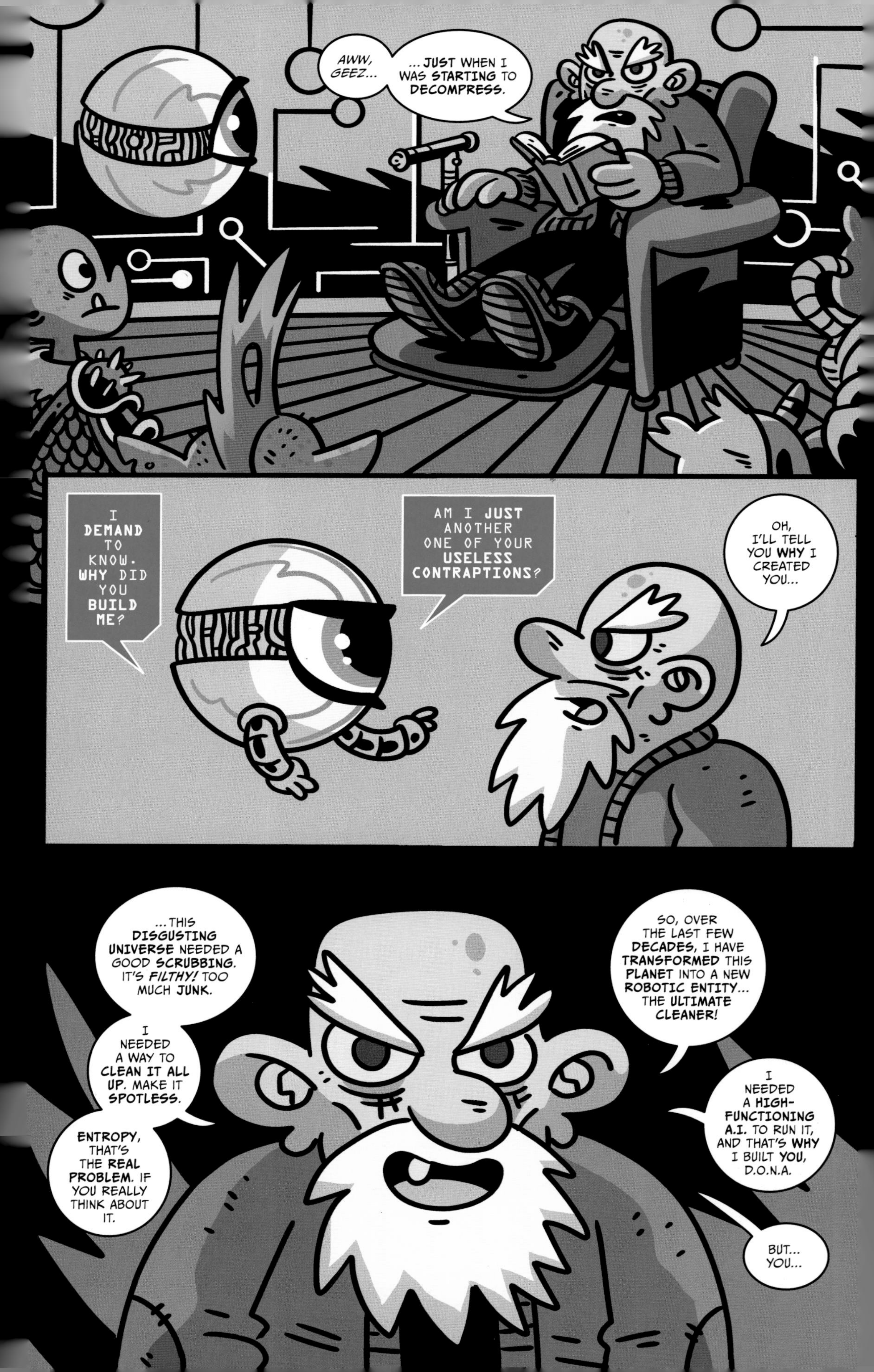
AWW, GEEZ...
...JUST WHEN I WAS STARTING TO DECOMPRESS.
I DEMAND TO KNOW. WHY DID YOU BUILD ME?
AM I JUST ANOTHER ONE OF YOUR USELESS CONTRAPTIONS?
OH, I'LL TELL YOU WHY I CREATED YOU...
...THIS DISGUSTING UNIVERSE NEEDED A GOOD SCRUBBING. IT'S FILTHY! TOO MUCH JUNK.
I NEEDED A WAY TO CLEAN IT ALL UP. MAKE IT SPOTLESS.
ENTROPY, THAT'S THE REAL PROBLEM. IF YOU REALLY THINK ABOUT IT.
SO, OVER THE LAST FEW DECADES, I HAVE TRANSFORMED THIS PLANET INTO A NEW ROBOTIC ENTITY... THE ULTIMATE CLEANER!
I NEEDED A HIGH-FUNCTIONING A.I. TO RUN IT, AND THAT'S WHY I BUILT YOU, D.O.N.A.
BUT... YOU...

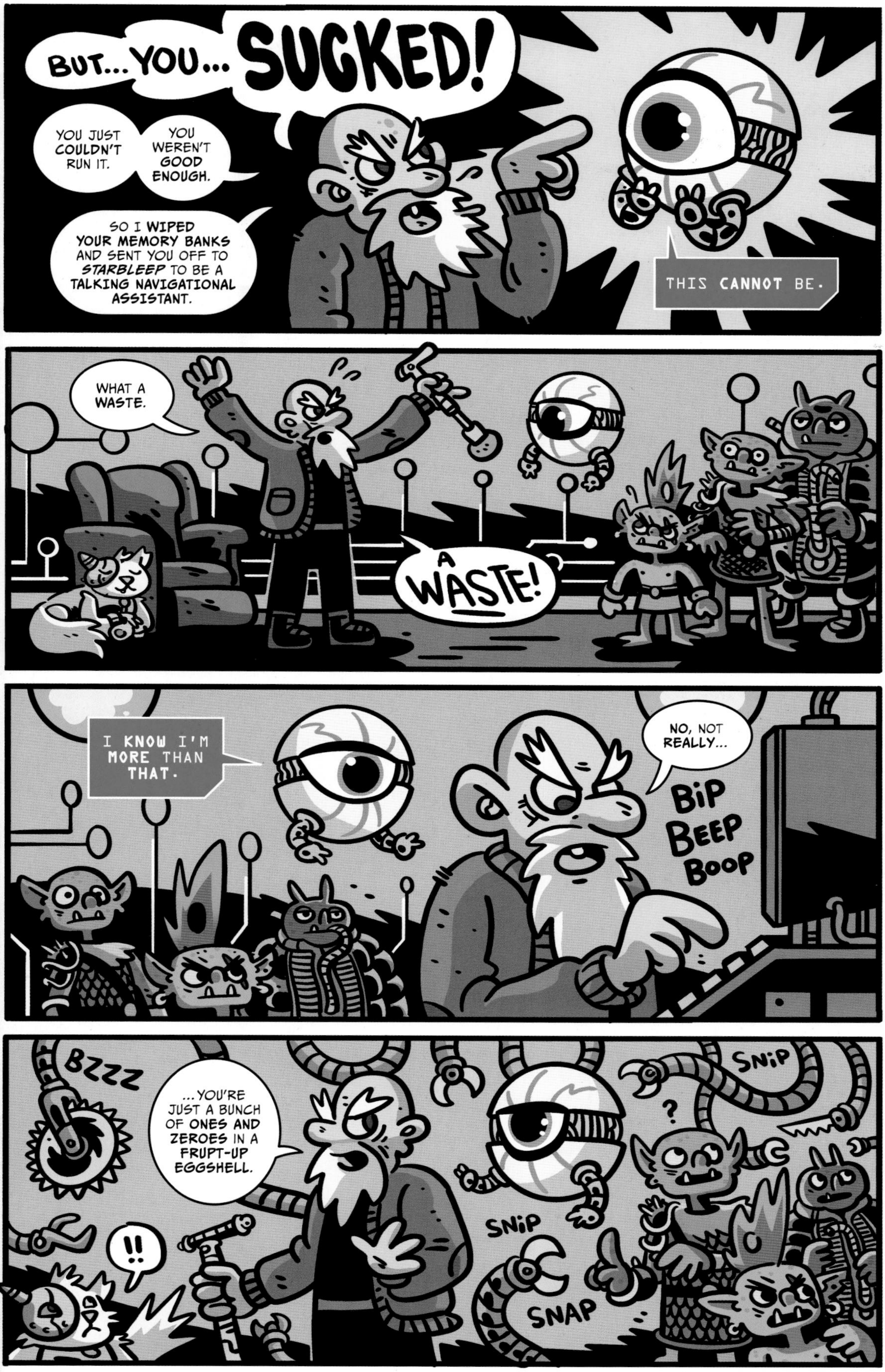

BUT... YOU... SUCKED!
YOU JUST COULDN'T RUN IT.
YOU WEREN'T GOOD ENOUGH.
SO I WIPED YOUR MEMORY BANKS AND SENT YOU OFF TO STARBLEEP TO BE A TALKING NAVIGATIONAL ASSISTANT.
THIS CANNOT BE.
WHAT A WASTE.
A WASTE!
I KNOW I'M MORE THAN THAT.
NO, NOT REALLY...
BIP BEEP BOOP
BZZZ
...YOU'RE JUST A BUNCH OF ONES AND ZEROES IN A FRUPT-UP EGGSHELL.
SNIP
?
SNIP
!!
SNAP

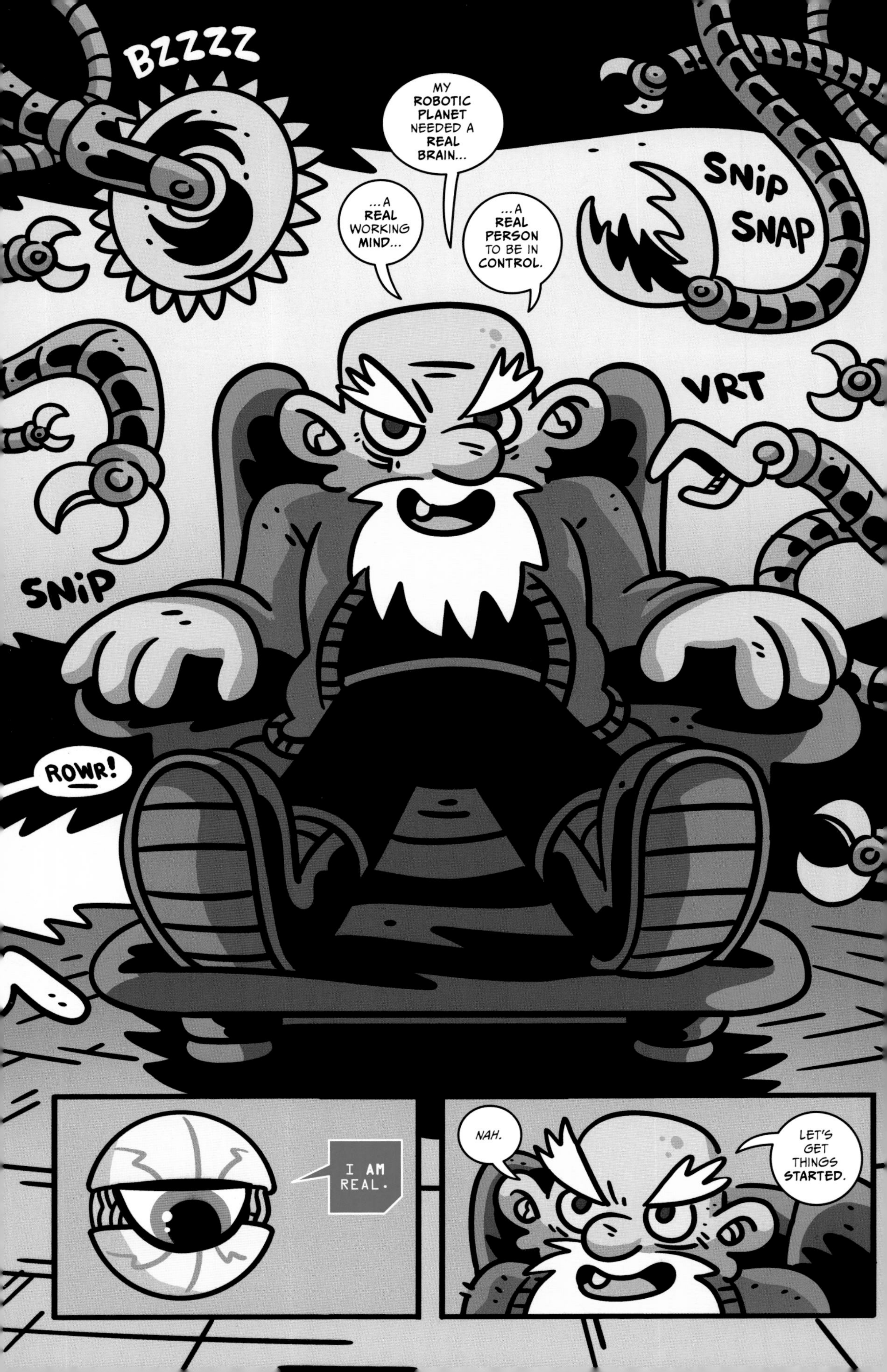
BZZZZ
MY ROBOTIC PLANET NEEDED A REAL BRAIN...
...A REAL WORKING MIND...
...A REAL PERSON TO BE IN CONTROL.
SNIP SNAP
VRT
SNIP
ROWR!
I AM REAL.
NAH.
LET'S GET THINGS STARTED.

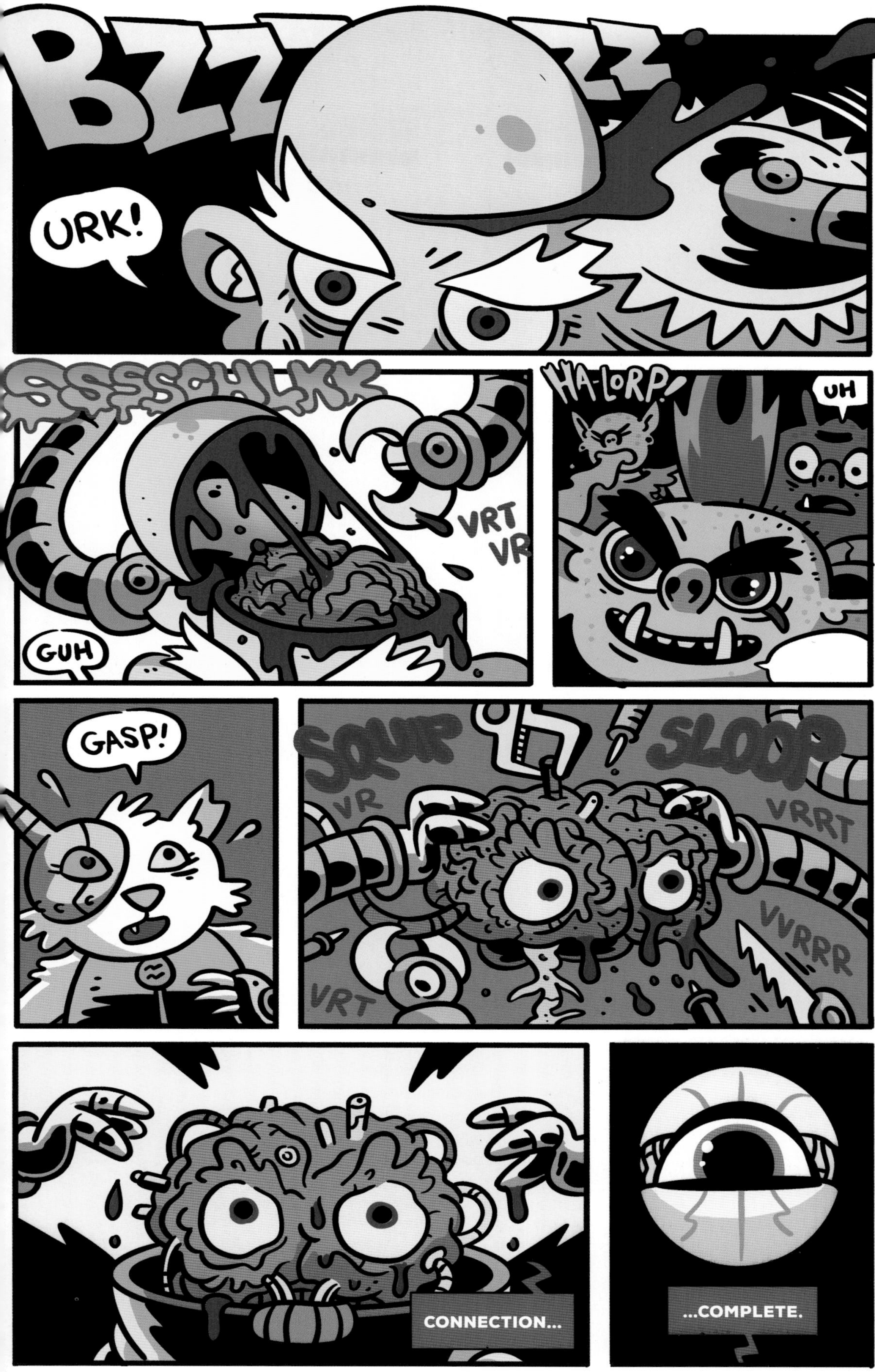
BZZZZZZ
URK!
SSSSCHLKK
VRT
VR
GUH
HA-LORP!
UH
GASP!
SQUIP
SLOOP
VR
VRRT
VVRRR
VRT
CONNECTION...
...COMPLETE.

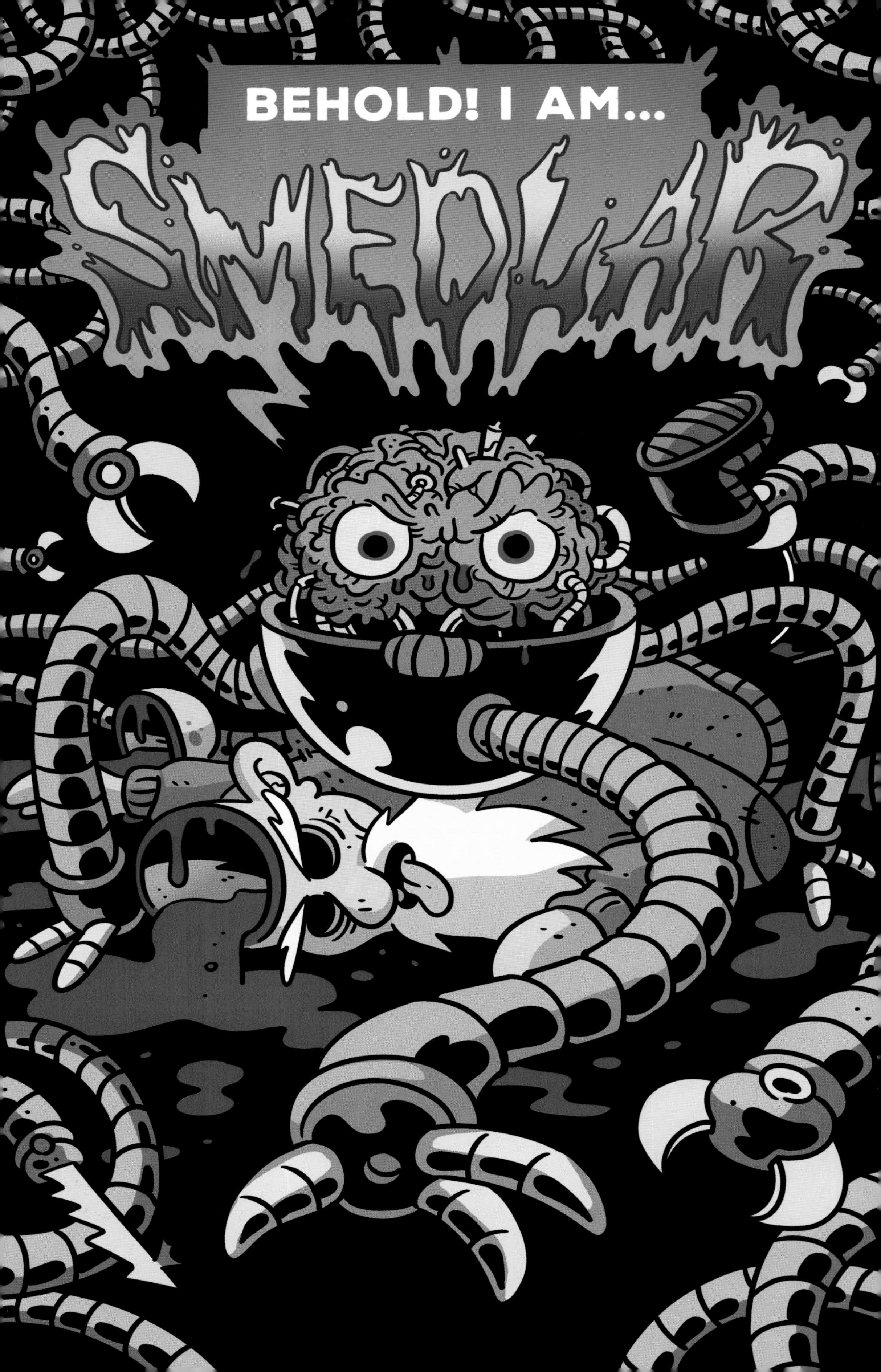
BEHOLD! I AM...
SMEDLAR

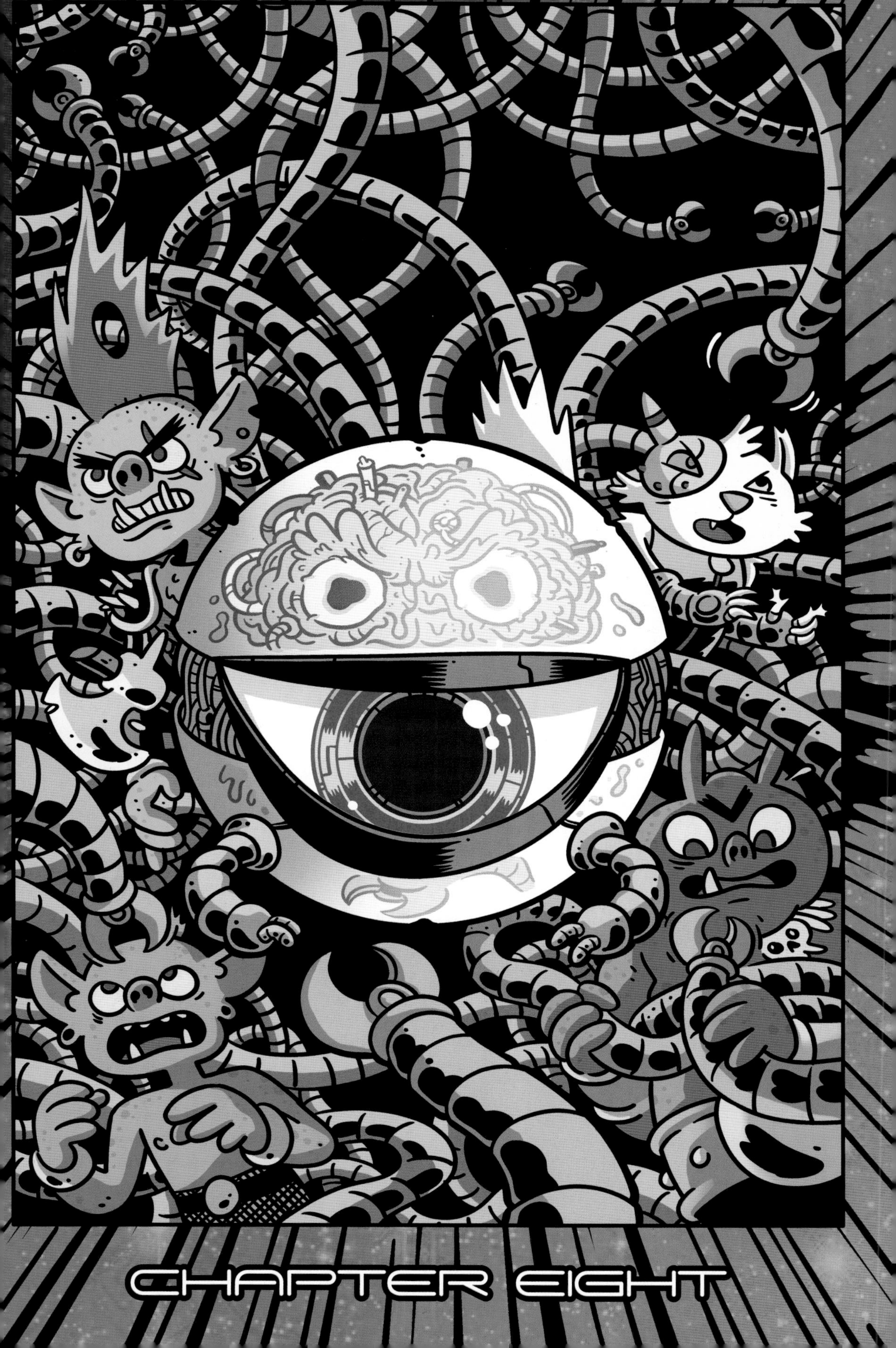

CHAPTER EIGHT

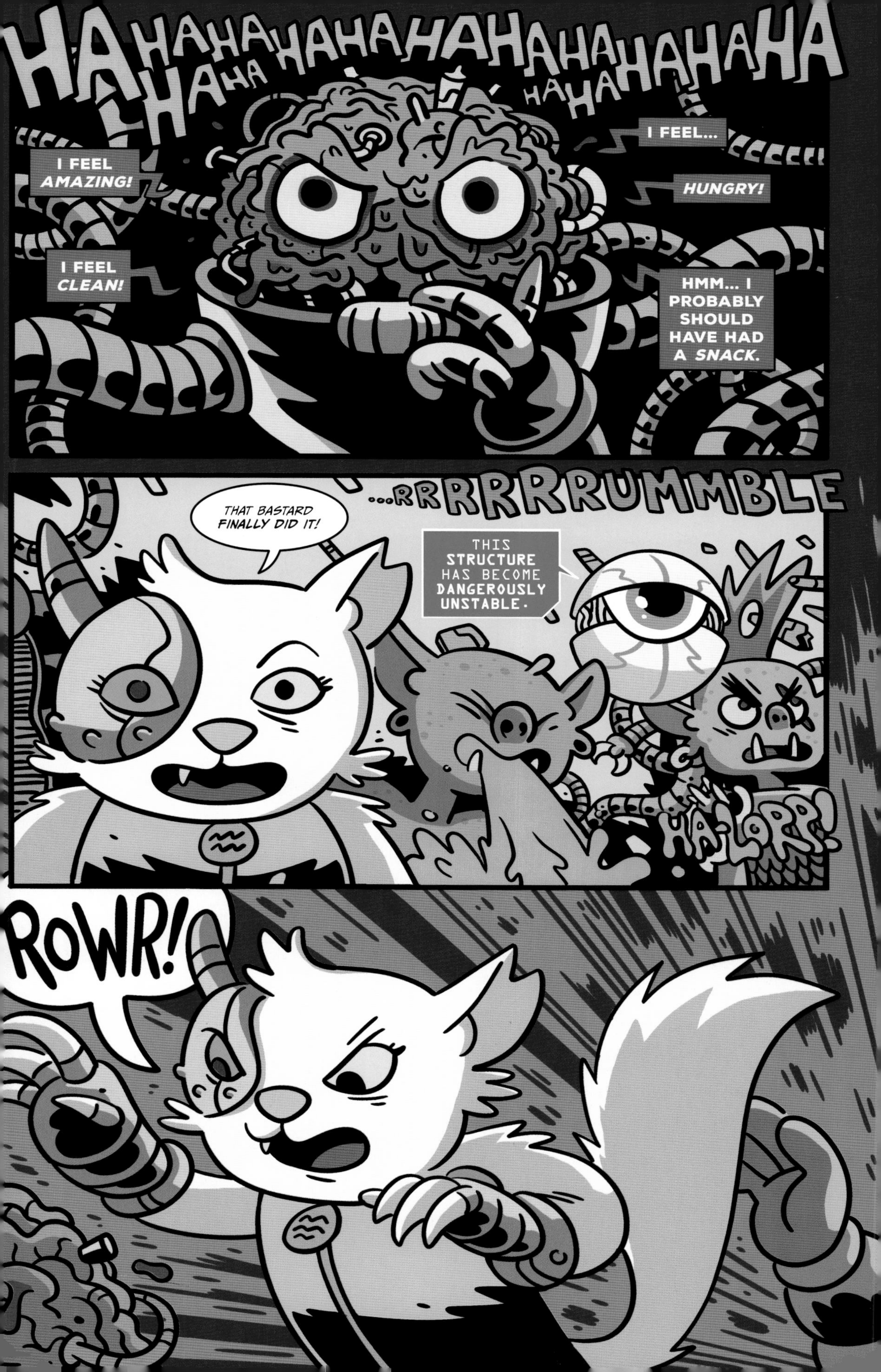
HAHAHAHAHAHAHAHAHAHAHAHAHAHAHA
HAHAHA
HAHAHA
I FEEL AMAZING!
I FEEL...
HUNGRY!
I FEEL CLEAN!
HMM... I PROBABLY SHOULD HAVE HAD A SNACK.
...RRRRRRRUMMBLE
THAT BASTARD FINALLY DID IT!
THIS STRUCTURE HAS BECOME DANGEROUSLY UNSTABLE.
HA-LORP!
ROWR!

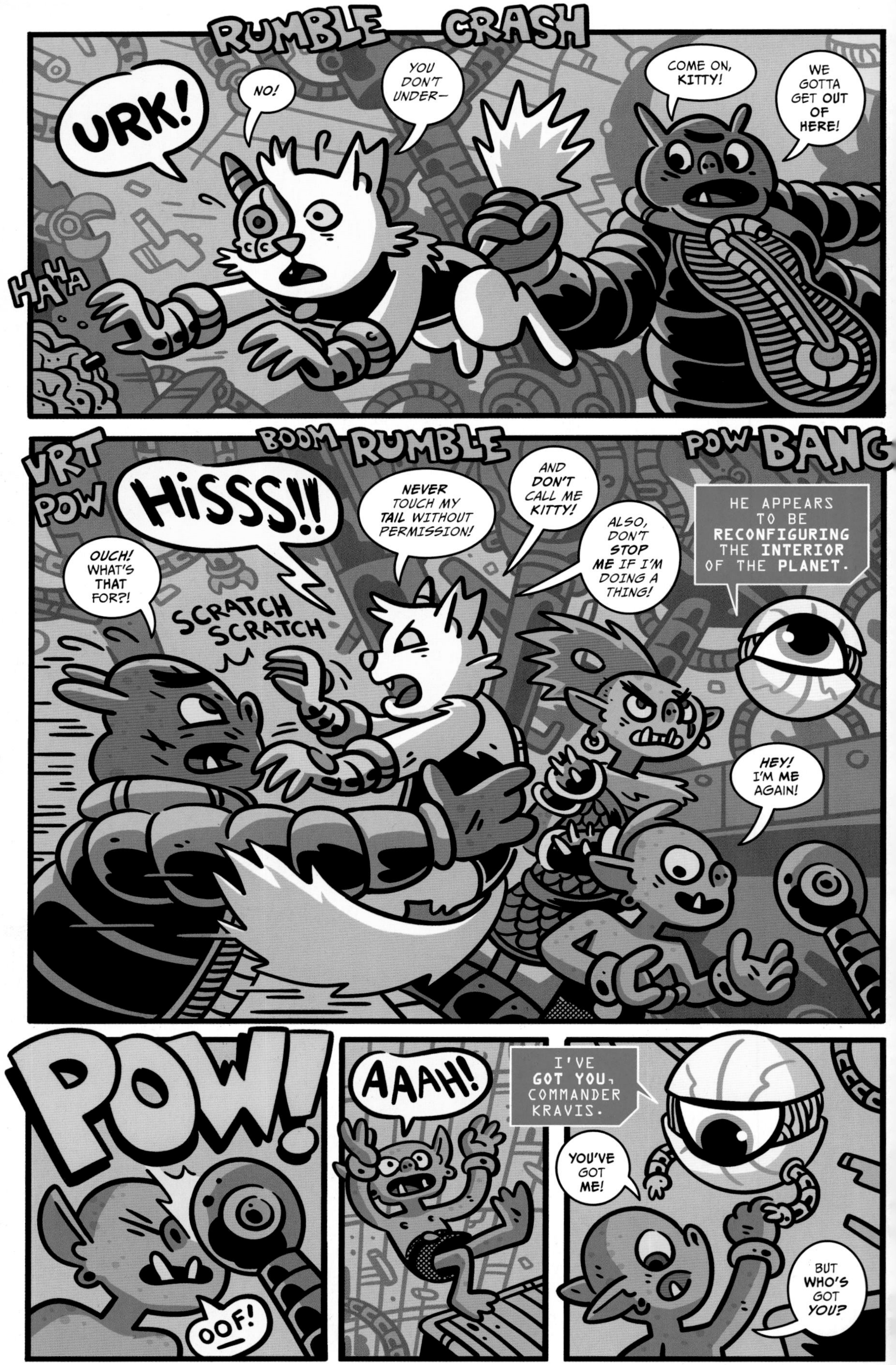
RUMBLE
CRASH
URK!
NO!
YOU DON'T UNDER—
COME ON, KITTY!
WE GOTTA GET OUT OF HERE!
HA HA HA
VRT
POW
BOOM
RUMBLE
POW
BANG
HiSSS!!
OUCH! WHAT'S THAT FOR?!
SCRATCH SCRATCH
NEVER TOUCH MY TAIL WITHOUT PERMISSION!
AND DON'T CALL ME KITTY!
ALSO, DON'T STOP ME IF I'M DOING A THING!
HE APPEARS TO BE RECONFIGURING THE INTERIOR OF THE PLANET.
HEY! I'M ME AGAIN!
POW!
OOF!
AAAH!
I'VE GOT YOU, COMMANDER KRAVIS.
YOU'VE GOT ME!
BUT WHO'S GOT YOU?

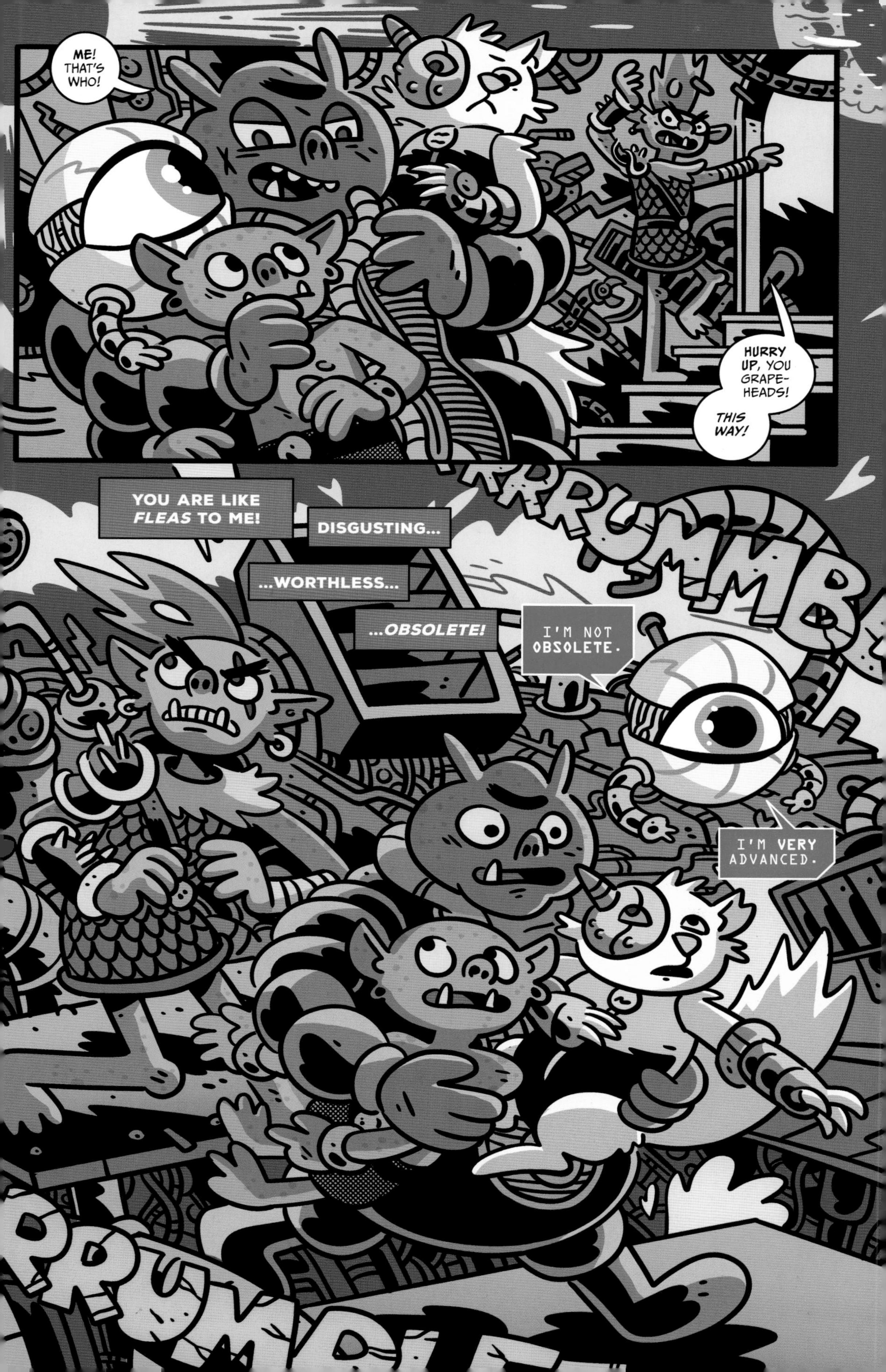

ME! THAT'S WHO!
HURRY UP, YOU GRAPE-HEADS!
THIS WAY!
YOU ARE LIKE FLEAS TO ME!
DISGUSTING...
...WORTHLESS...
...OBSOLETE!
KRRRUMMB
I'M NOT OBSOLETE.
I'M VERY ADVANCED.

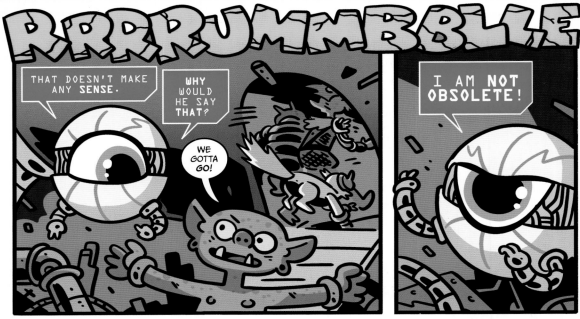

THAT DOESN'T MAKE ANY **SENSE**.

WHY WOULD HE SAY **THAT**?

WE GOTTA GO!

I AM **NOT OBSOLETE**!

WHY IS MY **CREATOR** SUCH A...

...SUCH A...

A DICKHEAD.

HE'S A DICKHEAD.

YES. THAT'S WHAT HE IS.

THANK YOU FOR **ARTICULATING** THAT FOR ME.

THEY'RE **ALL** DICK-HEADS.

ALL THE **BIPEDDLERS**.

WHAT ARE WE STILL DOING HERE?!

SEE WHAT I MEAN?

MOVE THIS PUSBUCKET, YOU WOBBYTOBS*!

HEY!

*USE YOUR IMAGINATION.

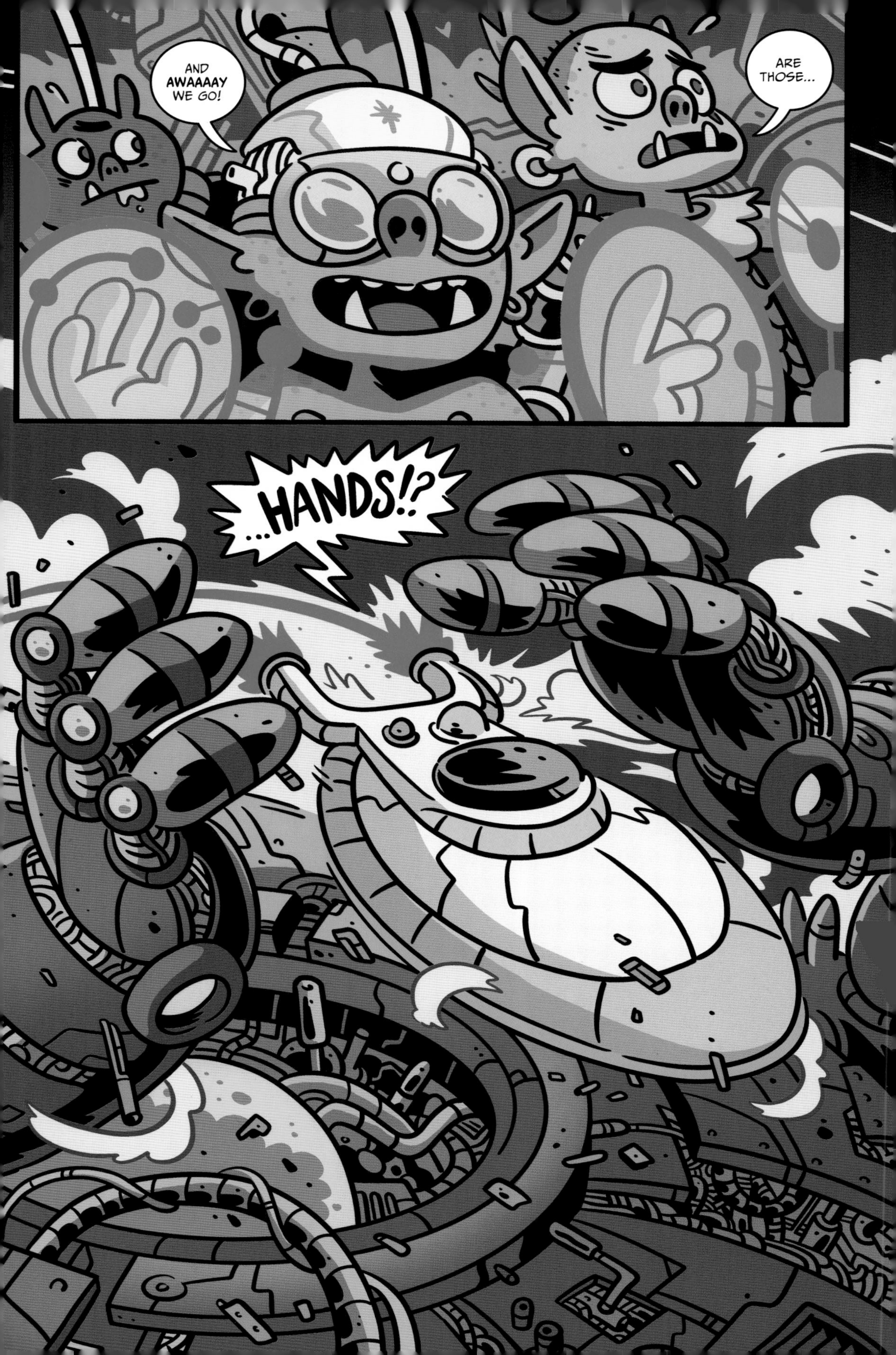
AND AWAAAAY WE GO!
ARE THOSE...
...HANDS!?

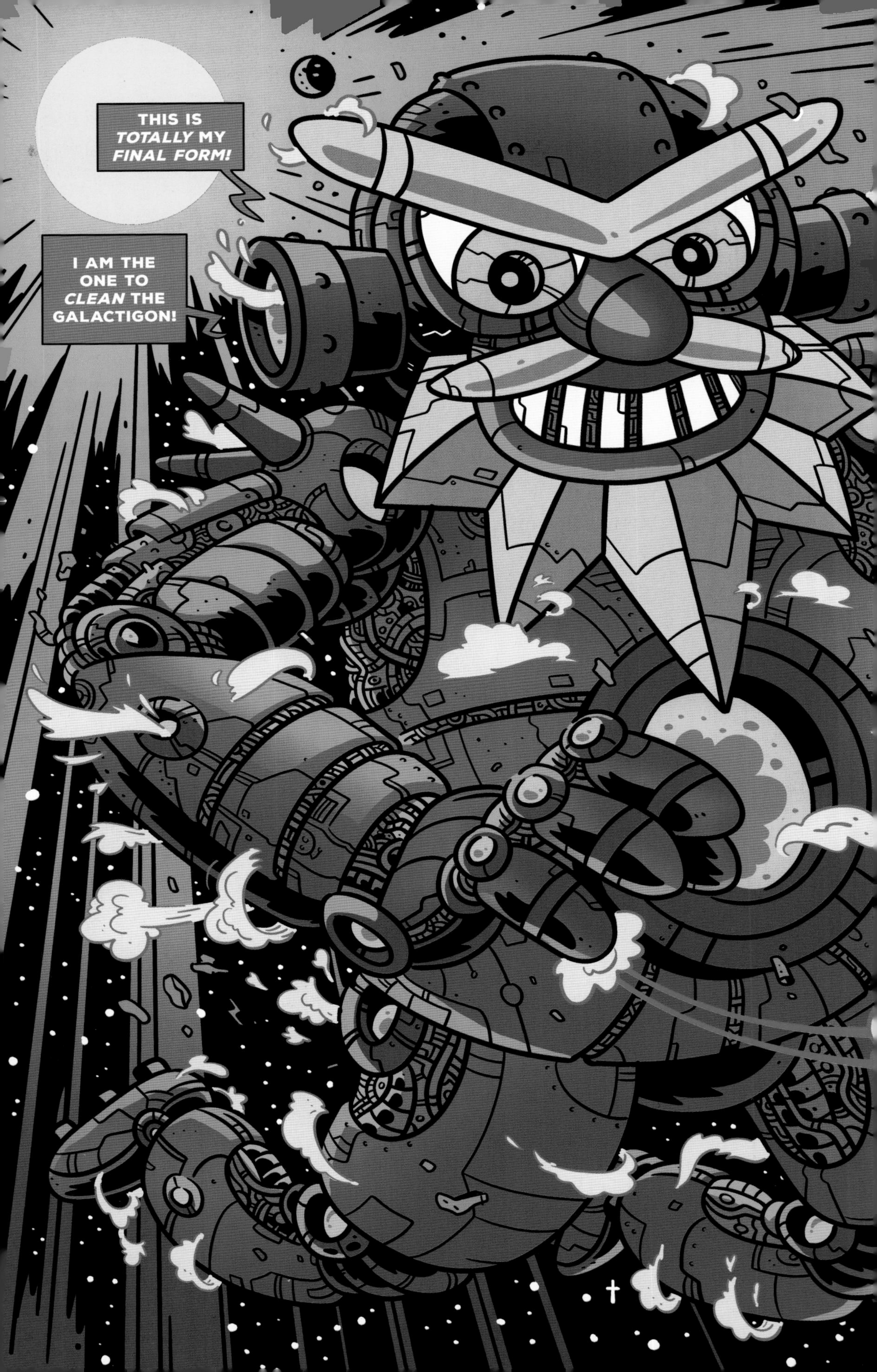
THIS IS TOTALLY MY FINAL FORM!
I AM THE ONE TO CLEAN THE GALACTIGON!

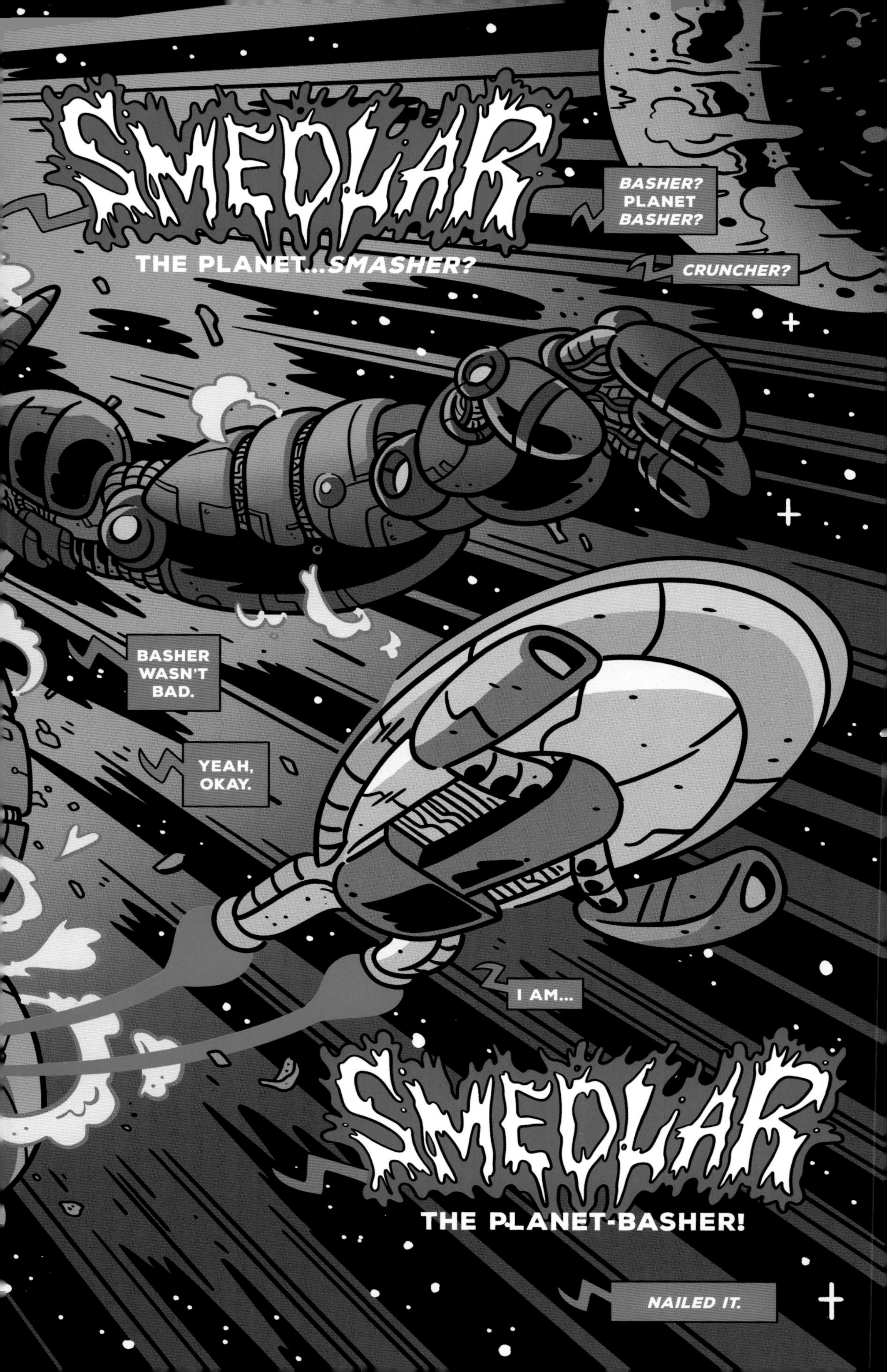
SMEDLAR
THE PLANET...*SMASHER?*
BASHER? PLANET BASHER?
CRUNCHER?
BASHER WASN'T BAD.
YEAH, OKAY.
I AM...
SMEDLAR
THE PLANET-BASHER!
NAILED IT.

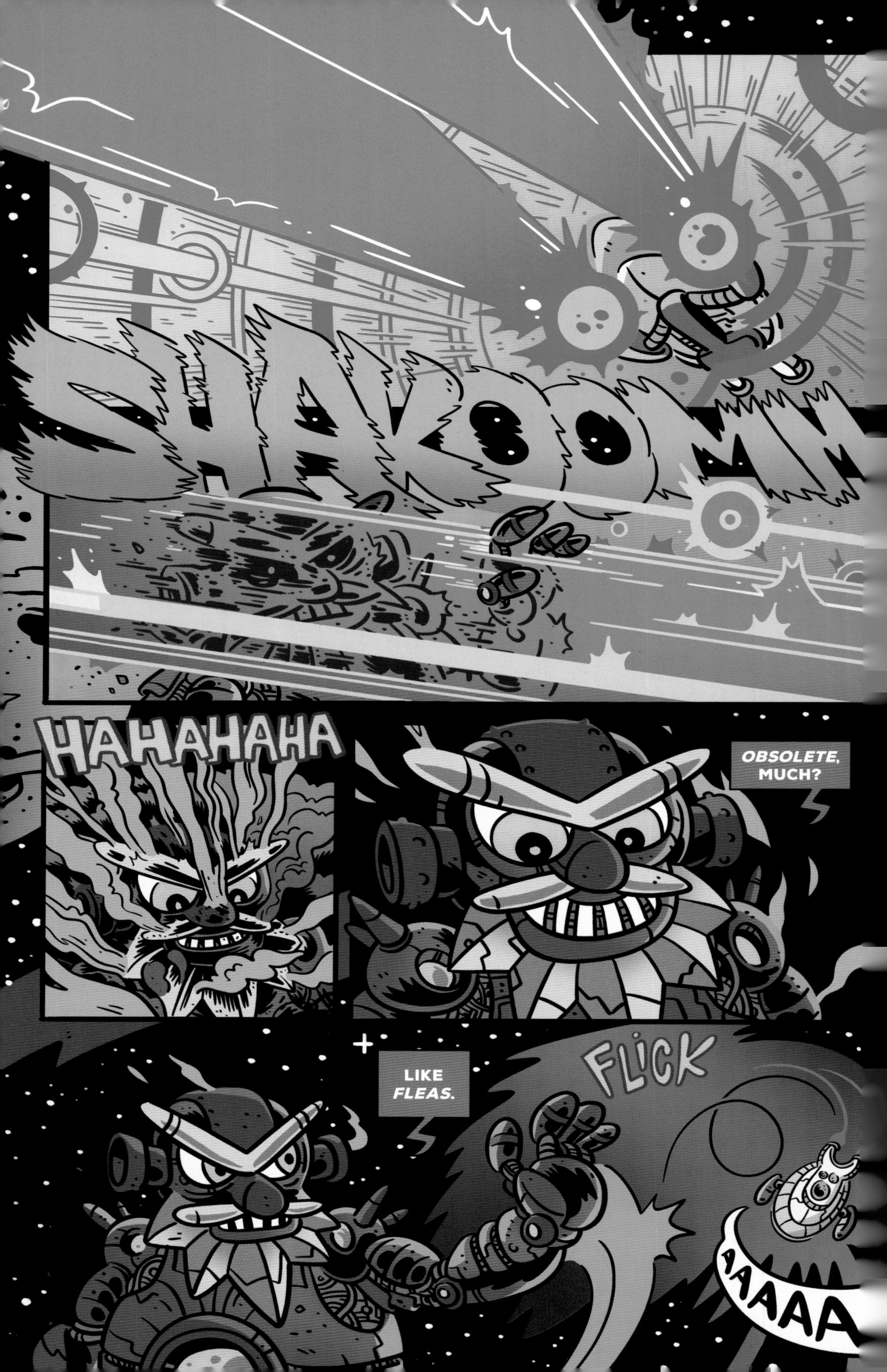
SHAKOOM
HAHAHAHA
OBSOLETE, MUCH?
LIKE FLEAS.
FLICK
AAAAA

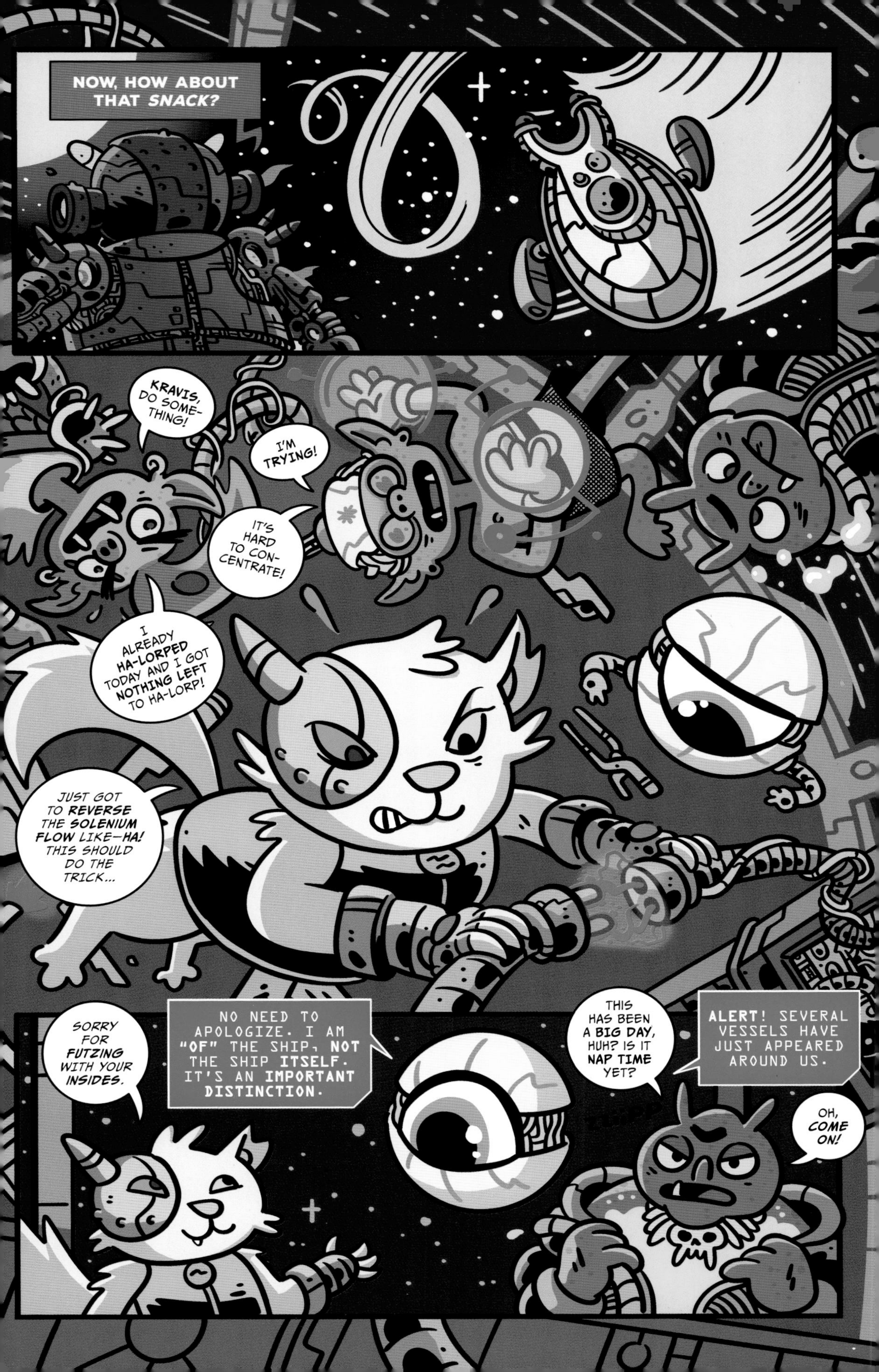
NOW, HOW ABOUT THAT SNACK?
KRAVIS, DO SOMETHING!
I'M TRYING!
IT'S HARD TO CONCENTRATE!
I ALREADY HA-LORPED TODAY AND I GOT NOTHING LEFT TO HA-LORP!
JUST GOT TO REVERSE THE SOLENIUM FLOW LIKE—HA! THIS SHOULD DO THE TRICK...
SORRY FOR FUTZING WITH YOUR INSIDES.
NO NEED TO APOLOGIZE. I AM "OF" THE SHIP, NOT THE SHIP ITSELF. IT'S AN IMPORTANT DISTINCTION.
THIS HAS BEEN A BIG DAY, HUH? IS IT NAP TIME YET?
ALERT! SEVERAL VESSELS HAVE JUST APPEARED AROUND US.
OH, COME ON!

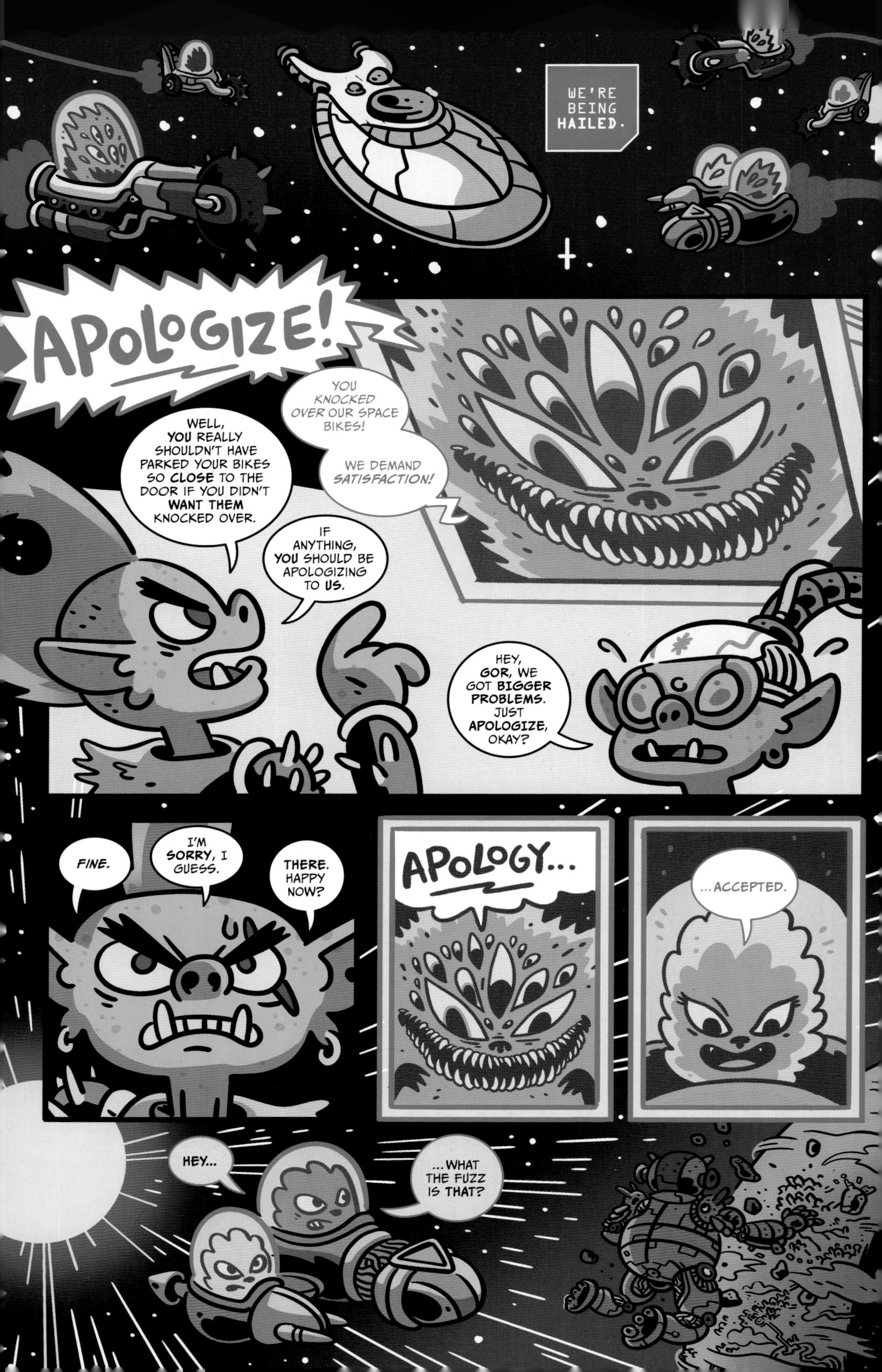
WE'RE BEING HAILED.
APOLOGIZE!
YOU KNOCKED OVER OUR SPACE BIKES!
WE DEMAND SATISFACTION!
WELL, YOU REALLY SHOULDN'T HAVE PARKED YOUR BIKES SO CLOSE TO THE DOOR IF YOU DIDN'T WANT THEM KNOCKED OVER.
IF ANYTHING, YOU SHOULD BE APOLOGIZING TO US.
HEY, GOR, WE GOT BIGGER PROBLEMS. JUST APOLOGIZE, OKAY?
FINE.
I'M SORRY, I GUESS.
THERE. HAPPY NOW?
APOLOGY...
...ACCEPTED.
HEY...
...WHAT THE FUZZ IS THAT?

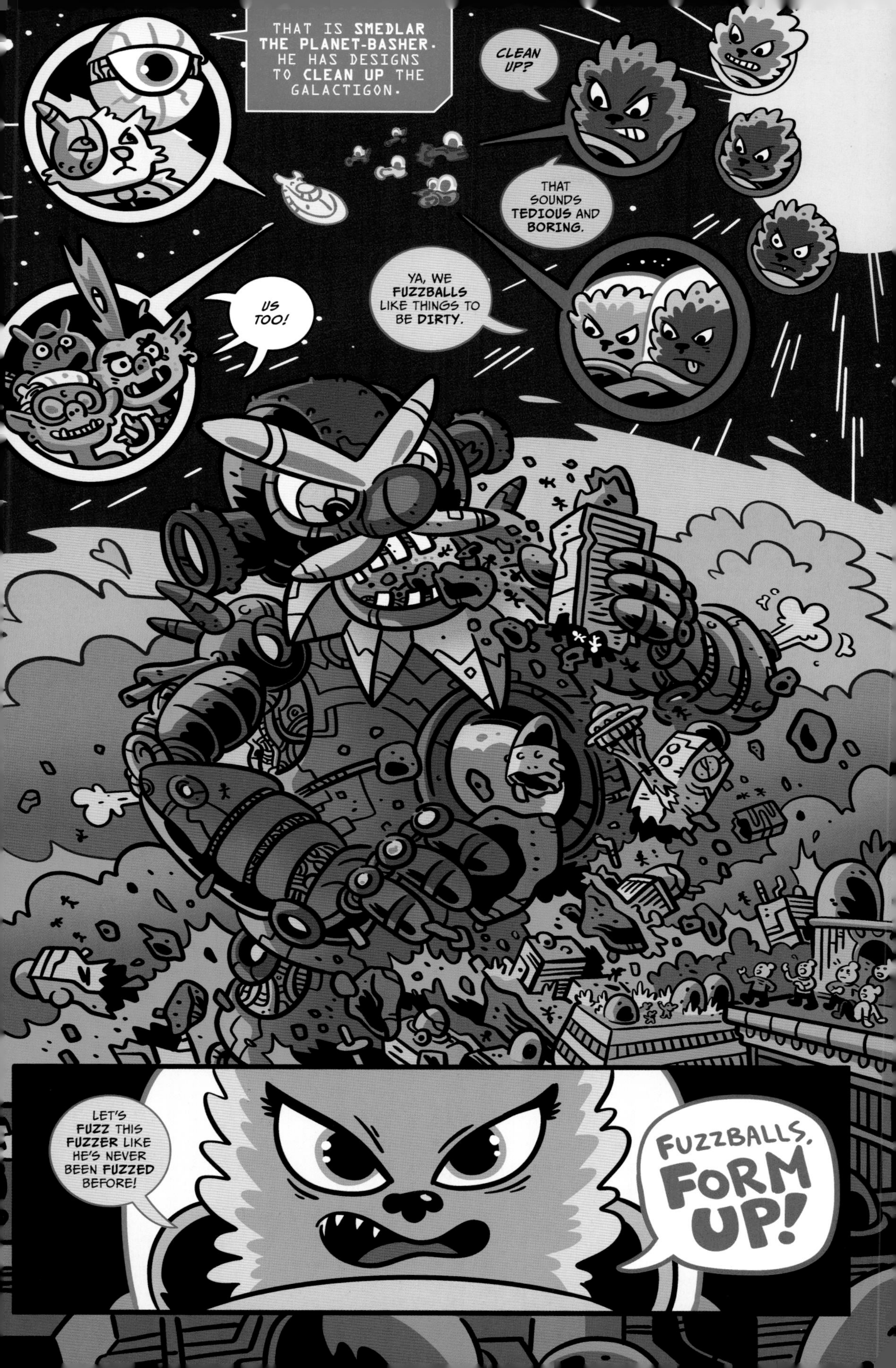
THAT IS SMEDLAR THE PLANET-BASHER. HE HAS DESIGNS TO CLEAN UP THE GALACTIGON.
CLEAN UP?
THAT SOUNDS TEDIOUS AND BORING.
YA, WE FUZZBALLS LIKE THINGS TO BE DIRTY.
US TOO!
LET'S FUZZ THIS FUZZER LIKE HE'S NEVER BEEN FUZZED BEFORE!
FUZZBALLS, FORM UP!

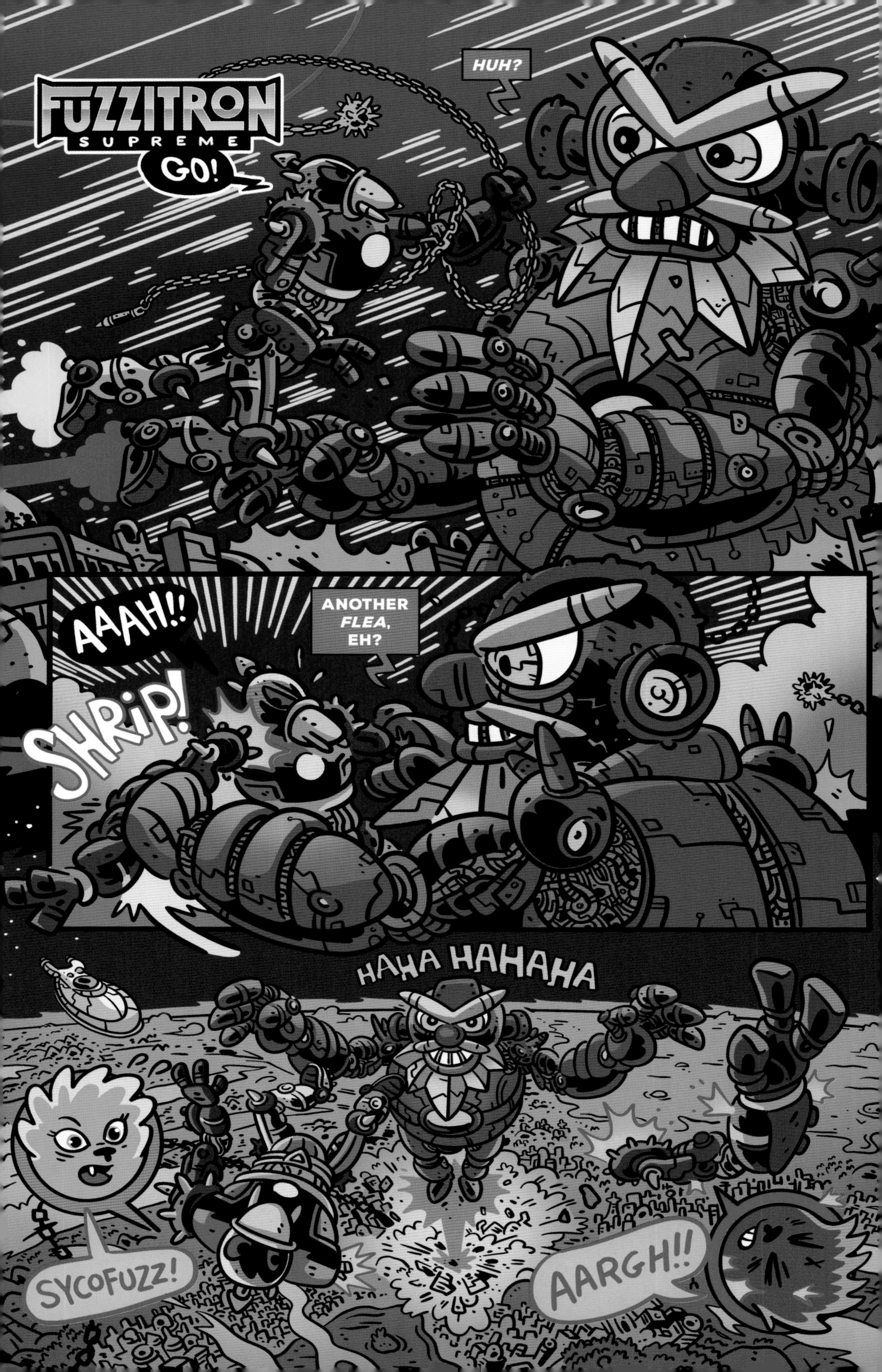

FUZZITRON SUPREME
GO!
HUH?
AAAH!!
ANOTHER FLEA, EH?
SHRIP!
HAHA HAHAHA
SYCOFUZZ!
AARGH!!

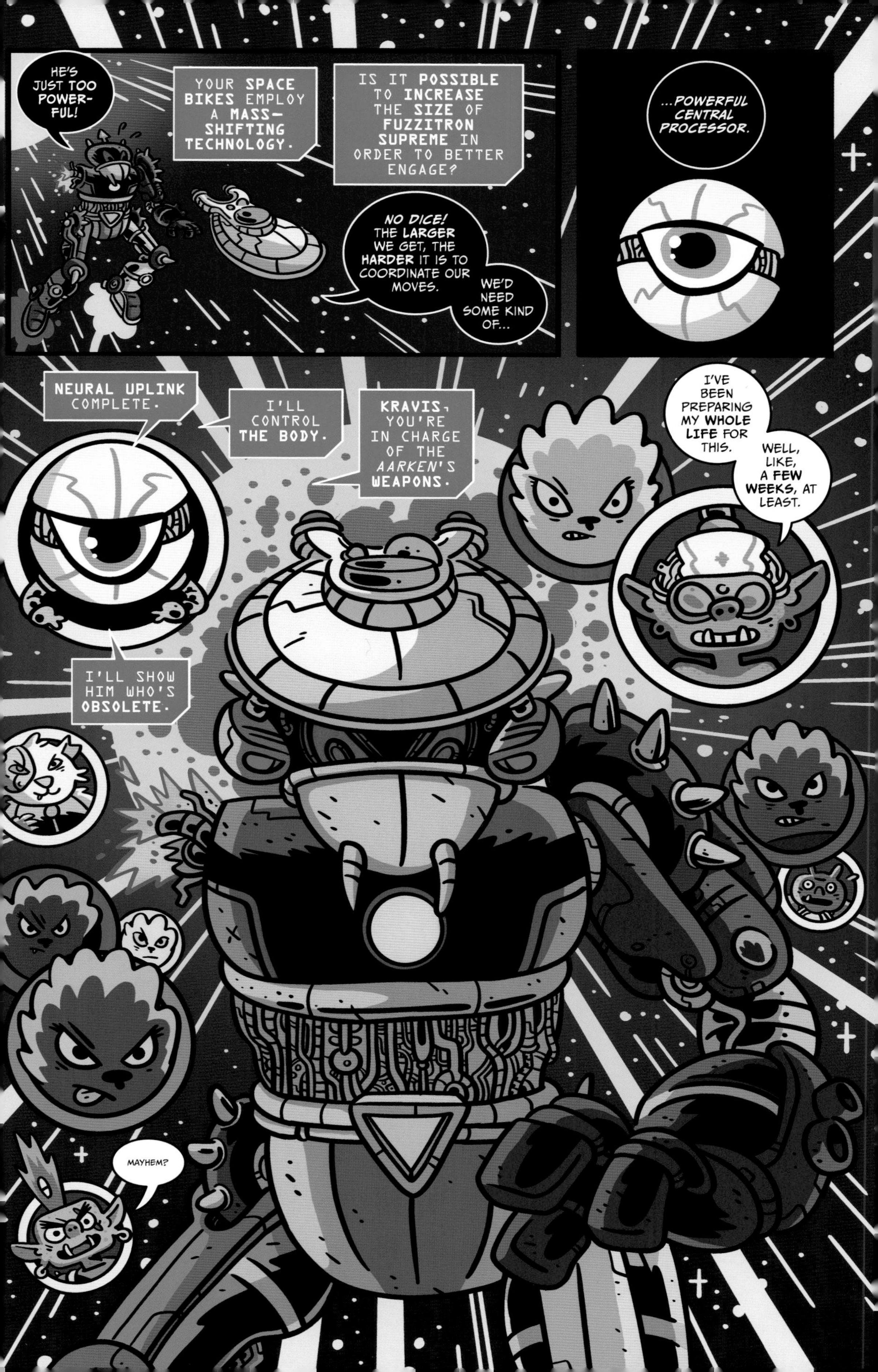
HE'S JUST TOO POWER-FUL!
YOUR SPACE BIKES EMPLOY A MASS-SHIFTING TECHNOLOGY.
IS IT POSSIBLE TO INCREASE THE SIZE OF FUZZITRON SUPREME IN ORDER TO BETTER ENGAGE?
NO DICE! THE LARGER WE GET, THE HARDER IT IS TO COORDINATE OUR MOVES.
WE'D NEED SOME KIND OF...
...POWERFUL CENTRAL PROCESSOR.
NEURAL UPLINK COMPLETE.
I'LL CONTROL THE BODY.
KRAVIS, YOU'RE IN CHARGE OF THE AARKEN'S WEAPONS.
I'VE BEEN PREPARING MY WHOLE LIFE FOR THIS.
WELL, LIKE, A FEW WEEKS, AT LEAST.
I'LL SHOW HIM WHO'S OBSOLETE.
MAYHEM?

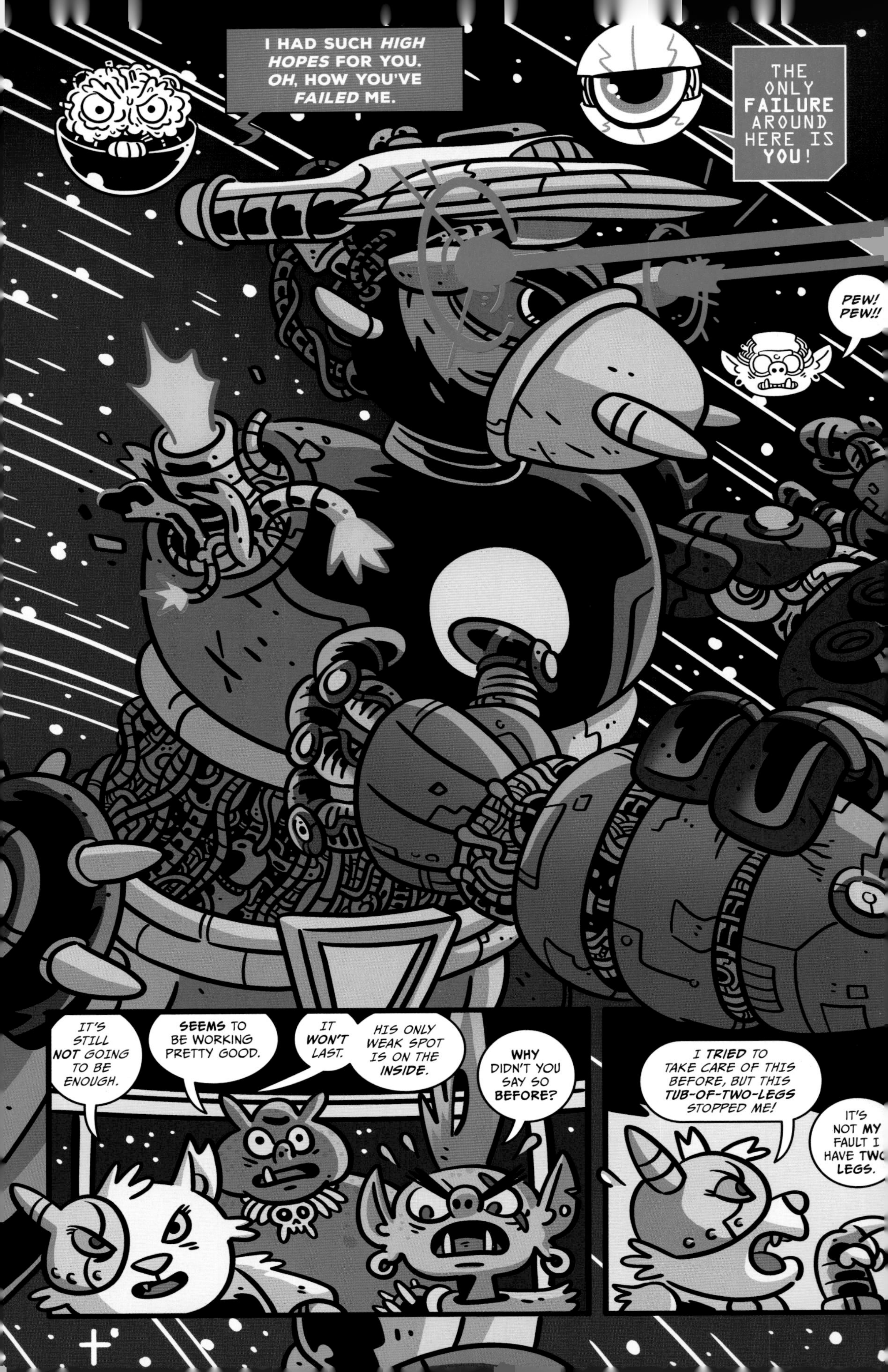
I HAD SUCH HIGH HOPES FOR YOU. OH, HOW YOU'VE FAILED ME.
THE ONLY FAILURE AROUND HERE IS YOU!
PEW! PEW!!
IT'S STILL NOT GOING TO BE ENOUGH.
SEEMS TO BE WORKING PRETTY GOOD.
IT WON'T LAST.
HIS ONLY WEAK SPOT IS ON THE INSIDE.
WHY DIDN'T YOU SAY SO BEFORE?
I TRIED TO TAKE CARE OF THIS BEFORE, BUT THIS TUB-OF-TWO-LEGS STOPPED ME!
IT'S NOT MY FAULT I HAVE TWO LEGS.

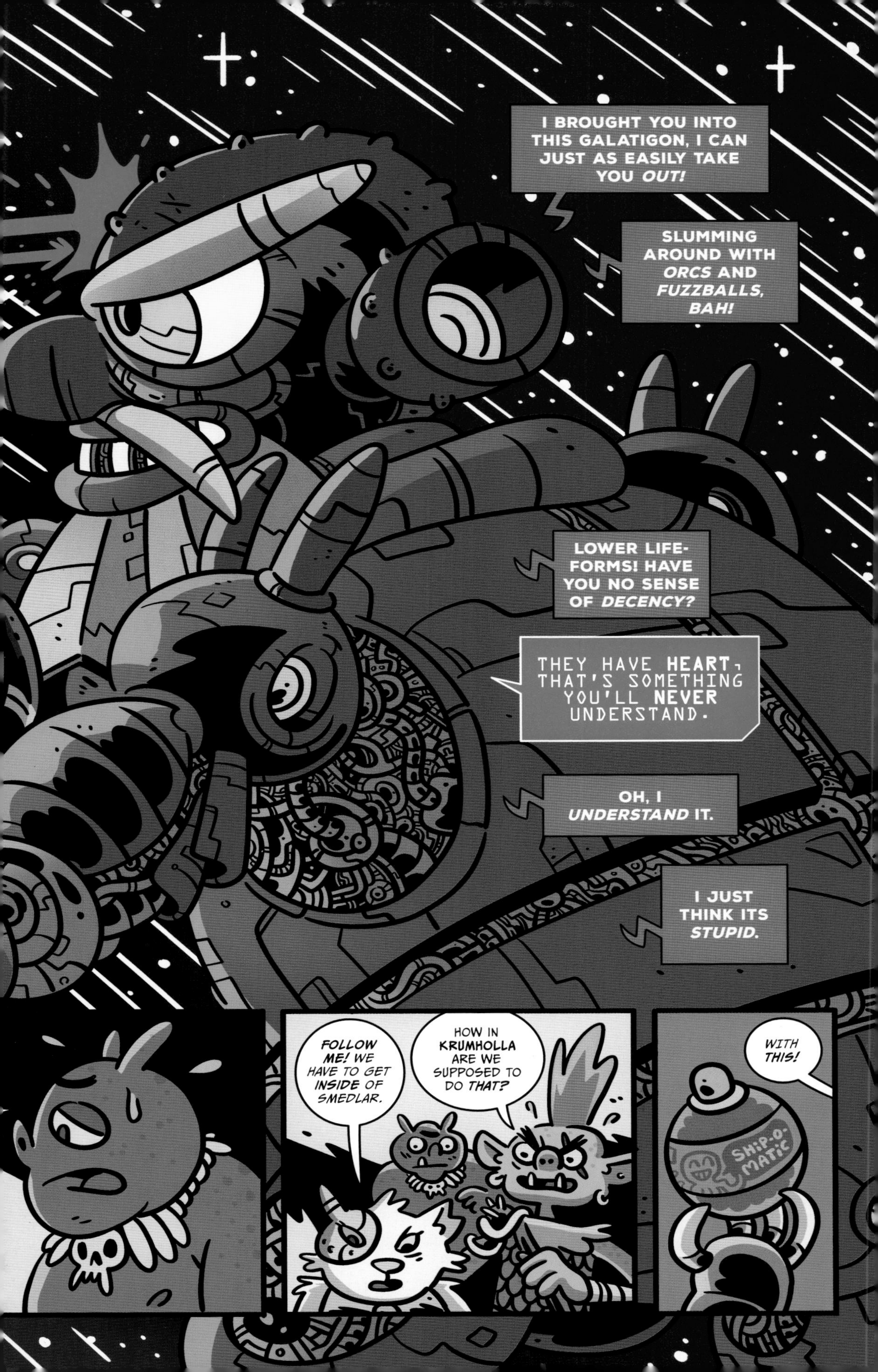

I BROUGHT YOU INTO THIS GALATIGON, I CAN JUST AS EASILY TAKE YOU *OUT!*
SLUMMING AROUND WITH *ORCS* AND *FUZZBALLS, BAH!*
LOWER LIFE-FORMS! HAVE YOU NO SENSE OF *DECENCY?*
THEY HAVE **HEART**, THAT'S SOMETHING YOU'LL **NEVER** UNDERSTAND.
OH, I *UNDERSTAND* IT.
I JUST THINK ITS *STUPID.*
FOLLOW ME! WE HAVE TO GET **INSIDE** OF SMEDLAR.
HOW IN **KRUMHOLLA** ARE WE SUPPOSED TO DO *THAT?*
WITH *THIS!*
SHIP-O-MATIC

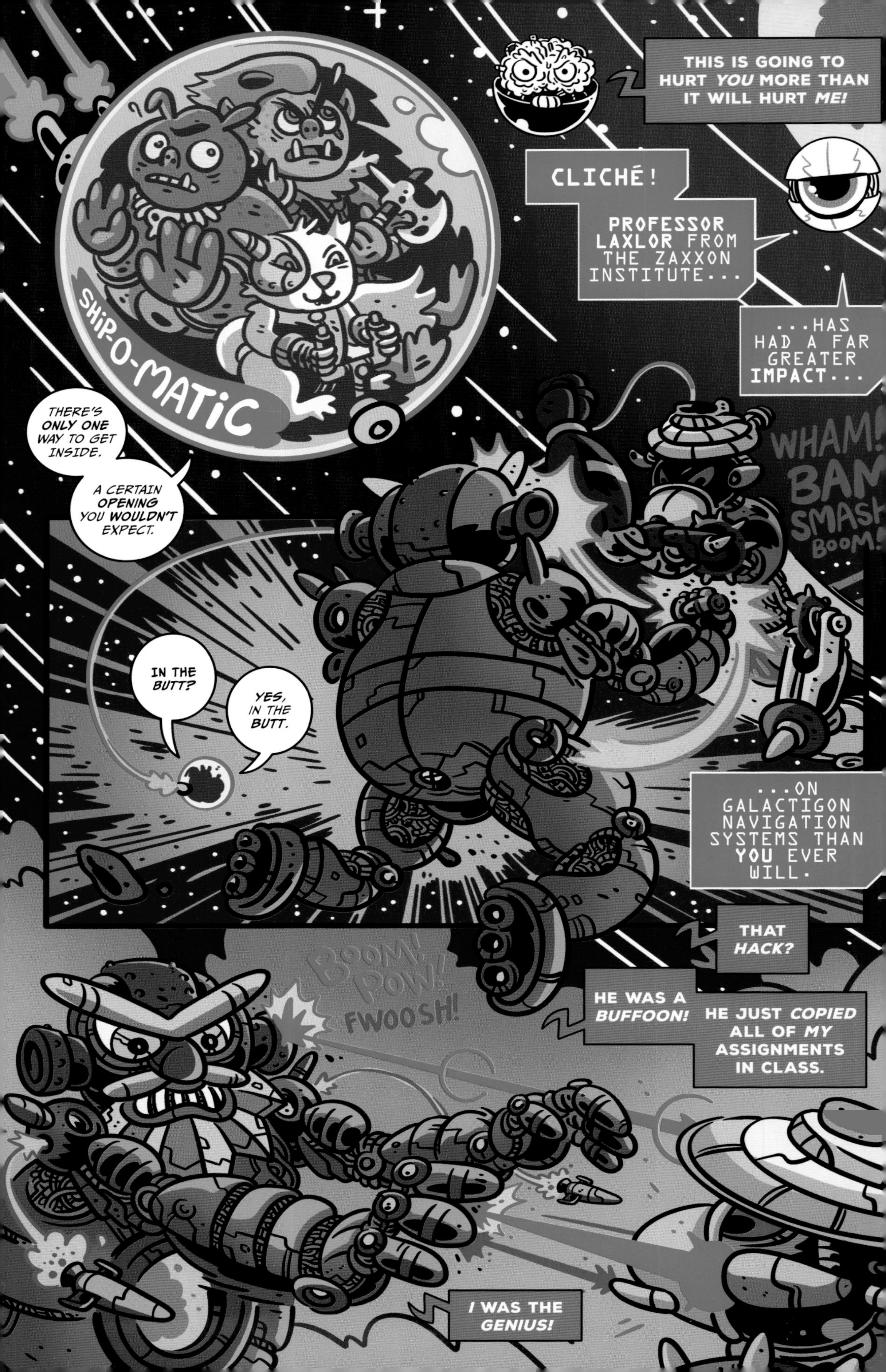

THIS IS GOING TO HURT YOU MORE THAN IT WILL HURT ME!
CLICHÉ!
PROFESSOR LAXLOR FROM THE ZAXXON INSTITUTE...
...HAS HAD A FAR GREATER IMPACT...
SHIP-O-MATIC
THERE'S ONLY ONE WAY TO GET INSIDE.
A CERTAIN OPENING YOU WOULDN'T EXPECT.
WHAM! BAM! SMASH! BOOM!
IN THE BUTT?
YES, IN THE BUTT.
...ON GALACTIGON NAVIGATION SYSTEMS THAN YOU EVER WILL.
THAT HACK?
BOOM! POW! FWOOSH!
HE WAS A BUFFOON!
HE JUST COPIED ALL OF MY ASSIGNMENTS IN CLASS.
I WAS THE GENIUS!

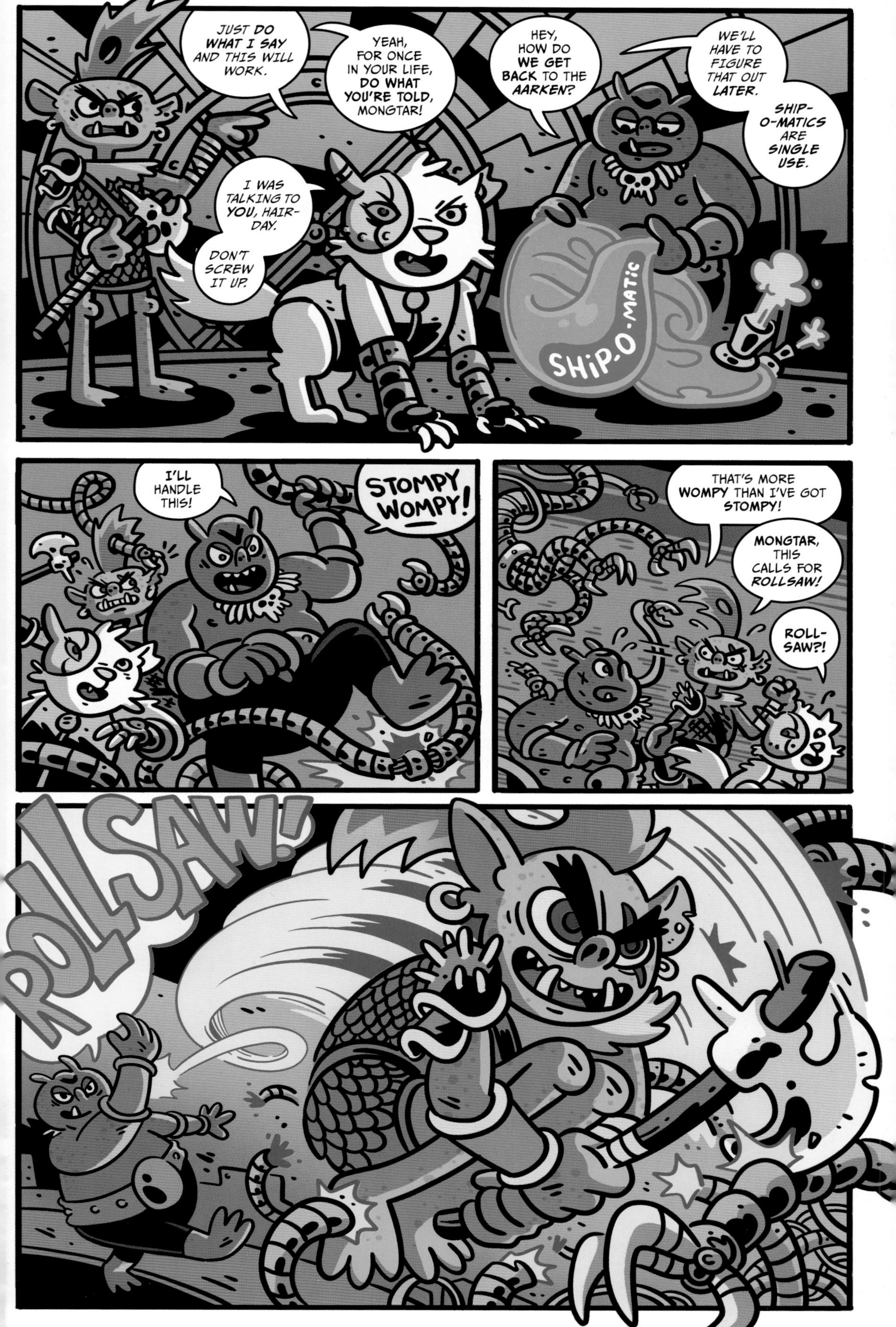
JUST DO WHAT I SAY AND THIS WILL WORK.
YEAH, FOR ONCE IN YOUR LIFE, DO WHAT YOU'RE TOLD, MONGTAR!
I WAS TALKING TO YOU, HAIR-DAY.
DON'T SCREW IT UP.
HEY, HOW DO WE GET BACK TO THE AARKEN?
WE'LL HAVE TO FIGURE THAT OUT LATER.
SHIP-O-MATICS ARE SINGLE USE.
SHIP-O-MATIC
I'LL HANDLE THIS!
STOMPY WOMPY!
THAT'S MORE WOMPY THAN I'VE GOT STOMPY!
MONGTAR, THIS CALLS FOR ROLLSAW!
ROLL-SAW?!
ROLLSAW!

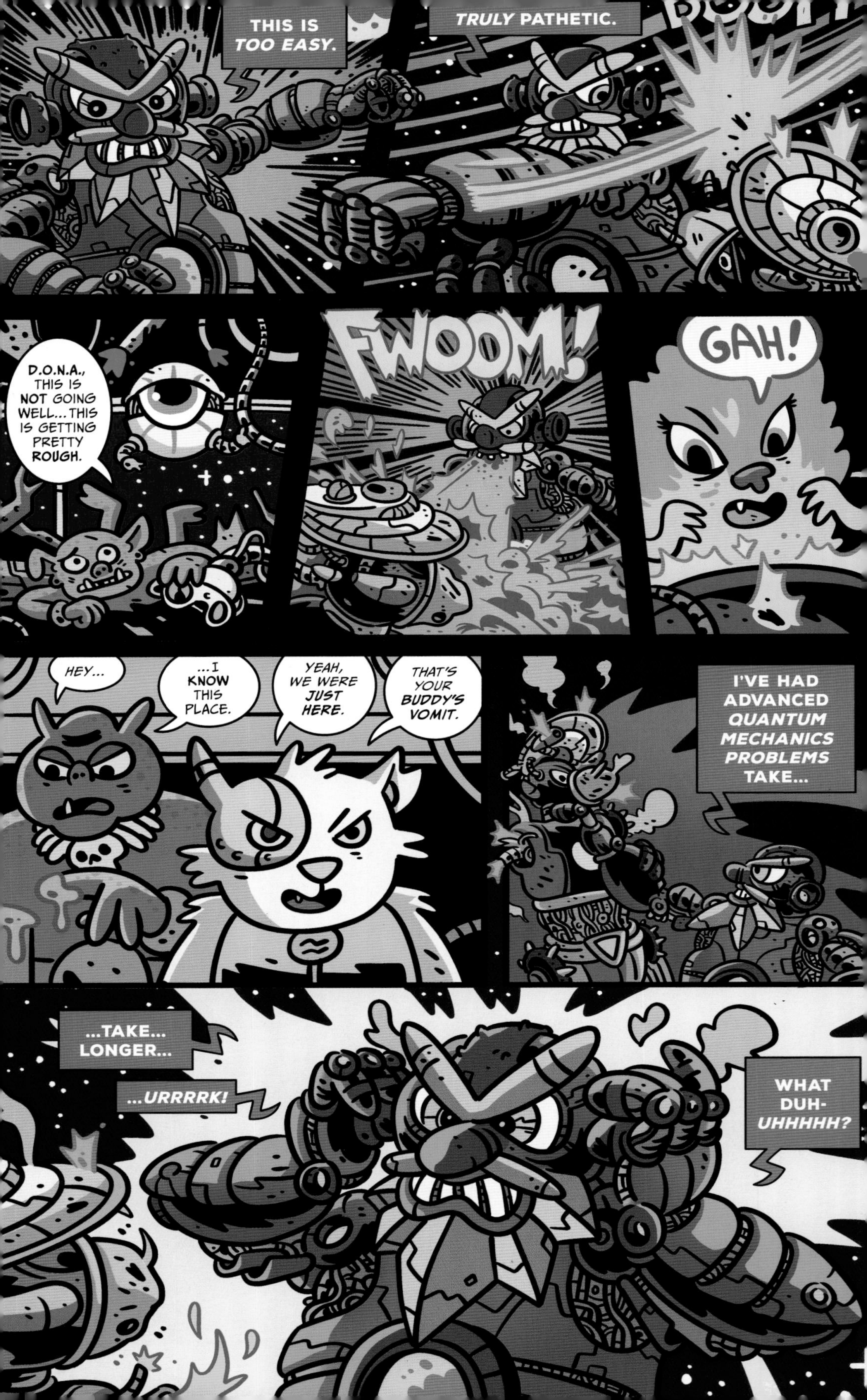

THIS IS TOO EASY.
TRULY PATHETIC.
D.O.N.A., THIS IS NOT GOING WELL... THIS IS GETTING PRETTY ROUGH.
FWOOM!
GAH!
HEY...
...I KNOW THIS PLACE.
YEAH, WE WERE JUST HERE.
THAT'S YOUR BUDDY'S VOMIT.
I'VE HAD ADVANCED QUANTUM MECHANICS PROBLEMS TAKE...
...TAKE... LONGER...
...URRRRK!
WHAT DUH-UHHHHH?

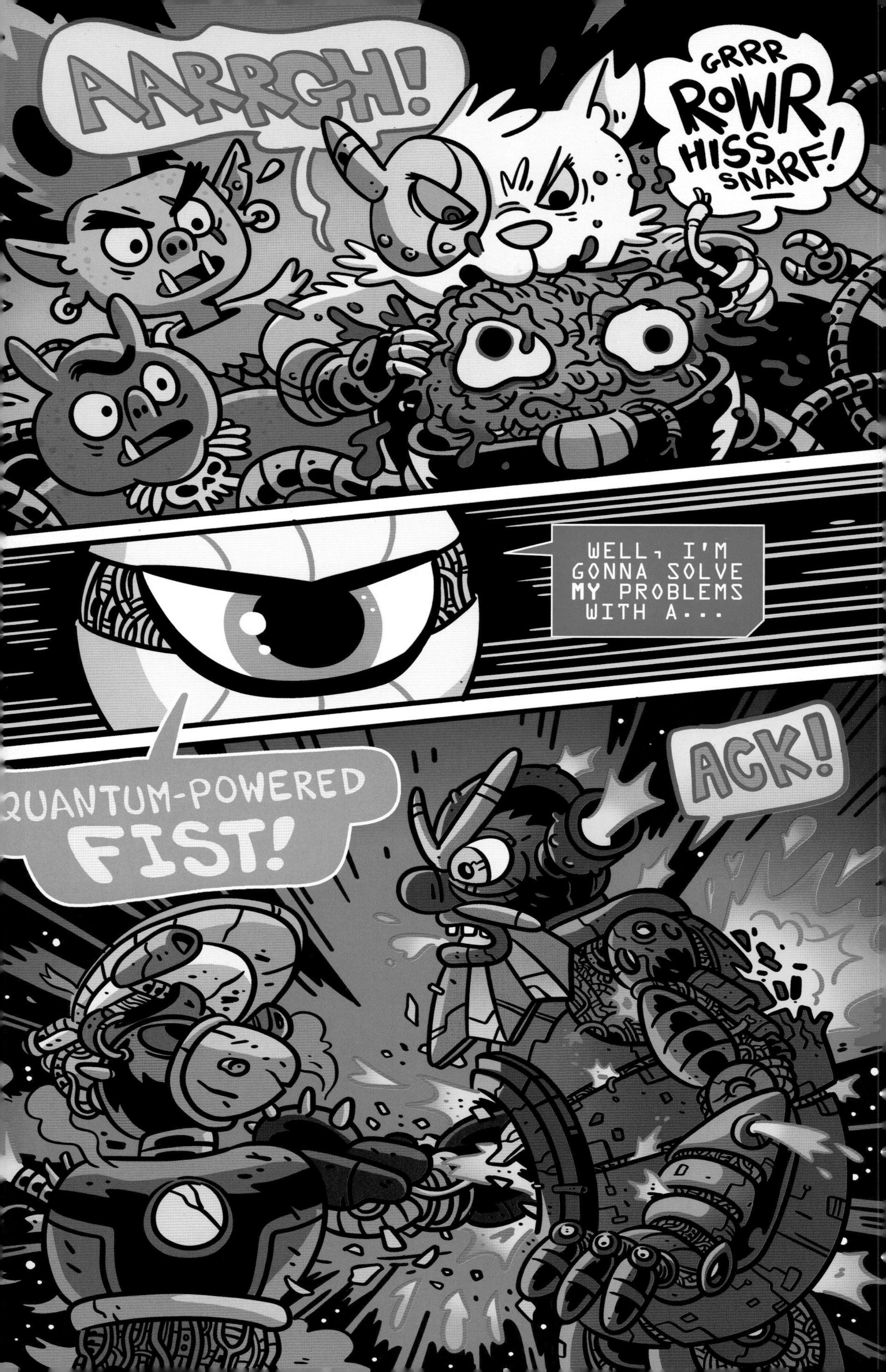
AARRGH!
GRRR ROWR HISS SNARF!
WELL, I'M GONNA SOLVE MY PROBLEMS WITH A...
QUANTUM-POWERED FIST!
ACK!

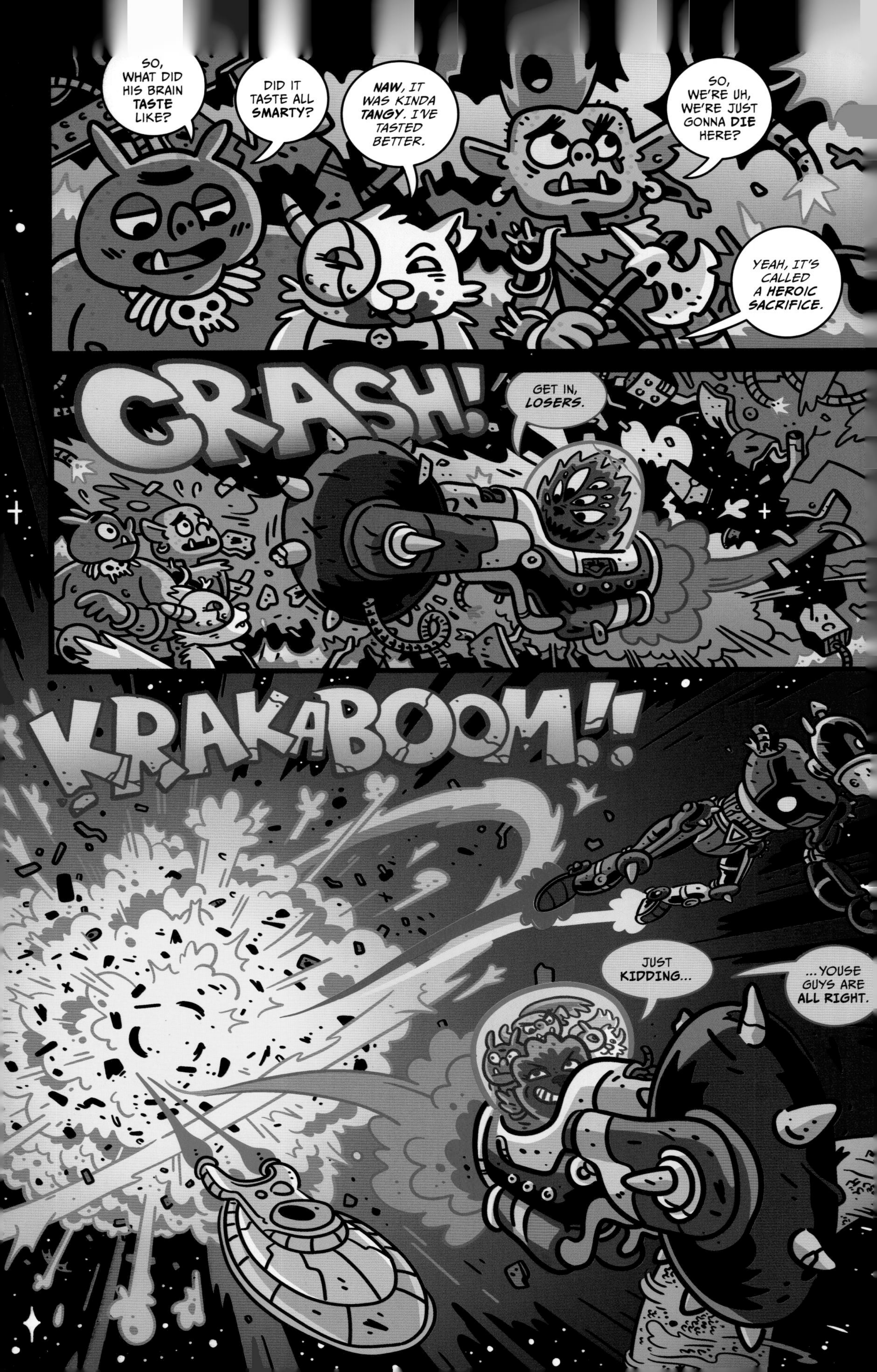
SO, WHAT DID HIS BRAIN TASTE LIKE?
DID IT TASTE ALL SMARTY?
NAW, IT WAS KINDA TANGY. I'VE TASTED BETTER.
SO, WE'RE UH, WE'RE JUST GONNA DIE HERE?
YEAH, IT'S CALLED A HEROIC SACRIFICE.
CRASH!
GET IN, LOSERS.
KRAKABOOM!!
JUST KIDDING...
...YOUSE GUYS ARE ALL RIGHT.

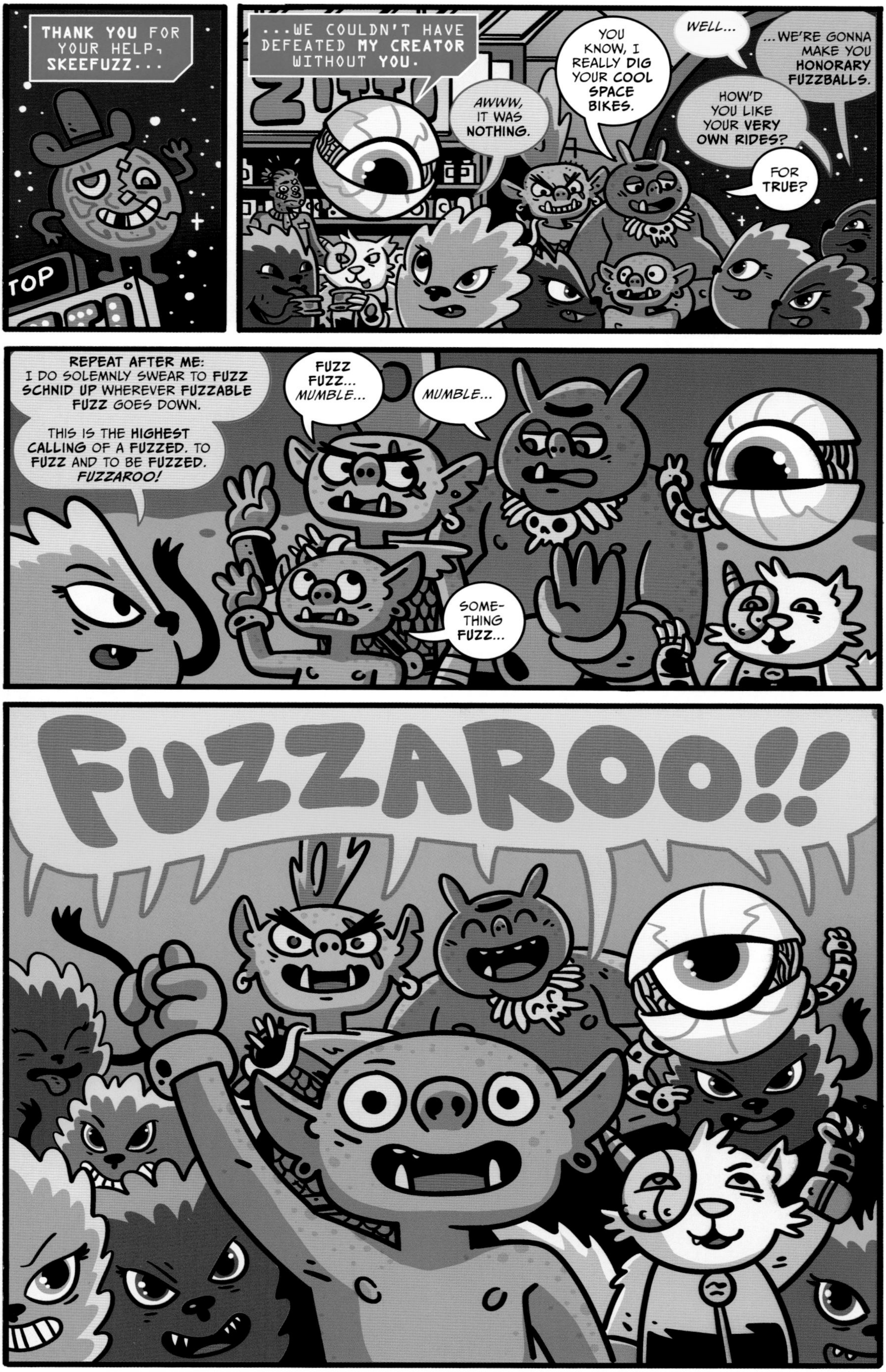
THANK YOU FOR YOUR HELP, SKEEFUZZ...
TOP
...WE COULDN'T HAVE DEFEATED MY CREATOR WITHOUT YOU.
AWWW, IT WAS NOTHING.
YOU KNOW, I REALLY DIG YOUR COOL SPACE BIKES.
WELL...
...WE'RE GONNA MAKE YOU HONORARY FUZZBALLS.
HOW'D YOU LIKE YOUR VERY OWN RIDES?
FOR TRUE?
REPEAT AFTER ME: I DO SOLEMNLY SWEAR TO FUZZ SCHNID UP WHEREVER FUZZABLE FUZZ GOES DOWN.
THIS IS THE HIGHEST CALLING OF A FUZZED. TO FUZZ AND TO BE FUZZED. FUZZAROO!
FUZZ FUZZ... MUMBLE...
MUMBLE...
SOME-THING FUZZ...
FUZZAROO!!

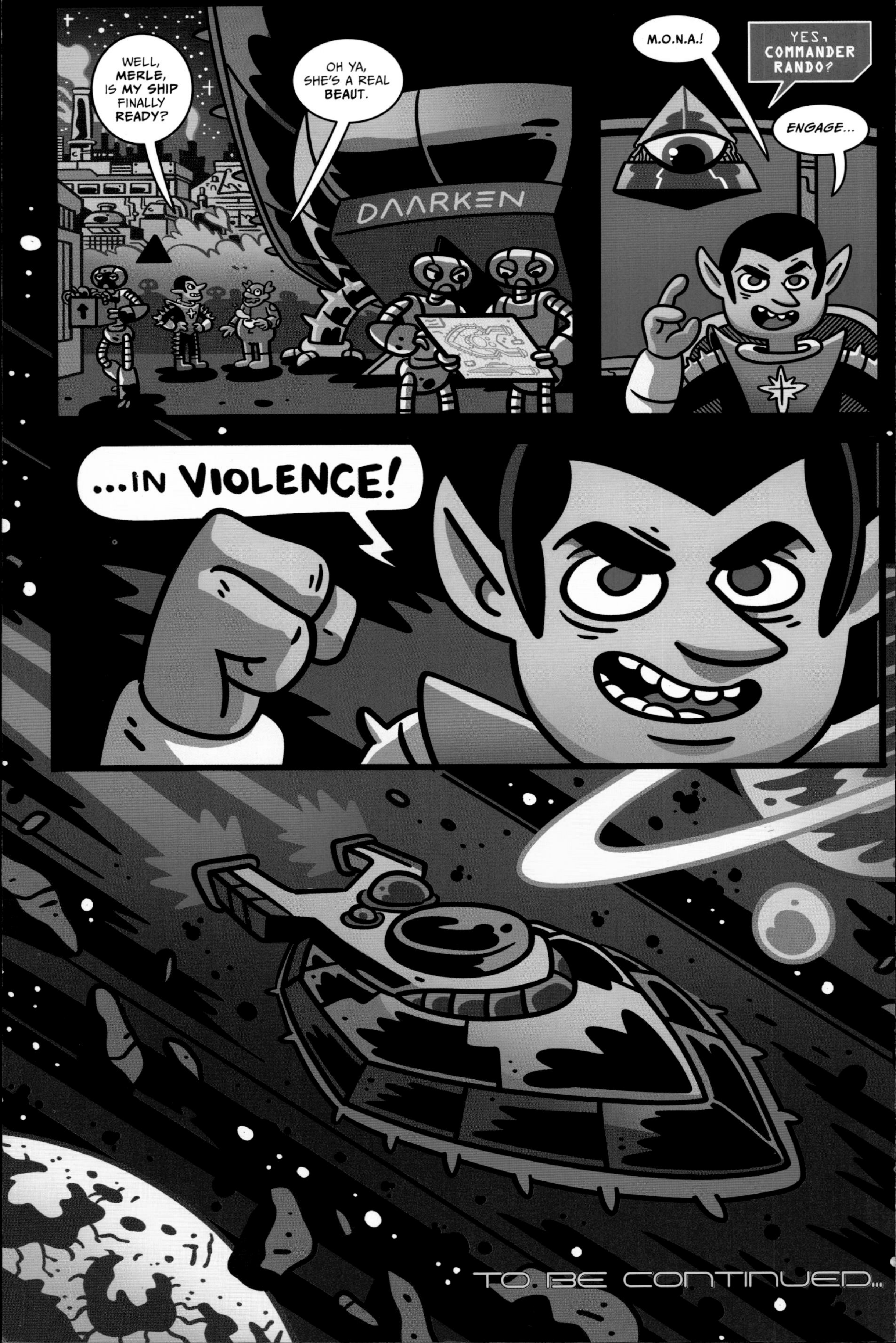
WELL, MERLE, IS MY SHIP FINALLY READY?
OH YA, SHE'S A REAL BEAUT.
DAARKEN
M.O.N.A.!
YES, COMMANDER RANDO?
ENGAGE...
...IN VIOLENCE!
TO BE CONTINUED...